WITHDRAWN

THE HEALING DANCE

ABOUT THE AUTHOR

Kathleen Rea is a certified psychotherapist with the OACCPP. She earned a diploma in expressive art therapy from ISIS-Canada, a certificate in psychology from Ryerson University and a master's degree in expressive arts therapy with a minor in psychology from the European Graduate School. A practicing therapist for the past twelve years, she is also a therapeutic performance facilitator, helping people express their life stories through multidisciplinary performance. Kathleen has taught dance therapy, dance improvisation, and contact dance at York University, George Brown College, and Niagara College. She also founded and runs the Wednesday Dance Jam. Kathleen has choreographed over forty works for her company REAson d'etre dance productions and for other organizations. Her award winning dance film *Lapinthrope* aired on Bravo Television and screened at numerous international festivals. Her production *Long Live* was nominated for three Dora Mavor Moore awards, including outstanding choreography. In 2010, Kathleen was co-winner of the K. M. Hunter Dance Award.

THE HEALING DANCE

The Life and Practice of an Expressive Arts Therapist

By

KATHLEEN REA, M.A., OACCPP Cert.

With a Foreword by

Stephen K. Levine, PH.D.

CHARLES C THOMAS • PUBLISHER, LTD.
Springfield • Illinois • U.S.A.

Published and Distributed Throughout the World by

CHARLES C THOMAS • PUBLISHER, LTD.
2600 South First Street
Springfield, Illinois 62704

© 2013 by CHARLES C THOMAS • PUBLISHER, LTD.

ISBN 978-0-398-08847-7 (hard)
ISBN 978-0-398-08848-4 (paper)
ISBN 978-0-398-08849-1 (ebook)

Library of Congress Catalog Card Number: 2012027884

With THOMAS BOOKS *careful attention is given to all details of manufacturing
and design. It is the Publisher's desire to present books that are satisfactory as to their
physical qualities and artistic possibilities and appropriate for their particular use.*
THOMAS BOOKS *will be true to those laws of quality that assure a good name
and good will.*

Cover Photo by Judee Bramm, Toronto, Canada, copyright 1997.

Printed in the United States of America
SM-R-3

Library of Congress Cataloging-in-Publication Data

Rea, Kathleen.
  The healing dance : the life and practice of an expressive arts therapist / by
Kathleen Rea ; with a foreword by Stephen K. Levine.
      p. cm.
  Includes bibliographical references and index.
  ISBN 978-0-398-08847-7 (hard) -- ISBN 978-0-398-08848-4 (pbk.) -- ISBN
978-0-398-08849-1 (ebook)
  1. Arts--Therapeutic use. 2. Art therapy. I. Title.

RC489.A72R43 2013
616.89'1656--dc23

                                                                    2012027884

FOREWORD

As parents, we may have the experience of suddenly looking at our child and realizing with a shock that he or she knows more than we do. This happened to me in reading Kathleen Rea's fine new book. Kathleen has taken what she learned in the training we offered her at ISIS Canada and the European Graduate School and integrated it into her own unique body-based way of doing expressive arts therapy. Her method is grounded on her own experience as a woman, as a professional dancer, and as a therapist.

One of the great strengths of the book is Kathleen's honesty and vulnerability as she writes about her own struggles. She describes her personal conflicts in a way that lets us see not only the pain she experienced but also the ways in which she found the creative resources she needed to find her way through.

We read first of the struggles that Kathleen had with her body-image as she dealt with issues of perfectionism and control. Her attempt to take charge after the chaos of her parents' divorce, combining with the strong cultural messages that are given about women's bodies, resulted in a battle between anorexia and bulimia that almost took her life.

Dance became her passion and her way to survive. From an early age, she was drawn to this mode of expression, and it ultimately became a lifeline that would lead her into a deeper and more profound relation with her own body and with the bodily basis of emotional life. At the same time, the world of ballet that was her chosen field became the demon that told her constantly that her body was not good enough and that she had to exercise greater and greater control over it. It was not until she found another way home through more expressive forms of dance, like contact improvisation, that Kathleen was able to use her body as a resource and a route to greater self-acceptance.

Finally, as a therapist, we read of Kathleen's own experiences with her clients, the ways in which, in paying attention to her own bodily sensations, she is able to find creative forms of therapeutic action that lead her clients into more fulfilling modes of expression. Kathleen's openness to her own body as well as her fine sensitivity to the bodily expressions of others are the foundations on which her therapeutic practice is built.

We can see all these realms of experience converge in the extended description of the therapeutic work she did with her client, Allen. Kathleen's own experience with bulimia gave her a special insight into Allen's addiction to food and the way he used it to give himself control over his life. At the same time, her artistic background as a dancer became a resource for the movement work she did with him. The "fussy dance" she learned in her dance work gave him the ability to go beyond the inhibitions that prevented him from engaging in bodily expression.

We also see how her training as an expressive arts therapist, her own therapy, and the experience she gained in her therapeutic practice provided not only the skills and knowledge that every therapist must have but also the conviction that the therapeutic process is possible, that beneath all our suffering is an enormous beauty waiting to be seen if we can unlock the doors that protect it from harm.

Ultimately, then, this is a book about beauty. As an artist, Kathleen knows the power of beauty as a cultural expression. Those of us who were fortunate enough to have seen her perform can testify to the beauty of her movement, the way in which her body seemed to exhibit a spiritual grace normally denied to us earth-bound mortals. But beauty for her was never about perfection of form; it always testified to an openness and honesty that is deeply emotionally touching in her work.

Similarly, the beauty that shines forth in this book does so because it is infused with love. Kathleen's therapeutic practice is grounded on the capacity to accept her clients completely for the beautifully flawed human beings that they, and we, are. Her work with them in the expressive arts is never for the sake of the art itself but for the way in which the arts can hold our beauty and show our inner light.

Reading this book, I can offer no greater tribute than to say that I wish I could have had Kathleen as my therapist. Unfortunately no matter how special we realize our children have become, they can never be the parents we wish we ourselves had. There is a time to let them go and to take satisfaction in seeing who they are. I am proud to be one of those who have helped this wonderful therapist come into the world. I hope that the reader will come away from this book with a living embodied sense not only of what it means to be an expressive arts therapist but also of how living a life based on openness and honesty can put us in touch with the beauty and love that is ultimately ours to come home to.

Stephen K. Levine

Stephen K. Levine, Ph.D., D.S.Sc., REAT, is Co-Director of ISIS Canada and Dean of the Doctoral Program in Expressive Arts at the European Graduate School. He is the author and editor of many books in the field of expressive arts therapy, including *Poiesis: The Language of Psychology and the Speech of the Soul, Trauma, Tragedy, Therapy: The Arts and Human Suffering,* and, with Paolo J. Knill and Ellen G. Levine, *Principles and Practice of Expressive Arts Therapy: Towards a Therapeutic Aesthetics.*

INTRODUCTION

My expressive arts therapy studio has a wooden dance floor and enough room to move around. The view from the window is a garden, overgrown and wild. There are patterned curtains and a comfy old couch. I have taken care to make it an inviting place, as opposed to a sterile office. People say it has a cottage feel, which suits me fine. *The Healing Dance: The Life and Practice of an Expressive Arts Therapist* is inspired by what happens in this room.

My clients dance, paint, play music, sing, write poetry, and act out scenes with the intention of overcoming psychological suffering. My practice is not just for skilled artists. We are all creators who create every minute of every day through the imprint we leave on the world – every time we take a step, we create a "footprint" on the earth. I help the everyday person discover his or her creative spark, which invigorates and shines a light on the dark path ahead.

The Healing Dance portrays the theory and practice of expressive arts therapy, as seen through my eyes. I combine my experience as an expressive arts therapist, dancer, choreographer, and educator with stories from my personal life to explain this broad and sometimes confusing field of science. My aim is to be informative and engaging, but most importantly, accessible. I wrote this book for students, practitioners, and anyone curious about the enlivening power of the arts.

As a ballerina, I strived to achieve an external ideal of artistic perfection, and this led to psychological break down. Years later as a choreographer, I discovered that portraying the truth of my suffering was a healing balm. From these experiences, I learned that the arts are a powerful agent of change that can hurt as well as heal. I spend a significant portion of the book describing the conditions that help guide the creative process towards therapeutic results.

Recovery from my eating disorder inspired me to see the body not as something to be controlled, but as the source of vitality and wisdom. This led me to cultivate a style of expressive arts therapy that focuses on body awareness as the source of creative inspiration. *The Healing Dance* presents a view of expressive arts therapy in which body sensations have a central role. This concept is not just presented as a philosophical view, but is given life through client stories and practical techniques. Using a step-by-step outline, I describe body-based expressive arts methods that I developed. I also explain techniques that enable the client to pace the intensity of his or her sensation-based therapeutic work so that it does not occur at a quicker rate than he or she is able to tolerate.

Throughout the book, I refer to theories and research in the field of neuroscience and how they may relate to expressive arts therapy. While not an exhaustive exploration of neuroscience, I offer suggestions as to why expressive arts therapy might be especially helpful in changing brain pathways.

Most art-based therapists believe in the value of maintaining their own artistic practice. Yet an artistic practice is so often sacrificed because of the time pressures of the job. For me, the two worlds of therapist and artist have become so interwoven that they are often indiscernible from one another. I would not be the therapist I am today without my dance and choreography practice, and I would not be the dancer and choreographer I am today without my therapy practice. I hope the reader comes to understand how these two worlds can support and enrich each other.[1]

For me, expressive arts are not just a form of therapy, but a way of living. *The Healing Dance: The Life and Practice of an Expressive Arts Therapist* demonstrates how to access the creative spark living in one's body that has the potential to ignite a fulfilling life.

ACKNOWLEDGMENTS

I have many people to thank for making this book possible. Most importantly, I could not have created this book without my clients, whose courage and creative expression have been among my greatest teachers. A special thank you to the client who inspired the "Allen" story that animates Chapters 2 and 3.

Thank you to the *Long Live* dancers who wandered into the unknown with me, and then generously hopped on board the chair-on-wheels. Your brave performance of the work gave me the chance to step back and witness it come to life. Special mentions to Suzanne Liska, who let me intermingle her own story with mine during the creative process; to Karen Kaeja for being a creative force in my work for the past ten years; and to Tom Brouillette for your eyes that so powerfully relayed to the audience the dad's internal struggles.

I acknowledge my teachers at ISIS-Canada and European Graduate School who opened the door to the wild and powerful realm of expressive arts therapy and encouraged me to explore. A special thank you Rowesa Gordon, Steve Levine, and Ellen Levine for being supportive of my career over the past ten years. I also appreciate my time as an assistant to Janine Hancock's arts-based supervision course at ISIS-Canada. Your seemingly fearless conviction gave me the confidence to trust the artistic process.

Thank you to Kimberly Way, Tina Chase, Maya Potter, and Ariel Brink for their valuable editorial feedback that helped the book reach the professional standard of which it was capable. I could not have completed the book without my husband, Jeff, who re-read every page ten times over, always asking me the same question: "What are you saying here?" I would tell him, and he would always respond with, "Now just write that." With this dialogue, Jeff helped me to arrive closer to the truth of what I wanted to say. I marvel at the fact that I married a man who naturally follows the expressive arts practices of asking non-directive questions, which allow the artist to find his or her own answers.

To my son, Wyatt, whose appearance at the end of the story in Chapter 4 gave it the best ending I could have ever hoped for.

Thank you to my family, especially my mother, Olja; my stepdad Mike; and my older sister, Lovisa, for your unwavering belief in me. Thank you to my dad, Craig, for being one of my biggest inspirations. I know you are looking down from heaven, and are really proud of me for writing this book.

Thank you to Michael P. Thomas for seeing the value in *The Healing Dance*, and for guiding me through the publication process.

To ensure my clients' confidentiality, many of the descriptions of session work in this book are composites of different clients' work mixed with typical representations of what clients tend to do in Kathleen's private practice. Where a client's actual session or series of sessions has been described, all defining details have been changed and the client's permission obtained. Clients were encouraged to review their segment and approve or make changes. They were also given the option to opt out at any point in the writing process.

CONTENTS

THE HEALING DANCE

Chapter 1

BECOMING A THERAPIST

I absorb every detail of the swan costume pictured on the back of my Anna Pavlova record. The coffee table is pushed out of the way and a large, open carpet beckons. The house is empty – a rare occurrence. Holding the record carefully by its edges, I gently ease it onto the turntable. Like most nine-year-olds, I'm usually pretty careless with my stuff, but this feels important and worthy of care. I gingerly place the needle onto the record; a single cello note hovers. More follow. My feet start to move and my arms float upward as my body becomes light. The living room walls disappear. Warmth builds. I turn and bend and move towards something unknown. It's risky – anything might happen. My heart feels big, like it might break into a million pieces. Goosebumps flutter up my spine as my swan wings spread and I feel air rush through my feathers. Then it hits me: a knowing that cuts through all else. I am the reincarnation of the great ballet dancer Anna Pavlova. Her love of dance lives on in me, and I am born to shine this love as bright as it will shine.

*****

I have found the perfect hiding spot to read my book, a window ledge alcove on the third floor of the National Ballet Company rehearsal hall. Here I will be safe from the judgmental eyes of colleagues who would probably laugh at a book called *A Woman's Worth*. The ballet world is not exactly friendly to feminists. I have a single Twizzlers candy hidden in my pocket. I slip it into my long sleeve and nibble on the end, hiding sweets like a kid even though I am twenty-four. It's my only source of calories in a day of nothing but Diet Cokes. My shoulders curl in. I have to return to rehearsal soon and the licorice feels like it has already made its way to my thighs. I dig my nails into my thighs creating large red scratches. My rehearsal mistress warned me last week about my weight.

She said, "You're a big-chested girl, so you need to be even thinner than the other girls." She continued, sweeping her hand over my collarbone, "I want to see more bones."

Back in the present, from my alcove, I hear music from the studio below – Swan Lake, one of the most gruelling ballets I have ever danced. I love it and I hate it. It's stunning, but for the *corps de ballet*, by the third act, it's a war field of bloody toes, hunger, and exhaustion. Just getting through it gives me a similar sense of accomplishment that I imagine climbing Mount Everest would. My rehearsal starts soon. I open the book I have been holding close to my chest and read:

> "What?" you say. "Me, a goddess?" Yes, I say, and don't act so surprised. You knew when you were little that you were born for something special and that no matter what happened to you, that couldn't be erased. The magic could not be drained from your heart. . . Sorry to tell you, but you had it right years ago, and then you forgot. You were born with a mystical purpose.[2]

These words are my nourishment for the day.

*****

I lean on the arm of my chair, chosen for its comfort – an important thing for a forty-something retired dancer with achy bones.

My client asks me, "Is it really possible to get better?"

"Well, it is possible. I had an eating disorder for ten years, and today I eat whatever I want, whenever I'm hungry. And I have learned to appreciate and love my body. But I understand what you are saying. I remember thinking I would never get better."

After a pause, I continue. "Do you remember a time when you were young? Before you started not liking your body?"

"No."

"Are you sure?"

She closes her eyes. "I think I remember something . . . I am very young. My mom helped me make a suit of armour out of cardboard. I wore it the whole day. I remember feeling so proud of how I looked."

"Can you describe that feeling?"

"Hmmm," she pauses for a moment before continuing. "It's hard to describe. It's like just . . . *being* . . . with no negative thoughts getting in the way."

"How about exploring this 'just being'? See if you can remember what it felt like to be that knight. How did you stand? What was your expression?"

She spends a few moments trying out different postures, finally settling on a lifted chest and a beaming closed-mouth smile.

"Now just stay with this posture and explore how it feels to move about the studio. See if you can welcome the knight back into your body."

*****

From a wild swan girl, to an image-obsessed ballerina waif, to a guide helping others, I have experienced the healing of hearts and minds. I've discovered that healing does not need to be a forward progression in which we continuously improve upon ourselves. Rather, it can be a falling back into ourselves, remembering and experiencing the current of life that pulses through us. It can be a coming home.

I will now take you back to the beginning and tell the full story of how I came home to my calling as an expressive arts therapist. I will describe pivotal life experiences that influence who I am as a therapist and the understanding I harvested from each. Many of the things that happened were challenging and didn't feel like they offered a harvest at the time. It was not until decades later that I realized how these experiences helped me understand, and have compassion for, the suffering of others. I needed to walk the path in order to be a guide for others on similar paths.

*****

Trying to Control the Uncontrollable

My sister and I are sitting with our parents in our living room. My Dad has asked us to stop playing and listen because he has something important to tell us.

"Your mom and I are not getting along and we . . ."

Adult words swept over my five-year-old self.

My dad finished with, ". . . and so I'm moving out."

I looked at him with disbelief. I would no longer be swung up on his shoulder when he came home from work. There would be no "Dad belly laughs" to fill the house.

"Are you leaving because I've been bad?" I asked.

He told me I was not to blame, but I did not believe him. I was sure that I could magically fix everything by being a "really good girl."

In the weeks that followed my dad moving out, my attempts to be a good girl did not bring him back. Grief overwhelmed me and I became too upset to eat. I remember lying in a big hospital bed with intravenous needles feeding my body while my parents stood on either side of me, yelling at each other. They were each blaming the other for my illness. I wanted to find some way to make them stop, but I couldn't find the energy to speak.

Rescuing Others Rescues Me

My bedroom was the barracks for a small army of stuffed animals. I had two shelves of them above my bed. My favourites were my raccoon, Brownie, and a grey seal named Sleeky. I wanted to cuddle with them every night, but I believed that all my stuffed animals were alive and had feelings; I didn't want any of them to be lonely. I understood how lonely felt. For months after my parents' separation, my mom was despondent. She would often close the door to her bedroom and play sad music on her guitar for hours. I only saw my dad every other weekend. I missed both my mom and my dad. I couldn't change what was happening to my family, but I could ensure that my stuffed animals were not lonely like me. In order to give equal snuggling time and love to each, I slept with them on a rotating schedule. Taking care of them helped heal my sad heart.

Art Can Hold Like a Mother's Hug

After my dad left, my mom found a job and went back to school to get her master's degree because she wanted to build a career that would support us. She left so early in the morning that by the time I awoke, she was gone. Not wanting my sister and me to feel abandoned, my mom drew whimsical cartoons in which our favourite stuffed animals went on magical adventures. Each morning we would find a new installment by our breakfast bowls. As I sat eating my cereal, I watched Brownie and Sleeky sail across the world in their magical boat, and I learned how a drawing could hold like a mother's arms.

Play Heals

The chaos of the divorce receded and life continued, only with two distinct households. My mom and new stepdad were thoughtful parents who encouraged our creativity. On the weekends, they spent hours helping my sister and me with art projects. They even let us design our own playhouse. There was no TV, just a playroom full of simple toys. My sister and I didn't need much. Mostly we played with dress-up-clothes and paper dolls, as well as entertaining ourselves for hours playing with buttons as if they were kings and queens fighting epic battles.

We stayed with our dad every other weekend. There were no toys at his place, but that didn't matter, because Dad was one big fun-machine who played "silly" with us like he was a child himself. He read bedtime stories that he acted out like a play. He took us on rock-climbing adventures, which my mom would never dream of letting us do.

I learned that play can heal a broken heart.

Perfectionism

My sister was born with feet that pointed inward. Our family doctor said ballet classes would straighten them out. My mom didn't have time to drive both my sister and me to separate activities, so we were both enrolled.

My sister's prescription for pink tights and leotards became my joy. Noticing my aptitude and love of dance, my teacher suggested that I audition for the National Ballet School of Canada. At the age of ten, I was accepted into their rigorous eight-year training program, which combined classical dance with academics. I went to school from nine in the morning until six at night, dancing three to five hours a day. Every student there worked towards transcending the limitations of the body through discipline and control. We were all drawn to the thrill of becoming the "perfect dancer."

My attraction to ballet did not just evolve out of a love of dance, but out of my desire to feel that I had control over my life. The strict rules instantly resonated with me because they provided a set of ideals to reach for, a magical recipe that, if followed, promised to make me "perfect."

This started an internal battle of expression versus perfection. In the world of perfect *pliés* and pretty *pirouettes*, was there room for me, the individual? What about the wild swan girl who danced so freely in her living room? Ultimately, the drive to conform to the ballet ideal overtook me and the memory of the wild swan girl dimmed.

Shame

His hand touched me. I didn't understand what was happening. I trusted him. My family trusted him. I didn't know his hands weren't supposed to touch in those places, in that way. When I began to understand, I shrank inward from shame. I learned to sneak into bed early. I shut my door tight in the hopes I would get no goodnight kisses. A secret kept; a silent imprint upon my body.

The Pain of Not Fitting In

I came home from school crying and my mom wrapped me in her arms. It was re-audition time at the ballet school. Every spring, a panel of teachers scrutinized our dancing; weeks later, we all received a letter either inviting us back for another year or "un-accepting" (i.e., dumping) us. It had been a tough year in other ways. With my new glasses, braces, and horrible headgear contraption to pull my bite forward, I felt like a dork. We were all expected to look like pretty ballerinas; instead, I was a bull's-eye for teasing. Much of the year my classmates had called me fat and retarded, following me around and copying every movement I made. Even my best friend switched camps and joined in.

"You don't have to go back there," my mom said. "You can quit and go to a regular school. It's such a hard thing you've chosen. I know you love to dance, but are you sure it's worth it?"

There was never a choice for me. It was a dream I could not give up.

Madness

One day while walking home from school, I heard a voice in my head tell me, "Don't step on a crack – something bad will happen."

What might happen? I wondered.

I started to imagine that my mom might die or a horrible tornado would tear down the house. I checked the window about a hundred times before I went to sleep that night, just to make sure there were no black clouds in the sky. I decided that I would never step on another crack, ever again.

It didn't end there. The voice came back and told me of more things I had to do in order to prevent disaster: chew my food twenty times before swallowing, sleep with my entire body under the covers, swallow ten times in a row before turning on a light. I performed all these rituals because I thought they would prevent illnesses, accidents, natural disasters, and crime. The list of potential disasters grew more horrible each day. Soon I was convinced that scientists were sneaking into my room late at night and doing experiments on me, and that my parents were trying to poison me. I was scared to eat, scared to go outside, scared to wake up, and scared to go to bed. I told no one, because even in the midst of this personal hell, I did not want to cause any worry.

Was I "mad"? Yes, I was mad at a crazy world in which dads moved away, friendly hands could take away innocence, childhood friends became bullies, and my chance to be a ballerina could be lost if a panel of experts decided my legs were too fat. These things made me angry, but my anger had no place to exist because it did not fit into my "good girl" image. With nowhere to go, it turned into madness.

I knew I was "mad" and was determined to get better, to be normal again. I picked a date two months in the future and marked it with an X on my calendar. I decided that if I could not get the voices to stop by that date, I would kill myself. I had even picked my method. There was a bottle of drain cleaner in the basement and I decided I would drink the whole bottle. I then began to fight for my life by trying to get the voices to shut up. Every time they spoke, I forced myself not to listen, to concentrate on something else. My will to live without madness was strong. By the date marked on the calendar, I had silenced the voices. I was once again a "normal girl."

> Having traveled the road to madness and back, I'm familiar with the path. I understand that no matter how counterproductive or "crazy" someone's behaviour seems, it's possibly the only coping method they have. I do not look at a "crazy" person and see craziness. I see through the surface layers to the sane desire to make it through. I see complex defenses that bend and twist back on themselves so many times that at first glance they seem crazy.
>
> I also believe that inside each of us is a "mad" person, and that part of life is finding a productive container for this madness. I eventually chose choreography as my container. The chaos intrinsic to the choreographic process is a type of insanity. During intense creative moments, I become mad as creative forces take over. A voice in my head tells me what the next dance move will be. I even welcome the repetitive rituals that were part of my former madness into the dance studio as inspiration for choreographic material.
>
> My journey into psychosis inspires me to help others find the right homes for their madness.

Having Someone on Your Side

At the end of the summer, right before school started, my older sister decided to give me a makeover. She said, "No matter what Mom or the orthodontist says, never wear your head gear in public ever again. And the glasses . . . go bug Mom about getting contact lenses and don't stop until she says yes. We're also going to my hairdresser, and then I'm taking you to buy new clothes. I'm going to make you look so cool, that no one will feel they have the right to bully you."

It was not the new outfit or hair that stopped the bullying. It was a new-found confidence that my sister fostered. I discovered that everyone needs someone to cheer for them.

The Body as the Enemy

As I went through puberty, I developed a curvy body that was considered too fat for the stage. Thus began the battle to conform my hips and breasts to the ballet ideal. The issue was simple: I was battling between who I was and who I wished I was.

My dissatisfaction with my body shape was not only influenced by the ballet world, but also by my family. My grandmother, an important role model, was preoccupied with her appearance and suffered from an eating disorder. Through several generations, the women in my family shared a history of sexual abuse that caused them to be ashamed of their bodies. Body shame was a learned thing, passed down from my grandmother, to my mother, to me. Added to this was the shame that came from my own sexual trauma. On top of this was societal pressure to be thin that was being delivered through billboards, magazines, and TV advertisements. It came at me from all directions. I was a child soldier walking through a body-image minefield.

I decided that the cure for my body shame was to become really skinny through excessive dieting. My aim was to be anorexic. At the start, it was a calculated career move, as all the accolades in ballet went to the girls who looked deathly thin. I didn't realize that my "career move," over time, would become uncontrollable and dangerous. I was borderline anorexic for about six months when an intense desire to eat overcame my willpower. I started having uncontrollable food binges, after which I would purge myself by vomiting. I wanted to be anorexic to escape my body, with its curves, appetites, and challenging emotions. In contrast, my binge eating was a return to the body, a secret indulgence of the cravings denied by my conformist ideal. I would diet intensely for days, and then a famished "creature" would seize control. In a trance-like state, I would binge on cakes, ice cream, and greasy foods until satiated. Emerging from my daze, I would purge myself, trying to erase all the calories I had eaten. My bulimia eventually overtook my anorexia as my wild side asserted its existence. Eventually, I was binging and purging up to eight times a day. My bulimia was like a secret and wild "lover" that soothed and caressed my soul amidst the stringencies of ballet life. The mortality rate of anorexia is extremely high compared to bulimia, so my secret lover may have saved my life by ensuring that I got the base minimum of calories I needed to stay alive.

Instead of fighting against the conformist ideals surrounding me, I fought against myself. It was another type of madness born out of the need to say no. Instead of saying no to the craziness around me, I said no to myself by hating my own flesh, and undertook self-harming by see-sawing between starving and overeating. The angrier I became with the world, the more I hurt myself. This gave me some comfort, because by self-harming, at least, I was in charge of my own suffering.

Space to Be

After graduation from the National Ballet School, weight fluctuation rendered me unemployable in the eyes of the ballet world. Colleagues, friends, and family encouraged me to quit because the dream of being a ballet dancer seemed out of reach. I then came upon a rare thing: a ballet director who was not obsessed with skinny dancers. He offered me a part-time position in his dance company. With less pressure to be thin, my eating stabilized. I stopped starving myself, started eating nutritious food, and rarely binged and purged. Although I still suffered from body-image issues, I was able to slim down to a performance weight that was natural for my body.

The director of the National Ballet Company of Canada came to see one of our performances. He liked my dancing so much that he offered me a job and, of course, I said yes. With this new job, I had achieved my dream of working for a world-class ballet company. I couldn't believe my luck.

The Pain and Joys of Conformity

On my first day of work at the National Ballet Company of Canada, the director called me into his office and told me I was fat. He accused me of gaining weight between being hired and my first day of work. I went home and weighed myself. I had not gained a pound! I was devastated and immediately began starving myself. A month later, at 5'6" and 105 pounds, my ballet rehearsal mistress (whom I secretly referred to as the Dragon Lady), told me I needed to lose just a few more pounds so she could see bones. Apparently, with my "larger" breasts (my cup size was B), I had to be even thinner than the other girls. I gave them bones, while in secret I binged and purged my nights away. Each morning, I put on my pink tights and faced the scrutiny of the Dragon Lady.

Life under such pressure was hard, but being part of an elite dance community with extravagant productions and performances throughout the world was enthralling. We were lavished with praise by those who saw us as the epitome of control and discipline. I was a part of the *corps de ballet*, a perfect conformity of women moving and breathing as if we were one. We bonded like a proud army, sharing the experience of bleeding toes, muscle fatigue, injury, exhaustion, and hunger. We developed an intimate understanding of each other's physicality and could mirror each other's breath, posture, and body movements. After hours of practice, there were moments of transcendence in which we achieved an ethereal unity of movement.

The prestige, the fancy costumes, and the camaraderie brought about through shared hardship were not the only things that kept me going. I also returned to my secret "living room dances." I snuck into the National Ballet studios late at night and danced in my own way, in my own world, safe from the scrutiny of any "dragons." The wild swan was still alive.

Dying from the Inside Out

I had spent most of the night eating loaves of bread with butter and quarts of ice cream, and had just finished throwing up into the toilet. I had successfully starved myself for a week after being told I might lose a role unless I dropped some weight, but tonight I had failed. I knew that it wouldn't matter how hard I tried to purge the calories; they had already made their way to my thighs. I lay on the bathroom floor holding a sharp knife and fighting the urge to cut the fat off my thighs.

I lay there until morning; the softness of my bed seemed too indulgent. The cold tiles and the cool metal of the knife resting against my thigh were somehow a comfort as I dozed. It was just the right match for how I felt.

In the morning, I awoke and prepared for work. I curled my hair into a bun as tight as I could, as if this would give me strength to face the eyes that would scrutinize my body shape. I looked in the mirror at my sunken face. I paused for a long time, looking into my eyes. I could see in them that I was dying – a soul death that would eventually result in a physical death if I stayed on the path I was on.

Paradigm Shift

During a performance tour of western Canada, I started to see everything double and was not able to withstand even dim light. Steroids cleared up the eye condition, but a series of medical tests were done that led to the diagnosis of Lupus. Lupus is a degenerative and chronic inflammatory disease affecting the eyes, skin, joints, blood, and kidneys. When the ballet company told me to be sickly thin, I had obeyed like a "good little soldier." Now that I had Lupus, it didn't make sense to be deathly thin. It was the first time that my health became a priority over my dance career. I found an eating disorder therapist and began the hard work of recovery.

Three months later, I received another shock. A Lupus specialist told me that I had been misdiagnosed: I did not have Lupus! I then faced a crossroads: I could go back to my eating disorder or continue my recovery. I chose life. I knew this decision could jeopardize my dance career, but coming face-to-face with a potentially debilitating illness helped me to see that my health was more important than anything else.

A shock that changes one's perspective is sometimes a much-needed thing.

Saying No

My eating disorder therapist suggested that I work on softening my steady stream of self-critique. This critique was not really my voice, but a repetition of the messages I received as a dancer. If I was going to recover, I had to find my own voice. What would my voice say? I wasn't sure I was ready to find out. Most of my life I had conformed to the "good girl" image. The thought of speaking my truth set off internal alarm bells because it ventured outside of this role.

My therapist suggested that I scream into a pillow to get out all the frustration that had built up from years of trying to reach for an impossible ideal. I tried to do this for several months, but always stopped short, my voice stuck in my throat. I described to my therapist how it felt as if I was standing frozen with terror on the end of a high diving board.

She asked me to imagine jumping off the high diving board over the next week.

"Visualize it all," she said. "The fear, the shakiness, and the sweaty palms. Visualize having the courage to jump. Then feel the air pass over your body and the water splash against your skin. Visualize coming up out of the water and being okay."

I did my homework, and the next week she had me do the visualization again, in her office. This time, however, as I imagined jumping, she wanted me to let out a scream. As I jumped in my mind, I overrode my "good girl" conditioning and screamed an animalistic "NO!"

That "no" represented all the no's I had never said.

Intervention

After a year in therapy, I reduced my binging and purging, but was still unable to stop completely. My therapist suggested that next time I felt the urge to binge and purge, I should call her and leave a message letting her know my plans. She went on to say that I should then go ahead and do my binging and purging anyway.

The day the urge to binge overtook me, I called as instructed and proceeded with my ritual. It wasn't the same! It didn't satisfy me. Letting someone into my secret ritual took away its power. It was like revealing I had a secret lover. With the intrigue of sneaking around gone, I realized I did not even like this lover. Allowing my therapist into my secret world enabled me to see the binge/purge cycle from the outside, instead of just getting caught up in it. From this new view, eating lots of food and then making myself puke seemed like a useless thing to do.

I never binged and purged again.

Recovery Has Repercussions

I spoke with the National Ballet Company, telling them I was in recovery from an eating disorder and might gain weight, but I would try to get back to my performance weight as soon as possible. Shortly after this, the company went on tour to Washington, DC. After we returned, the artistic director told me I had been far too fat to appear onstage during these performances, but because there were so many injured dancers, they were forced to keep me in the performance line-up. As a result of this, he informed me, I had embarrassed the entire nation of Canada on the international stage!

Five weeks later, they fired me.

I had feared that my recovery might put my job at risk, but the reality of it actually happening was still a shock. I felt like Eve being cast out of paradise for eating too many apples. I was being thrown out of a world I had tried to fit myself into for the past fifteen years. I felt shame that my body size was an embarrassment and grief at the loss of my job, but there was also a sense of relief. The Dragon had released me.

The Habit of Thought

The first thing I did with my newly acquired freedom was to stop dieting. Yet my obsessive thoughts about food still ran though my head continuously. I could not even listen to a friend talk because I was so busy counting calories, planning what I would eat, or chastising myself for eating too much. I lacked presence in life because 90 percent of my brain was busy dieting, even though I was no longer trying to lose weight. There was a safety in these obsessive thoughts; they protected me from the inherent risks of truly engaging in life.

I had a vague feeling of having done something like this to myself before. Then it hit me. My obsessive dieting thoughts were similar to the voices and obsessive compulsive rituals I experienced when I was twelve. If I had been able to silence them before, surely I could do it again. I used the same tactic as before. Every time my presence slipped away into diet la-la land, I would wipe the obsessive thought away and think of something else more productive. Gradually, there was more and more of myself available to focus on doing life-invigorating things.

Today, obsessive thoughts about dieting still surface, but instead of taking up 90 percent of my thought space, they take up about 5 percent. They also now run at such a quiet level that even when they surface, I hardly hear them. They tend to visit during times of stress. It's my "old" way of trying to control my world in order to deal with the chaos of life. Now, rather than seeing the obsessive thoughts as an indicator that I need to diet, I see them as an old friend who has come to help out. I say to this old friend: "sit down at the table with me and let me tell you of other ways to deal with this crazy life."

A New Type of Beauty

I still needed to dance, but I wanted to find dance forms other than ballet. As part of my search, I began to participate in dance improvisation workshops. The people in the classes were mostly untrained dancers, who focused on expression and internal body rhythm rather than technical proficiency. I attended my first workshop with the snobby attitude of a professional ballerina, thinking I was the only one in the room who had the ability to dance.

As I watched people move, however, I was humbled. There was no technique, no perfected form. In its place was unfiltered expression. In that moment, I realized that beauty in dance did not require technique or the perfect body. An honest presence of body and soul in movement were all that was needed.

In my work as a choreographer, I hire dancers of all sizes, shapes, dance styles, and levels of training. I like to see myself as an ambassador who helps people see beauty in the unique and "imperfect" nature of each individual.

In the studio, I will often give dancers tasks that are seemingly impossible. They will, as professional dancers do, work on it until it is perfect. They will show me and I will say, "No, no, no. It's too perfect. Too in unison . . . too technical . . . too comfortable . . . too good." I get upset because they look too perfect, and perfection doesn't properly express our messy human nature.

I will send them back to work and say, "Try to move in unison, but do so imperfectly . . . use your technique, but always let there be cracks in it so you do not hide behind a wall of perfection."

The Need to Tell My Story

A few months after leaving the National Ballet Company, I choreographed a solo dance work inspired by my descent into and recovery from bulimia. To create this piece, I had to overcome the disease's tendency for secretive behaviour. I designed an empty mirror frame that I danced on, through, and around. I wore *pointe* shoes, glued to clunky bathroom scales, and created monologues that told my story of strug-

gle against body-image expectations. During the solitary creative process, I discovered a new internal strength: a creative drive that super-
seded the "timid me." There was no intention to please, only a wish for
truth. In the studio, on my bike, or at home doing dishes, I was in a
state of reverie as I acted out my solo in my mind. When I fell out of
this trance, the "timid me" imagined being shamed and ridiculed for
the subject of the piece. So great was the need to tell my story, however, that I could not stop.

The plan for the end of the dance involved me stripping down naked
in near darkness and then running off stage. On opening night, I took
off my clothes as planned, but the light got brighter instead of fading,
revealing my naked body to everyone watching.

"What the hell happened to my lights?" I asked my lighting designer after the show.

"Ah," he said, "I changed them! It has greater impact this way. It was-
n't right for the piece to end with you still in hiding."

Many of my ballet friends came to see the show and broke down crying as they watched. It was not just my story; it was also their story. I
forgave my lighting designer for the brightly-lit ending when I read the
following review: "In the final hymn of freedom . . . Rea revealed her
beautiful naked body, more lush than the world of ballet would allow,
and made her run to a new life."[3]

My eating disorder piece took me so far out of my usual state of being that I couldn't understand and assimilate the experience in the context of how I saw myself. Who was this beautiful and powerful woman
who could speak out against oppression and suffering with bravery and
grace? It certainly didn't feel like me. I was going to have to meet *her*
many more times before I could accept that she was me.

Choosing a New Path

As part of my recovery, my eating disorder therapist coaxed me into
doing some expressive arts in our sessions. As well, my experience creating and performing my eating disorder solo instilled faith that the arts
could be a form of therapy. I was intrigued enough to consider training
in this field, but I was not sure if I wanted to be a therapist. How could
I help others when I had recently been so "messed up" myself? Never-
theless, I enrolled in a three-year Expressive Arts Therapy training program because it allowed me to indulge in my passion for the arts and

gave me the opportunity to regroup. After having had such a strong direction for the past fifteen years, I was frightened to be without one. Expressive arts gave me something to hold onto as I let ballet recede into my past.

As part of my training, I was required to explore visual art, poetry, drama, and music. Due to my lack of experience in these art forms, I had low self-expectations, which fostered freedom from self-critique. While I had cared about being a great dancer, I didn't care how well I wrote, acted, sang, or painted.

In my previous career as a ballet dancer, the extreme roles and behaviours expected of me were externally defined, even to the point of regulating my body to an outside ideal. In my expressive arts training, expression came from within and was not judged. This freedom was exhilarating, though the lack of structure was frightening. Being accustomed to strict, pre-determined boundaries, I had no practice in navigating my classmate's free-flowing emotional expression. I frequently felt overwhelmed in the midst of such expressive freedom. I was facing the challenge of becoming my own person.

Not Letting Go of My Passion

During the first year of expressive arts training, the ballet director who had hired me fresh out of school – the one who didn't mind womanly curves in his dancers – asked to me to work with him again. I told him I could not because I was quitting dance forever. He said, "I know something about you that you don't yet know about yourself. You're like me: your love of dance is part of your being; it's in your cells. And just as you can't live without breath, you cannot leave dance. You might need to say you're quitting, but I don't believe it."

He was right. I could not turn away from this love. After only one year in the program, I left expressive arts therapy training. Rather than return to the ballet world, I chose to become a modern dancer. I felt the expressive, more natural style of modern dance was better suited to my body and personality. It was a relief to leave my therapist training. I felt overwhelmed by the challenge of knowing myself and others so deeply. I still had more growing up to do before I would be ready for such a career.

I decided to pursue work in Europe. After a gruelling two-month audition tour that included thirty dance companies, however, I returned to Toronto with only a few francs in my pocket and no job offers. In desperate need of money, I took a job serving snacks at the YMCA. I will always remember that one rainy afternoon when I stood in the steaming kitchen, a ladle of soup in one hand and a phone in the other. "A dancer is injured and they want you to fly to Innsbruck tomorrow to start work."

The next day, I was a modern dancer in a large state-run Austrian theatre that included performance artists of various disciplines (dance, opera, music, theatre, and visual arts) working under the same roof. This was very different from North America, where the artistic disciplines tended to be separate entities dispersed across a city, all competing for survival. In Austria, I was part of a multidisciplinary artistic community that worked together as a whole and thrived because it was so highly valued. My butcher, my doctor, and even the checkout clerks at the grocery store were all interested in my dance career and attended my performances. Audiences cared so passionately about the arts that during shows they would cheer loudly when pleased and boo when dissatisfied. As I rode the rickety old theatre elevators every day, I would hear a wisp of a song, a snippet of dialogue, or a flow of notes as I passed by each floor. The hustle and bustle of a healthy arts community was glorious to behold.

Practicing New Ways of Being

I found freedom in moving to a city where no one had preconceived ideas about who I was. In Toronto, I was typecast as a demure, graceful dancer. I was changing, though, and this image no longer matched me. Without any preconceptions, the Austrian dance company saw me as a "powerhouse" and cast me in commanding roles. My company in Austria, allowed enabled men and women to play more diversified gender roles. I found myself being fitted for a man's suit many times in costume fittings. I threw myself into roles that required me to be authoritative, bitchy, masculine, or sensuous. Asserting myself on stage became practice for asserting myself in everyday life.

There Is Nothing Wrong with Me

The women in the Innsbruck dance company, including me, were a healthy range of body sizes and shapes and were never pressured to diet until a former ballerina of the Vienna Opera took over the company. The week she arrived, she called the female dancers into her office and told us we were all fat and had to drop weight for the upcoming premiere. In my former world, when a director told you to lose weight, you did it quickly without question in order to keep your job. After the meeting, I sat slumped in my dressing room chair, my chest caving in with a familiar sense of shame. I began to plan the details of a restrictive diet. Around me, my colleagues started to make jokes about the director being so skinny and how she wanted us to look like her. This was a new approach: laugh at her instead of being scared. Then it hit me: there was nothing wrong with me. There was something wrong with her. I didn't need to do anything.

"She's crazy," one coworker announced. "The best thing we can do is to make a pact that none of us will diet. What can she do, fire all of us?"

In solidarity, we agreed. On the night of the premiere, our director told us how good we looked onstage because of our dieting. We had not lost a pound! I believe we looked beautiful because we were being ourselves, gloriously and unapologetically. She mistook this confidence for weight loss, because the "measure of skinny" was the only paradigm through which she understood beauty.

Sensory Living

I used my time in Europe to let loose, have fun, and fully indulge in the European lifestyle, with its delights of food, wine, and time with friends. I rented an apartment in a castle with a window overlooking an elegant courtyard. I rode my bike to work every morning, breathed in the clean air, and basked in the splendor of the Austrian Alps.

My friends treated authority and the pressure to fulfill social norms with a healthy dose of irreverence. I took part in escapades that I would never have dreamed of in Toronto. We dined and dashed, we snuck into private pools to go swimming, and we partied into the night without thinking about the next day. The social setting was so relaxed; plans and activities emerged out of spontaneous desires. This was in direct contrast to my North American big city life, where everything was planned well in advance. After so many years of having a Spartan work ethic and wasting time on binging, purging, and counting calories, I was finally learning to play, have fun, and indulge my senses. Sitting on the window ledge in my castle room, the texture of the well-worn wood beneath my legs, hearing the sounds of the church bells and smelling the snow on the mountains made me feel alive. A new world beckoned.

"Listening" with My Body

One day a friend knocked on my apartment door.

"Our car is just outside," she said. "We have one extra seat and we are heading to a retreat on the mountain."

These were my non-dance friends, who were always inviting me to weird hippie-style retreats, and I always pretended that I was busy. I was about to tell them that I had plans, but then a new spontaneity overtook me and I surprised myself by saying yes. I stepped into the unknown and took a seat in their car. The unknown in this case was contact dance, a form of improvised dance based on martial arts, in which physical momentum is used to create dance movements between two people. I entered a studio full of dancers, some professional and some hobby dancers, with hesitation. At first I was confused. There did not seem to be any set steps or even a particular aesthetic they were going for. As the workshop progressed, I realized there was an aim – to attune one's body to the motion of another and see what happened. This *listening* to my own movement and the movement of another enlivened my senses. I was dancing purely from my intuition, rather than trying to become something I was not. Analytical thought receded as I surrendered to awareness. Self-critique disappeared. I was finally free.

Pain as a Guide

Ironically, I found freedom in dance just as my joints started to say no to my dance career. Years of repetitive motions had taken their toll.

"You have cartilage damage in your knees," my doctor said. "It's permanent, and you shouldn't dance anymore. There just isn't enough cartilage left."

In the moments that followed his proclamation, everything was suddenly so pronounced. The sheen of the light board that held my X-rays. The tone of the doctor's voice, very matter-of-fact and slow. The hum of the overhead fluorescent lights as the doctor turned them back on. The way he stood up and left, closing the door behind him. The world moved in slow motion as a huge shift in identity hit me fast. I tried to comprehend this new information: this was not an injury that was going to get better. After torn ligaments and muscles, tendonitis, and bruises, all of which had healed, I had finally come up against my stop-point. My dance career was coming to an end.

Letting Go

An hour after returning from my life-changing doctor's appointment, I re-enrolled in expressive arts therapy training. Once again, it was something to hold on to. I resigned from my dance job in Austria and said goodbye to my European dance career, the friends I had made, my castle apartment, and the smell of snow on the mountains. I packed up my belongings and moved back home to Canada.

With virtually no job skills, I found a minimum-wage job at a large bookstore, where I picked up and reshelved books in alphabetical order. The greatest thing I got out of this job was learning that I was probably dyslexic. A few years later I was tested and found out I did, in fact, have such a learning disability. After dancing in a vibrant European theatre, my next job was filing books while not being able to keep track of alphabetical order. Looking back, this contrast is funny to me; at the time, it was devastating. I remember crying many a time in the Home and Garden section, somewhere between M and those confusing XYZs. That section induced the most tears because without my dance career, I felt like I had lost my home.

My self-esteem took another blow when, after having lived on my own for ten years, I was forced to move into my parents' basement due to financial constraints. The contrast between the vital, artistic life I left in Europe and my anonymous life in Toronto was extreme. My dance career had made me feel like a somebody; without it, I felt like a nobody.

Many dancers do not make it through the transition from career dancer to regular citizen. When all you know is dance, you do not know yourself in any other way. Many former dancers succumb to drugs or alcohol, or even kill themselves out of grief. So many do this, in fact, that an entire center was set up in Toronto to help them transition. This center gave me counselling and paid for one-third of my expressive arts school tuition. The great irony is that the Dragon Lady (yes, the one who wanted to see bones) was running the center at the time. It was she whom I had to consult for career advice and who gave the stamp of approval on my schooling grants. In this context, she was actually very nice to me and no longer required that I be deathly thin. I think she realized that looking anorexic was not exactly good advertising for a therapist. I was surprised to discover goodness in someone I had once so strongly vilified.

With the Dragon Lady's help, I asked myself: what is left when my body doesn't work? What is left when I lose my livelihood? What is left when I lose all that I have known?

Even though most days I felt lost and without an identity, I began to get an inkling of a different awareness: with everything stripped out of my life, I had a sense that what was left behind was my essence – the thing that stayed intact regardless of what else changed around it. With everything else disintegrating, I became aware of this fixed center. The person I thought I was fell away, and this left room for me to meet who I really was.

Thank goodness that my expressive arts training was there to hold on to while I took these uncertain steps. At the start of each class we had check-ins, where we would say how we were doing in the most honest way possible. It was a place to be, without apology. We were all in transition, shifting into our new identity of *therapist.* I was comforted by our shared experience. My grief was also soothed by letting myself get lost in the creation of paintings, sculptures, or poems.

Altered Reality

I booked double knee surgery with a well-known surgeon who operated on elite athletes. A long wait list meant that I had a year before going under the knife, but I didn't mind, because I needed to get some dancing in while I still could. The little cartilage I had left did allow me to dance, albeit in pain, for a few hours a day. I promised myself I would take care of my knees after surgery so that I wouldn't injure them further, but I saw the time before going under the knife as an opportunity to push through pain to fulfill my dream of doing a one-woman show.

A friend told me of how she was bedridden with pneumonia, so was unable to save her favourite tree from being cut down by her landlord. I decided to use this story as inspiration for a solo. I worked secluded in the dance studio for hours on end; so intense was my process that at times I entered a state of consciousness where I seemed to feel my body on a cellular level. I felt movements and shifts in the layers of my muscle tissues, oxygen flowing through my blood, my heart pounding.

My secluded creative process was a "glorious madness" that drew me into its thrall. Swept up, I pounded my body to its limits. When my piece premiered, whether a result of my intense and painful creative period or just bad luck, I was sick with a high fever that turned out to be mononucleosis. The piece had a vocal component that consisted of restricting my breath. The line between reality and performance blurred as I fought for breath both in real life and as part of the choreography. In my fevered state, my skin felt transparent. I believed that the audience could see inside me because I was too weak to put up a defense. Performing while I was so sick was stupid and dangerous, but I was so caught up in getting my last dance in that I disregarded common sense.

As I lay in bed for the next few months recovering from my illness, my emotions were fluid; I alternated between tears and peace. I didn't have the strength to repress my feelings, and would just ride their flow. My whole life, I had pushed myself to achieve; now I was so weak all I could do was follow the current. After so many years of hard work, it was like floating on the gentle undulation of ocean waves.

Love

I spent the end of my convalescence at my family cottage in northern Ontario. My friend put a mattress on the covered deck so that I could sleep in the shade during the day and still enjoy the outdoors. One day, while I was dozing, a wasp flew up the sleeve of my pajamas and stung me on the chest.

My hands and feet immediately started to burn as if they were on fire and I jumped up, took a few steps, and collapsed. As I drifted in and out of consciousness, I became filled with a sense of peace and joy that replaced the initial shock of the sting. I heard the commotion of my friend running for help, trying to drag me into her car, and giving me mouth to mouth resuscitation, but this all seemed distant. I felt so happy.

I thought, "This dying thing isn't so bad. I could go right now and it would be okay."

I opened my eyes. From the spot in the forest clearing where I lay, I could see tree branches swaying in the wind. Within the rustle of the leaves, I heard laughter.

"Ah, angels," I mused as I floated up towards them.

As I continued to approach, I realized that they were so beside themselves with giggles that they could hardly speak.

I asked persistently, "What's so funny?"

Finally, one angel composed herself enough to speak.

"We've been trying to send you a message for so long, and it's such a simple thing, really. It's so easy for us to understand. So easy for us to do. We giggle because we can't fathom why it's so hard for you. So hard for humankind."

"What is the message?" I asked.

I sensed I was being pulled away from them, so I asked again, with urgency, "What's the message? I need to know before I go back!"

"The message is that you just need to love yourself. All of yourself. The good and the bad. It's really that simple."

Their voices faded into wind as they said, "This is your chance to get it right!"

I felt a tug, a pull, and a crash. I hit the ground like a falling meteor. The shock of being back in my body caused me to pee my pants. My head rested in my friend's lap.

"Don't worry . . . I'm back," I said to her. I heard the paramedics arrive. The first lesson in loving myself completely turned out to be dealing with the shame of having peed my pants!

Soon after my near-death experience, I came across the following passage in Bob Trowbridge's book, *The Hidden Meaning of Illness*:

> Some of those who have had near-death experiences perceive God energy or the energy that they meet as light. Some describe it as love. If we think of the spirit flowing through mind to connect to the physical, we can think of that spirit as love. Whatever spirit-suppression devices we have are suppressing love. If we remove those devices, love can create miracles. That which is the greatest suppressor of love is fear. Love and fear cannot occupy the same space. . . . Overcoming fear and moving towards love means changing our beliefs and attitudes so that we can give up false protection, remove armour, and knock down the walls of our fortress. Love makes us vulnerable . . . [yet] one of the great paradoxes of love is that the more vulnerable we are, the safer we are.[4]

In my ballet career, I was taught that beauty and success came from whipping oneself into top form and that pain was a means to an end.

The end goal was never reachable, however, because it involved an absolute perfection that was not possible, so I never felt wholly satisfied. When I heard the angels laugh, I felt loved so completely that every part of my being was satisfied.

After my near-death experience, I did not find self-acceptance completely. What followed and still follows is a *process* of learning to love myself.

A few months after my near-death experience, I choreographed a full-length modern ballet with ten dancers. The memory of the angels' love helped me see my choreography in a new way: I let go of my usual critical attitude and became totally enraptured with the dancers and the piece I was creating. During the premiere I sat in the audience, admiring the different nuances that came with each dancer. The piece was a living, breathing, ever-changing entity for which I felt unconditional love. This love was not some ego-driven state that blinded me from seeing the piece's weaknesses; I could see it was not perfect, and I loved it anyway. This sense of love did not thwart my drive to improve my craft. It helped me see how my choreographic work could be fostered, like a child.

The Vulnerable Human Body

I worked the entire day before my double knee surgery, dancing in a film that involved a gruelling fourteen-hour shoot. We were filming outdoors and were unlucky with weather. As thunder rumbled around us, the director said, "Let's wrap up and continue the shoot tomorrow." I had to keep reminding everyone that there would be no dancing for me tomorrow. I did not mind the long hours, the wind, or how the cold made my knees ache, because all these things kept my pre-surgery anxiety at bay.

The next day, surgery preparation involved stripping down to the bare minimum: no make-up, no glasses, no clothing.

"Why no underwear?" I asked. "You guys are operating on my knees, aren't you?"

"No underwear for all surgeries from the waist down," decreed the nurse.

I climbed on the table and the nurses stretched out and tied down my arms. They then put blow-up tourniquets on both legs; as they inflated, my underwear-less legs spread apart. My surgeon walked into the room and started to make social chit-chat.

I was worried he did not remember I was a dancer, so I blurted out, "I used to dance with the National Ballet Company. You've operated on many of my colleagues."

"Oh, you're a dancer?" he asked as he scanned the various monitors around the table.

I began to recite all the ballets I had danced, trying to let him know the extent of my career. I desperately wanted him to see me as a "somebody," not just another patient. The anesthetic cut me off halfway through my list.

Many hours later, through a drugged haze, I heard my doctor telling me how the surgery went, but I couldn't concentrate on what he was saying. I fought towards awareness in time to hear him to say, "It was really bad in there. Your cartilage is rubbed down to the bone. I did the best I could, but it will not be enough. Your dance career is over."

My drug-addled brain thought only one thing: "Oh, thank God. I can finally let go. The war on my body is over!"

And with this relieving thought, I went back to sleep.

Synesthesia

I was in a room full of expressive arts trainees when I first noticed it. We were dancing together and suddenly my senses became heightened. Sounds were amplified. I felt air pass over my skin as I moved. Then I noticed that each person in the room had their own "hum": a silent note or vibration made up of a series of harmonies that created their own unique hum. The frequency of each person's body-hum had some elements that stayed the same and others that changed according to shifts in their emotions. Once I could make out a person's hum, I was flooded with images: a bird flying over a corn field, a young girl standing alone in a clearing, a fire in a cavern. These images were like metaphors that gave me a sense of each person.

At times, this heightened awareness felt similar to madness, because I could not understand it in the context of my literal world. After my childhood psychosis, I guarded myself against any thoughts or feelings that weren't based in reality. My near-death experience had been crazy, but I did not let this concern me because it was an isolated event that could be blamed on the effect of wasp venom and a lack of oxygen. Sensing the hum of the people in my class, however, disturbed me because it was a crazy thing that had made its way into my everyday life.

A few weeks later, also in a group dance exercise, I experienced a creative energy that felt infinite. It was like the hum of everyone in the room, maybe even everyone in the world, came together to form one hum. It was the world's hum.

These experiences were a perplexing anomaly that I gradually grew more comfortable with. I noticed that I could feel a person's hum only when in a state of "being in the moment," with no thought of the past or future. This state of grace also involved a deeply felt appreciation and acceptance of others. In this state, the sum of me and those I worked with was greater than each of us, as our energies seemed to play off each other.

Eventually, I began to see the hum as simply a way I sensed and collected information about the world. It also became useful in my work as a choreographer and therapist. As a therapist, this hum helped me attune to others. As a choreographer, the images and sensations that accompanied the hum were creative inspiration.

Synesthesia is a neurologically-based condition, thought to affect as many as one in twenty-three, in which stimulation of one sensory or cognitive pathway leads to automatic, involuntary experiences in a another sensory or cognitive pathway. People who report such experiences are known as synesthetes. An example of a synesthete is Evelyn Glennie, a famous deaf percussionist who sees colours when she *listens* to music. Another recently identified type of synesthesia involves hearing sounds in response to visual motion. This form of synesthesia is called visual-motion-to-sound synesthesia and possibly explains the phenomena of the hum I experience.[5, 6]

The Body Knows

I was on the road back to the wild and mystical swan girl I used to be, but there was still tightness around my heart that I could not let go of. My family had many secrets. Bad things had happened; people were too ashamed to ever tell anyone, so they kept those things secret. These secrets lived in our family's house – sensed by all, at some unconscious level, but never referred to. Our house was a weaving of untold stories, kept tightly protected in the name of preservation. I was part of this weaving, playing my role, having my secrets, not knowing how to unwind myself. Then something remarkable happened.

One of the "secret keepers" found the bravery to tell his story, which became the catalyst to unravel many other secrets as family members started to tell their truths. I learned that sexual abuse traumas, kept secret in the older generation, had reoccurred in my generation. I had so many questions. Had the younger generation unconsciously arranged their lives to experience the same trauma and then kept the same secrets? Was the experience unconsciously passed down from one generation to the next? I marvelled at humankind's tendency to unconsciously move to the familiar, even if it is harmful. I began to understand the innate human desire to repeat conflicts in the hope of creating an opportunity for redemption.

The days following the disclosures were unsteady for me. Everything I thought I knew about myself and my family had changed. Even though the changes were for the better, the ground I stood upon felt like it was moving. One morning, I lay in a hot bath in my parents' house, exhausted from the flow of emotions. As I stood up, I fainted and hit the back of my head on the toilet tank. When I regained consciousness a few seconds later, I was fine except for the bump on my head. I left the house without knowing that I had caused a hairline fracture in the porcelain toilet tank. A few hours later, the fracture cracked wide open and gushed water for ten hours. I flooded all three floors of my family house. I was awestruck by the idea that just as my family had metaphorically washed itself of its secrets, I had managed to accidentally wash the family home.

My family's secret-keeping caused me to reflect on my body's reaction to my family story. In secret-keeping, I tended to favour restricted postures, such as a tense chest and throat. It was as if my body had the job of physically holding the secrets. Once the secrets were told, I had a much greater capacity to breathe and move. While some of the secrets that were revealed were ones I had been keeping, others were secrets I had not been aware of. Even though I didn't know those secrets existed, I realized once they were told that my body had known. I had intuition and gut feelings that manifested as subtle physical reactions like holding my breath whenever certain subjects were broached. My body had been reacting to the hum of family trauma without me even being consciously aware of it. The night my family told their stories, it was as if my lungs sighed with relief, saying, "Yes, that's what I knew, but I had no words to explain it."

I learned that the truth lives in our bodies.

Trust

I couldn't dance full-time any more or earn my living as a dancer, but I could still do contact dance improvisation because it allowed me to practice listening to my body's signals and find ways of dancing that did not aggravate my knees. I discovered that Toronto had a vibrant contact dance scene and began participating in weekly dance jams. I wasn't always successful in dancing pain free – sometimes my desire to dance overrode my limitations and I would limp out of the studio with sore knees. Eventually, I was able to improvise within my body's limits, with relatively little pain. I didn't feel the same excitement as when I used to leap around the stage with technical perfection, but I began to feel a different type of satisfaction, which came from an attentive and intimate awareness of my body.

I also became interested in the relational aspects of dance. When I moved with a partner, I was invigorated by the challenge of maintaining physical and emotional contact. I discovered that dancing in an emotionally-closed state diminished my ability to follow the movement of another, while emotional openness expanded this ability. An improvised dance can never be repeated, thus the dance jams were a rich practice in letting go of each moment so that I could surrender to the new moment arriving. This surrender was practice in placing trust in myself and others.

Gentle Transformation

My favourite teacher from my expressive arts master's degree studies was a man who taught from his heart. He was wise and stern and an artist in his own right. He could hear the most troubling story of hardship and woe and, rather than retreat, step in closer to offer support. As we students expressed our sorrows through the arts, his heart stretched big enough to be with all of us.

One day he approached me.

"All your transformations are very well and fine," he said, "but each was achieved through a catastrophic event or by the tenacity of your will. Did you ever think that you don't need to get fired or almost die or flood your house in order to transform?"

He spoke to me of a transformation that was slow, gentle, and attentive – transformation that was based upon love and compassion.

"With those knees of yours," he told me, "you cannot even run anymore. It's time to stop chasing everything and let things come to you, instead. Don't be a moth fluttering too close to the flame. Fly back and let the light warm your body, not burn it."

Many years later, I heard rumors that he struggled with alcohol addiction. I had noticed that he occasionally drank heavily and I wonder whether his advice to me came from a personal understanding of the dangers of flying too close to the flame? Just as those we vilify are not all bad inside, those we idealize are also a mix of positive attributes and flaws. Those with the gift of a deep heart sometimes do not know how to carry the burden of their gift. I decided I would not become a casualty of my deep heart. I would learn to fly in the warmth of the fire instead of getting burned by it.

Arriving Home

While I studied expressive arts therapy, I never admitted to myself that I wanted to be a therapist. I really enjoyed the courses and worked hard at my studies, but I was unsure about whether or not I could actually do the job. I wondered if my sensitivities to life would overwhelm me, and if I was ready to take on the responsibility of being a guide to others. I worried about the challenges of balancing my artistic pursuits with my life as a therapist. I even wondered if taking on the role of a therapist might somehow damage my ability to choreograph. If I opened my heart to help others, would it soften my creative edge?

There was a gentle, yet persistent calling within me to use my knowledge and expertise to guide others, however. It wasn't like my calling to dance, which from a very young age felt like a bullet constantly speeding through me. My calling to be a therapist was different: it was a soft voice that I had to lean into in order to hear.

Upon graduating from my studies, I received a call from a woman who wanted to work with me. I thought, "Well, it would be silly to refuse her. After all, she wants to work with me."

She was soon followed by other clients, and thus began my practice.

A few months later, I remember sitting in my chair listening to a client describe an interaction she had had with a friend.

She said, "I told my friend that my therapist had said . . ."

As she was completing her sentence I thought to myself, "I wonder who her therapist is?" And then . . . Boom! It hit me, like a weight dropping onto my body. She was referring to me! I was her therapist.

I have been a therapist ever since.

Chapter 2

A MAP OF HUMAN EXPERIENCE

Allen

A man rounds the corner. As he approaches my studio, I notice his imposing silhouette. I open the door and he steps inside, his arm trembling as he reaches out to shake my hand. His large size catches me off guard at first, but up close I see he is just a person, like you or me, who is searching for answers.

"Hi," he says, "I'm Allen."

My inner voice cheers for his bravery. I know how hard it is to round that corner and reach out a hand. He sits down and begins to tell me about himself. As I settle into my chair, my professional training and practice, combined with my personal life experiences, all sit with me. They form my understanding of humanity. They are my "ground."

In this chapter, I will tell the story of Allen's initial steps into expressive arts therapy, but first I will describe the influences that form my ground.

INFLUENCES THAT FORM MY GROUND

Thirty years of dance training and performance taught me that my body is a source of wisdom. Rather than "think" my way through a performance, I learned to quiet my mind and let my body take the lead. When I did so, I discovered enhanced abilities: I understood the rhythm of the music more intuitively, my movements felt evocative, and feelings and images arose from sensation, feeding my artistic expression. When in this dance trance, I often finished performances not fully aware of what had occurred, but with a sense of having taken a journey that was highly satisfying. These experiences did not just happen within me. They reached out into the world and connected me with the audience more completely.

As a dancer, I learned to follow the rhythm and instincts of my body. As a teacher and choreographer, I wanted to share this knowledge with others. I did not want dancers to be soul-less arms and legs moving in intricate steps. I wanted them to feel truly alive in their bodies, and to transmit this liveliness to the audience. Many believe such vibrant stage presence cannot be taught. They see it as indefinable, something that one must be born with. I believe we all have the ability to shine, and that accessing and following our body-based intuition awakens this ability. I began to ask dancers to perform steps "messier" so cracks would open in their technique, allowing their human nature to emerge. Working with highly trained dancers in this manner felt dangerous, because it pushed against the perfected ideals of the professional dance world. I borrowed exercises from expressive arts and improvisation-based theatre that helped dancers surrender to their body instincts. I experimented with using images and metaphors to inspire movement, opening up the power of the imagination to enliven the body.

At first, I made detailed choreographic and teaching plans. As I helped dancers trust and follow their bodies from moment to moment, I began to trust myself as a teacher and choreographer in the same way. I began to devise class structures and exercises spontaneously. I would arrive in the studio, get a sense of the dancers, and, without knowing where I was heading or why, I would begin. Trusting my intuition like that was a humbling experience. I could never grab onto what I thought I knew, but instead followed a knowing that arrived with each breath. I discovered that following intuition led to dance that was more sensitive, honest, and dynamic than my thinking brain could create.

During my expressive arts therapy studies, I realized that my experience as a professional dancer influenced who I was as a therapist. I discovered that when I followed the lead of my body, I gained a clearer understanding of therapeutic dynamics. My body felt like a satellite dish that was collecting information. Sympathetic body shifts such as changes in my muscle tension and breath gave me valuable insight into the emotional world of both myself and my client. Sensations such as tightness in my chest, heaviness in my heart, or a desire to fidget became physical clues that informed me as a therapist.

Reflection upon my personal life also helped me understand the role my body played as a guide. When I was a young girl dancing alone in my living room, I was at home in my body. Although I later tore myself apart trying to achieve the perfect ballet body, a part of me never forgot how alive I felt in those living room dances. The chaotic behaviour of bulimia was a cry against ballet's perfected ideals, an uncontrollable body-based wisdom asserting its need to be heard. Eventually, I walked the road home and learned to be at peace with my body. Both successes and failures were teachers throughout my work of coming home. I now know something about this road; my work now is to be a guide for others trying to find their road home. All guides need a "map" that helps them help others find their way. The map I use was created through a mixture of resources, both professional and personal. It formed over the past ten years as I gained experience as a therapist. There are three parts to it:

1. Body-Based Wisdom
2. The Self in Relationship to the World
3. Wellness and Dysfunction.

MY MAP
PART ONE: BODY-BASED WISDOM

My sense of body-based wisdom originates in common gestures and actions. It is not just me that craves to know my body-home; we all unconsciously call ourselves home through our movements. When feeling loving emotions, we frequently reach for our heart. A hand on the stomach and a queasy look often accompany the statement, "I have a bad feeling about this" – it is a "gut" feeling literally arising from one's belly. Even if we are out of practice, our legs seem to remember how to ride a bicycle as if they had a memory and intelligence all their own. A person will slap his head when an idea comes to him, indicating that ideas are "up in our heads." I remember a commercial for a hospital fundraiser in which people receiving bad news from their doctors were hit by a wave of air that knocked them off their chairs in slow motion to demonstrate how a life-threatening diagnosis can feel like a strong hit to the chest.

Not only actions fill in the "body-home" map; colloquial sayings and clichés do so, as well: her spirits were "lifted," his heart was "crushed," she "lost her ground" in the argument, she was so surprised it "knocked her socks off," an idea "struck" him, they "fell" in love, she "felt butterflies" in her stomach, there was "a frog in his throat."

These gestures and sayings portray our bodies as wise tellers of our personal stories. This pushes against traditional Western understanding, which exclusively values wisdom that arrives through intellectual thought: influential seventeenth century philosopher René Descartes believed that mental phenomena (thoughts and consciousness) were of greater value and separate from the trivial nature of the body.[7] This belief is often referred to as the mind/body split. Hundreds of years following Descartes, science began to understand the brain as the generator of thoughts and the control center for the body through the study of brain injuries and advances in surgery. When technology for scanning the brain was invented, scientists were able to map out areas activated during specific experiences. For example, the limbic part of the brain is active during emotional responses and the frontal region of the brain is active during problem solving.[8]

As we better understood the brain's role, mental phenomena were no longer believed to exist outside our bodies, but to arise from our heads. While consciousness was now seen to live within us, Western society still minimized the role of the body from the head down. A new divide was seen to exist between the brain, where mental phenomena arose, and the rest of our body, which was seen as a mindless machine activated by the brain. An educational science website explains to kids:

> [The brain] is the site of consciousness, thought and creativity! Different parts of your brain do different things. Some areas receive messages from sense organs, others control balance and muscle coordination, and still others handle speech, or emotion, memories, or basic motor skills, or complex calculations. You may think your heart is where you feel emotion, but it's really your brain. You may think your legs take you down the street, but it's your brain instructing the muscles in your legs to move. Your eyes may take in light and an image may be projected onto the pupil, but it's your brain that interprets what you see . . . you get the picture.[9]

Understanding the significant role of the brain and how it functions has enabled us to better diagnose and treat many diseases. For those who can afford it, Western medicine has nearly doubled life expectancy.

As a map of human experience, however, the traditional Western view has large gaps. It is disconnected from the ways in which we actually feel and sense life through our entire body. Telling a woman who is "falling in love" that it's all happening in her brain insufficiently describes why her heart feels like it is going to burst. When we minimize our experience of life to mechanical descriptions of function, we leave little room for dialogue about the mysteries of the human soul. The traditional medical model has forgotten that we need a language that describes the breadth of human experience. Aboriginal and shamanistic healing practices understand this human need. They focus less on the mechanics of our physiology and more on the story of people's lives. They have much to teach us about taking care of the soul/body.

There is hope for a meeting of the minds between the traditional scientific view and the ways in which we actually experience life through our bodies. Through advancing technology, neuroscience researchers have discovered neuropeptides and developed an understanding of how they function. Neuropeptides are molecules used by brain neurons to communicate with each other. One can see neuropeptides as sparks in our brains that ignite different "brain engines." There are more than a thousand different neuropeptides, including endorphins and adrenaline; each triggers a specific physiological effect.

Internal thoughts, feeling states, and emotions cue neuropeptide responses. Every time you have a thought or feeling, your body releases a corresponding neuropeptide that revs up a specific area of the brain, which then triggers a specific physiological response. An example is waking up with a sense of doom because you're pretty sure you're going to fail your driving test, which is scheduled for today. This thought causes a release of neuropeptides that make your heart race and cause you to sweat. If you have these types of stressful thoughts consistently over a long period of time, they will eventually take their toll on your body and result in stress-related health problems. Conversely, a more positive outlook will likely improve your health over time.[10, 11, 12, 13] There is also growing data from the field of psychology that further establishes the relationship between emotional stress and ill physical health. Numerous studies have linked emotional stress to depressed immune response, leaving people vulnerable to a myriad of diseases and illnesses.[14, 15]

Neuropeptides are the bridge between thoughts, emotions, and physical reality. The mind–body connection has become an established truth. Even the most conservative doctors have started to consider the multifaceted and non-linear influences of the psyche in the explanation of physical health and disease.

Since our body acts like an imprint of what is happening in our thoughts and emotions, one might think that heeding the wisdom of body sensation would be of high priority in our society. This is not the case, as most still see our thinking brains as the chief source of intelligence that guides our lives. I believe brain intelligence is just one form of body-based wisdom; there are many others centered in other areas of the body. For example, we can make decisions from our hearts, or let our legs tell us when to stand up from a chair. Some would say that it may *feel* like your body has an intelligence of its own, but these things are actually directed by your brain. However, in the 1980s, Candace Pert, then a section chief at the National Institutes of Health in the U.S., made a fascinating discovery that could explain how more than our heads might be involved. Most scientists had assumed that neuropeptides were exclusively produced by and housed in the brain. Although neuropeptides are primarily produced in the brain, Candace Pert discovered that every tissue in our body (including our muscles and organs) also produces and houses them.[16] It may be possible that our organs do not simply receive their "marching orders" from the brain, but have some type of awareness that they communicate back to our brain through neuropeptides. Yes, what I am saying is that an organ like your heart may contribute to your understanding of the world. Perhaps we do not exclusively interpret life through intellectual brain processes, but use our entire body as a "thinking brain" that helps us understand our world. Neuroscience is mapping the molecules of human consciousness, and it may in the future confirm what body-based practitioners have known all along: we interpret life through our entire body.[17, 18]

While neurobiology may provide a scientific explanation for a body-based experience of life, when I am with a client, I am more interested in focusing on the stories their body is telling them. Clients will say, "I feel like I am floating through life," or, "I feel heaviness in my heart," or, "There is a knot in my shoulders screaming at me." They will describe how they crave movement, saying, "I want to run away from it all," or, "I want to grab it by the horns." They describe images from their dreams that have physical impact: "I was standing on a mountain, looking out at the expansive view, and I breathed in the beauty," or, "I was climbing in a dark tunnel that became so narrow, my body could hardly move." I want to draw each client closer to these experiences so they can connect with their body as a source of wisdom.

Six Forms of Body Wisdom

After many years of working in this manner, I have sorted body-based experiences into six categories, each of which is concentrated in a specific "home" in our body:

- **Action** – experiencing life through movement. The home of action is the physical movement of the limbs, torso, and orifices.
- **Inner Body** – experiencing life through an internal sense of our organs, muscles, posture, and how we hold or release our breath. Shifts in our inner body are felt throughout the entire body, but often concentrate in intuitive sensations in the digestive-tract area and referred to as "gut" feelings. The home of inner body is, therefore, the gut.
- **Physiology** – experiencing life through changes in physical health. This includes the health of our organs, the wear and tear of cartilage, inflammation, and reactions to stress such as sweating, as well as more mundane physiological events such as a sense of tiredness, which lets us know it is time to go to sleep. The home of physiology is the sensation of health, ranging from vitality to illness.
- **Thought and Imagination** – experiencing life through images, sounds, and words that play out in our heads. The home of thought and imagination is, therefore, the head.
- **Emotion** – experiencing life through the range and interplay of our feelings (happiness, sadness, grief, anger, joy, jealousy, resentment, remorse, etc.). Emotions are felt throughout the body (for instance, in clenched fists when angry, or a smile when joyful), but often concentrate in sensations in the heart or chest area. The home of emotions is, therefore, the heart.
- **Spirit** – experiencing life through the energy or life-force present in oneself and in all living things. The home of spirit is the sensation of one's body energy or life force.

As with any system of categorization, it is important to not feel too bound by its structure. Although for clarity's sake, I have divided the different forms of body-based experience into distinct categories, they actually overlap and blur together. One can see how this blurring together happens in the way emotions and thoughts cue physiological changes through neuropeptides. We receive messages from the different forms of body-based experiences every minute of every day. The experience that leads us at any given moment depends on the focus of our attention rather than whichever body-based experience is "speaking out" the loudest. For instance, hugging an upset friend involves movement (*action*), but we are drawn to hug through compassion (*emotion*). Trying to solve a difficult math problem might cause one's body to become tense with concentration (*inner body*), but solving the problem is mainly an intellectual process (*thought/imagination*). Each type of experience offers its own distinct wisdom that can guide our lives. Let's examine each of these wisdoms in more detail:

1. The Wisdom of Our Actions (concentrated in the sensation of physical movement of the limbs, torso, and orifices)

Body action includes all physical actions, including moving our arms and legs, walking or running, and even kissing. Body action wisdom is challenged when we learn a new sport, dance, or exercise. The wisdom of our actions can be felt when our legs seem to decide for themselves the right moment to rise from a chair, or when one's body recalls previously acquired abilities through action, such as remembering how to ride a bike once your feet hit the pedals. In my dance career, I often thought I wouldn't be able to recall the steps of a dance, but when I heard the music, my legs would remember, on their own, the entire sequence of steps. As a therapist, I often let the wisdom of action lead me when I turn off my "thinking brain" and let my body lead in a playful dance with a client.

Different issues arise for clients when they move in a session, as opposed to sitting on the couch. They are actively engaged: they sweat, their hearts speed up, and their breathing adjusts accordingly. Instead of just talking about their lives, they are physically engaged. This helps them follow the wisdom of their actions. We naturally crave movements that are a satisfying match for our internal world. For example, if I am sad, the most satisfying movements are often those that represent my sadness. Sometimes clients feel numb and do not know how they feel. If they let themselves move spontaneously, they can gain awareness of their emotions. A woman moving freely might suddenly find herself making loud stamping sounds, and realize she is angry. Through movement, she accesses feelings she might not have noticed had she remained on the couch.

Anna Halprin, a pioneer in the therapeutic dance arts writes:

> [My] approach to teaching movement is based on the belief that when we begin to use the language of movement rather than the language of words, a different kind of image and emotion arises, which bypasses the controlling and censoring mind. Words label what we already know; expressive movement reveals the unknown. Sensations, feelings, emotions, and images that have long been buried in our bodies are revealed through movement. This is also useful for shifting old patterns, habits, and destructive belief systems.[19]

Once, a client came to me with complaints about his boss giving him an impossible workload. The client saw himself as a powerless victim, helpless in the face of his boss's unfair requests. The client and I decided to explore this issue through role-play to get a better understanding of it. I played the role of "the boss" by holding a large exercise ball and running at him, yelling, "Here is another project for you to do! I need it done by tomorrow!" while aggressively pressing the ball into his space, pushing him around the studio. As I continued to chase him, I dropped my role several times and said, "Feel what your arms want to do. Let your arms respond." Eventually, he began pressing against the ball and ended up pushing me around the studio while saying, "No, I won't!" He was surprised by how good it felt and how easy it was to do. The following week he reported that he told his boss that he was too busy to take on any new projects. His boss agreed, passing the extra work to another person. The ability to push back had been frozen inside my client; by following the wisdom of his body action, he got it flowing.

2. The Wisdom of Our Inner Body (concentrated in the gut)

The realm of the inner body includes subtle shifts in breath, muscle tone, and posture, and focuses on how body movements and our organs feel from an internal perspective. Through inner body sensations, we connect to our intuition, or "gut feelings." By intuition, I mean a sense of knowing that arrives without concrete clues (for instance, knowing something without exactly knowing why or how we know it).

When meeting a person for the first time, you might feel tightness in your gut, which makes you feel that you can't trust him or her, even though you don't understand why or how you know this.

Eugene Gendlin, a body-based psychologist, writes about the value of internal sensations in his book *Focusing*:

> So little attention has been paid to this mode of awareness that there are no ready-made words to describe it, and I have had to coin my own term: *felt-sense*. . . . A *felt-sense* is not a mental experience but a physical one. . . . [It is] a bodily awareness of a situation or person, or event. [It is] an internal aura that encompasses everything you feel and know about the given subject at a given time – encompasses it and it communicates it to you all at once rather than detail by detail.[20]

Sandra and Matthew Blakeslee, in their book *The Body Has a Mind of Its Own*, provide a neurological perspective to Eugene Gendlin's felt-sense. They describe a neural map, made up of a series of neural pathways in our brain that keeps track of all the different areas of one's body, such as legs and arms. Included in this map is an area dedicated to how one's body feels internally and, more specifically, how one's organs feel. They explain:

> [You have a] body map of all your body's innards. This is your primary visceral map, a patchwork of small neural swatches that represent your heart, lungs, liver, colon, rectum, stomach, and all your various other giblets. This map is uniquely super-developed in the human species, and it gives you a level of access to the ebb and flow of your internal sensations unequaled anywhere else in the animal kingdom. . . . These visceral inputs to the psyche are the wellspring of the rich and vivid emotional awareness that few other creatures even come close to enjoying.[21]

I once worked with a man who was frustrated with the fact that he frequently said yes to things he did not want to do. He explained that in the moment of being asked a question, such as, "Would you like to go out for lunch?" he would become bewildered. Whenever this happened, his reflex answer was "yes." This frequently led to anxiety, as later on he would realize he had really wanted to say "no." Over several sessions, he practiced being aware of his inner body sensations. One day I asked him to try an experiment: when someone requested something of him, he could say, "Can I get back to you on that?" I then asked him to spend a few minutes connecting with his inner body sensations. During this "checking-in" time, I suggested he could imagine saying "yes" and "no" and feel how his body reacted to each. He did this, and reported it had been much easier to figure out when he didn't want to do something. He said, "I noticed my stomach braces and tightens, and this lets me know it might be a good idea to say 'no thanks'."

3. The Wisdom of Our Physiology (concentrated in the sensation of health, ranging from vitality to illness)

Body physiology is the system of organs and chemicals that regulate our health. Body processes affecting our health are continually occurring and can be seen as a poetry that is expressive of our state of being. When we feel, think, and act, our bodies respond with changes in blood flow and body chemicals: the heart beats faster, the breath slows down or speeds up, we get nervous stomachs. Over time, these physiological reactions can form patterns that affect our health.

Shifts in body physiology, including illness, are a normal and unavoidable part of life. We are constantly influenced by our physiology, from the simple feeling of being tired, which informs us that we need to sleep, to the trauma of a heart attack that may be the catalyst for life change. In my case, the eroding cartilage in my knees forced me to rethink my dance career. In these ways, physical symptoms can be "tough love" teachers that push us towards new things.

If we are interpreting the wisdom of our physiologies, I don't believe it is helpful to blame people for their health problems, or to create categories of emotional disturbances that lead to certain diseases. I once read a self-help book that explained how knee problems were always a repercussion of not being able to stand up for oneself. This predetermined categorization minimized and immobilized the meaning of my knee pain. I would much rather be open to the multitude of stories my symptoms may be telling me. I consider myself, as the owner of my body, the most qualified expert in this discovery process. Our body's physiological responses, if given consideration, can expand past symptoms to become unique and intricately crafted poems that guide our lives with the images and feelings they elicit. These poems are not always pretty or easy to listen to, but hold many truths.[22]

I once worked with a retired circus performer who could not concentrate during a therapy session because of pain in his hip. He explained that the pain was chronic and quite bad at times, making it very difficult to walk. I suggested that he pay attention to the pain as a way of getting to know it better. He placed his hands on his hip and closed his eyes. After some time, I asked him if he noticed any images or sensations. He described how his leg felt tight and stuck; it craved to move freely. I invited him to show me, through movement, what the tightness felt like. He began to move around the studio, purposely exaggerating the awkwardness.

"My legs want to run," he said, "but they can't."

He let go of his hip and, even though his legs continued to move stiffly, his arms reached out and moved like a bird circling and playing with the wind. I was moved by the grace of his arms "flying" over the top of the painful awkwardness. In the following sessions, he said that the pain in his leg did not go away, but somehow his relationship with it had started to change.

"I realize I can still 'run.' Maybe not with my legs, but in other ways. Knowing this, I feel less angry about the pain. And this puts me in a better frame of mind to figure out what I need to do to take care of it."

I also worked with a woman who had recovered from several heart surgeries. During one of our sessions, she formed a pouch using clay and then poked numerous holes in it. When I asked her about the sculpture, she said it was her heart, which had been poked and prodded by doctors for so many years. This clay figure, representing her illness, was sitting there on the table, a short distance away from her, creating space for a dialogue.

She spoke to the sculpture, saying, "I am afraid you may get sick again."

I then asked her if the sculpture had anything to say.

After thinking for a moment, she turned to me and said, "The pouch with all the holes is afraid no one will like it because of its failings." As she spoke, tears welled up in her eyes. She was forming an emotional relationship with her illness rather than ignoring it. Through this relationship, she discovered truths about how her illness made her feel.

Connecting to one's emotions might help people stay physically and psychologically healthy. A phenomenon occurred in England, in which after Princess Diana's death, there was a significant reduction in health-care costs. In particular, the number of hospital trauma admissions and patients treated for depression and stress lowered by ten to fifty percent. This effect was named the *Diana Effect*. Researchers deduced that the community crying and grieving done *en masse* gave the nation a much-needed emotional catharsis that resulted in improved wellbeing.

They also figured that the better people felt, the less likely they were to injure themselves and end up in the hospital trauma ward.[23, 24] Predicting exact outcomes of emotional releases is not possible. The client who made the clay pouch may or may not have experienced an improvement in her health as a result of expressing her emotions. At the very least, the dialogue with the clay sculpture represented movement towards feeling alive despite what that aliveness brought her. We will all inevitably experience sickness and death in our lives. Facing this vulnerability can be scary, but can also bring a sense of peace, since we are no longer running from the truth.

4. The Wisdom of Our Thoughts and Imagination (concentrated in the head)

Our thoughts and mental images feel like they arise from our heads. People "lost in thought" often say they are "up in their head" and may even roll their eyes skyward as if to signal the movement of consciousness upward. When a person says she is "up in her head," she may be trying to recall a to-do list, engaging in deep contemplation, figuring out a problem, or daydreaming about lying on the beach. Thoughts and mental images are the play material of our imaginations and the key to creativity and ingenuity. Western society highly values the process of analytical analysis. This form of being up in one's head is the central force in Western society and the basis for engineering, architecture, and scientific breakthroughs. But analytical analysis without creative imagination will fail to inspire and hatch new ideas. In my practice, both analytical thoughts and the imagination are considered valuable wisdom in the therapeutic process: analytical thought can help us to cognitively understand why we do the things we do, and our imagination helps us expand past what we see in the present to imagine a new future.

In Western society, traditional schooling tends to focus on filling children's minds with words, numbers, and facts and does not train and foster creative ingenuity. Traditional intelligence tests seek to connect rational answers to set questions, and, as such, do not necessarily measure the depth and imaginative capabilities of our intellect. Expressive arts therapist Paolo Knill once said that psychological illness is a failure of our imagination, in that we become incapable of imagining a way out of our suffering.[25, 26] People come to see me, an expressive arts therapist, to train and strengthen their imagination. Suffering is an unavoidable part of life, but through creative ingenuity we can find resourceful ways through.

In my recovery from bulimia, I embarked on a creative **rethinking** of my life. I began to rethink my **perception** of self by no longer basing my self-esteem on how thin I was. I began to **understand** that bulimia was not a random occurrence, but was my "natural self" asserting its need for expression in the face of ballet's strict ideals. Once I **recognized** this, I was a step closer to unravelling the food addiction that had held me captive for so many years. I **realized** that my self-judgmental thoughts were actually destroying me. I began to let go of my perfected ideals and replace obsessive thoughts about dieting with thoughts that were more life affirming. I began to **daydream** about running a dance company in which, rather than enforce perfected ideals, I would let each dancer be uniquely themselves. Over time, I realized this dream. Rigid thought processes had held me prisoner for many years, but I was able to recruit the power of my *mind* as an ally, instead of an enemy, in the process of healing.

As a therapist, my key focus is to help people become more embodied. In so doing, however, I don't want to undervalue being up in one's head. Clients come to me because they want to feel more connected to their bodies. Frequently, they refer to being "up in their heads" as if it is something bad that they must fix or eradicate to achieve their goals. It is as if they feel like their body begins from the neck down and does not include the head!

"Is it possible," I ask, "to appreciate your intellect as you pursue increased connection to your emotions and embodied living? Is it possible to use your head wisdom as an ally in your process?"

Your head is a part of your body and deserves just as much credit as other sources of body-based wisdom.

5. The Wisdom of Our Emotions (concentrated in the heart)

We can feel and express emotion everywhere in our bodies (anger in clenched fists, sadness in heavy shoulders, or happiness in excited feet), but the key place that emotions seem to concentrate is our heart area. This is evident when a person who is emotionally moved puts his hand on his heart, as if to hold back the flood of feelings.

Awareness of our emotions colours and informs our experience and gives depth to our lives. Emotions help us to know what we want more or less of in our lives, in much the same way as the physical pain of burning our hands teaches us not to touch fire. Being aware of your emotions, and those of others, helps guide your actions and has a direct influence over your ability to respond effectively to your environment.[27] As seen in the *Diana Effect*, connecting to and expressing an emotion such as sadness may ward off depression and make us less accident prone.

When we emotionally "numb-out" as an escape against the intensity of our feelings, we disconnect from the guidance our emotions could offer. One client described how she had been feeling emotionally numb since her mother died the year before. The thought of feeling her emotions terrified her. Through painting and poetry, she began to express emotions in little increments, with greater and greater ease over time. Eventually, she tried more physically expressive art forms. While doing a breath exercise one day, a flood of tears arrived. She curled into a ball and cried, beating her fists against a pillow. She said afterward that it was as if she was crying for all the losses in her life, both big and small: crying for the death of her mom, crying for her stolen laptop, even crying for the freshly squeezed orange juice she had spilled that morning. The following week, she told me that after weeping like she had, everything looked different. She explained how she had never given the trees in the park much thought, but that day as she walked out of my studio, she suddenly saw them as if for the first time. She was struck by how beautiful they were. Her emotions were in a state of flow that allowed her to see through the eyes of her heart and be moved by the beauty of the trees.

6. The Wisdom of Our Spirit (concentrated in the sensation of one's body energy or life force)

I believe that the wisdom of our spirit resides in our body's energy; you are especially connected to this wisdom when you sense your energy in relationship to the world. This relationship helps you understand your place within the larger picture of humanity. It helps us all understand that while we are separate entities, we are also part of a larger whole. This enables us to see beauty in the patterns of life. We may have spiritual experiences when walking in the forest and call it Nature;

when joining with others in a social justice rally, we may call it community; when playing a particularly good game of hockey, we might call it "the zone"; when practicing yoga, we call it prana; when involved in an intimate relationship, we call it love; when in prayer, we call it God.[28] Spiritual wisdom is concentrated when a meditative focus is reached, be it through physical achievement, prayer, love, or reverie.

Spiritual wisdom is an important entity in my work, because without its presence, people suffer alone. If someone cannot sense their own life force, they will not feel connected to the energy of the world, the people around them, or depending on their beliefs, God. They become cut off from the understanding that they live within the collective human experience.

At my dad's funeral, I experienced a meditative moment. It was as if connecting threads fell upon the world, joining me to others who were grieving. I was not alone – we were all in this together. Others felt what I felt. In therapy, sometimes a sense of spirit also expands into the studio, gently covering and connecting everything and enabling myself, my client, and the art we create to be connected to the "we."

There was a study that correlated meditation with a sense of the universal "we." Magnetic resonance imaging was used to measure brain activity in both monks and university students while they meditated on compassion. During the meditation, regions of the brain involved with keeping track of what is "self" and what is "other" became less active and regions of the brain associated with empathy and maternal love became more active.[29, 30] The monks, more practiced at meditation, demonstrated a greater degree of change. This study demonstrates how a spiritual practice such as meditation may help one let go of the sense of "I," so that one can feel a greater sense of the "we." Please note, when I say "spiritual practice," I refer to any practice that helps us reach states of reverie. It does not matter how one chooses to reach this state, be it through sport, nature, church, temple, art, relationships, cooking, meditation, altruism, or political action.

I once helped a youth choreograph a dance piece based on her life story. She wrote a poem depicting how isolated she felt. She recited it while kneeling and swirling her arms at a large blue silk cloth that another youth held behind her, like a wall. She kept trying to reach through this "wall" as if searching for somebody out there to hear her words. We tried different arrangements of the piece until it finally happened – we were in the "zone": it felt like her every move and every word was guided by a smooth and knowing energy. Her dance became unmistakably about all of us, even though it expressed her unique story. Each of us in that room understood how she felt: all alone, searching for a hand to reach out to. It was her story, but it was also our story. It was the world's story.

MY MAP
PART TWO: THE SELF IN RELATIONSHIP TO THE WORLD

Allen

Allen has arrived in my studio and we now sit facing each other.

The first part of my map tells me that Allen has a wealth of wisdom inside him and that the key to accessing this wisdom resides within his body. Part one of my map also tells me that shifts of sensations that occur in my body during our sessions can be a guide that can illuminate the therapeutic process. Before I unfold the story that sensation can tell us, however, I need to enter Allen's world.

"Tell me about yourself," I say, breaking the uncomfortable moment of silence.

In quick, awkward phrases, Allen says, "Well, I'm a computer programmer. I'm sort of creative, even though I work in a cubicle. I make up these virtual worlds and stuff, but really at the end of the day it's all just a lot of geek stuff. I mean, I wouldn't say the guys at work are a bunch of artists, and they'd surely have a good laugh if they knew I was here. . . . I remember I liked painting when I was younger. . . . Anyways, I don't like talking about myself much. Never have. It wasn't much encouraged in my family. . . . I found your flyer at a café and was intrigued enough to stick it on my fridge. I looked at that flyer every single day for a whole year. And then, I finally called, and now, here I am."

He looks down at his hands and then stares out the window. "But I need help with some stuff. . . . Some things just aren't working. I thought this type of therapy might be good because I could draw and stuff instead of sitting around talking about myself."

I wait in silence for Allen to continue.

I feel like fidgeting. I feel the urge to look out the window instead of at Allen. Given how awkward this moment is for me, I guess it is even more uncomfortable for Allen. Talking about himself isn't a frequent occurrence in his world.

The World Out There

Like the rest of us, Allen is not completely autonomous, but functions in relationship with the world. In saying "world," I refer to all that occurs outside of a person and makes up their physical surroundings, including other people and their actions. From our first breath, our dependence on oxygen puts us in a relationship with our physical surroundings. With this breath, we begin a life-long "dance" between ourselves and the world. It is a dance that is inescapable and that can range from sublime to horrific.

This is how I see the steps in this dance unfold. There are a multitude of things occurring around us. Sight, touch, taste, smell, and hearing act as a bridge connecting us with all that is out there.[31] We receive this sensory input continuously, and interpret it through the wisdom of our actions, inner body, physiology, thoughts/imagination, emotions, and spirit. We then affect the world through the outward force of action and energy. All the steps in this dance occur continuously and simultaneously.

As a therapist, I will gradually get to know Allen's dance with the world. I will hear stories about his family, work, and life goals, as well as how the world influences him. I will also experience his interaction with the art-studio world (me and the art room), which will probably mirror how he interacts with the world outside therapy.

Allen

"What things aren't working?" I ask.

Allen takes a deep breath and dives in, as if to get it over with quickly.

"Well, I can't remember the last time I felt good. It seems like years ago. And I have this problem I don't talk about." He pauses. "You see . . . I secretly binge eat. I mean, I sit down and eat tons of food – not healthy food, but really 'bad for me' food. And I always feel like shit afterwards. No one knows I binge." He looks down. "But hey, people must wonder why I am the size I am, but no one says anything."

By society's standards, Allen would be considered overweight, even obese. However, I like to see everyone just as they are. For me, he is "Allen-sized."

"I turned thirty this year and it really scared me. I always thought my life would be great if I could just lose weight. Like there was always this promise of something just around the corner that would make my life perfect. But then I realized this is it. There is no perfect life waiting for me. There's just me and my big body. Women see me walking down the street and they pull their purses close. I'm like a big monster to them. It wasn't supposed to turn out this way. I've got things I want to do and, with my food problems, I'm at a standstill. Even worse, it might stop me dead in my tracks. You know, my dad was overweight, too, and he died of a heart attack when he was my age. That's enough incentive to get me off my ass and in here. . . . You see, I just can't keep going like this. . . . It feels weird telling you all this," he says and cringes. "But I guess that's the point of therapy, isn't it? To stop pretending."

MY MAP
PART THREE: WELLNESS AND DYSFUNCTION

Allen has just told me that he feels unwell and he has come to see me because he wants to feel well. The third part of my map illuminates this "well" thing that Allen searches for.

I believe wellness is a state of dynamic flow that invigorates our lives. It is a place of sharing between the psyche and the body that incorporates the world, but does not eradicate suffering. In fact, it helps us to be present with the pain that life brings us. Luckily, this dynamic flow also opens us to joy and beauty and helps us feel alive throughout life's ups and downs.[32, 33]

For someone to experience wellness, they do not need to be in perfect balance. In fact, there are valuable imbalances that can invigorate a person's life and create unique nuances that enrich our lives. For example:

- someone with overly keen senses can find enjoyment as a chef or wine taster
- a person with a predominantly intellectual way of seeing life may make important scientific discoveries

- an artist can be enriched by their singular focus on understanding emotional nuances
- a writer may enjoy a hermit-like existence in order to finish a book

There is nothing wrong with these types of idiosyncrasies, which bring a flavour and diversity to life that would be sorely missed if everyone was perfectly balanced all the time. Clients often talk about wellness as being a state of perfect balance they are trying to achieve. I often challenge them by asking, "Why not go in the other direction and find exactly the right *imbalance* that will invigorate your life and lead you to your passion?"

If wellness can include imbalance, variances in flow, and suffering, then the presence of these cannot be used to define dysfunction. Unlike these normal ups and downs of life, dysfunction tends to be a defense or a way of relating that is stuck in a continuous self-harming cycle. For instance, a person dealing with loss may disconnect from their emotions because facing their grief feels too overwhelming. They may then never let go of this protective stance and years later still be in a state of emotional disconnection. This challenges their well-being, because emotional wisdom needed to interpret and mediate life is being damaged or blocked.

I once spoke to a man who was taking a dance workshop with me. It often happens with therapists that people sense we are good listeners and tell us their life stories. It was such with this new acquaintance of mine. He told me that he used to love going out dancing with his wife, but when both of his sisters died in a car crash, he stopped dancing entirely. He explained how he had been afraid that moving freely might open things up emotionally and cause him to fall apart.

"I learned to keep my body still and not to feel," he explained.

He told me his coping strategy was hard on his wife, who frequently expressed frustration that he was emotionally distant. He spent five years in this state. Finally, his wife gave him an ultimatum: learn to feel again or risk losing her. So there he was, at a dance workshop with me, learning to move again and deal with the feelings that arose. This man's story is an example of a persistent pattern of coping that can undermine someone's life.[34]

I frequently refer to such patterns as the "amazing" way a client organizes his or her life in order to survive. Dysfunctional behaviour, at its starting point, is most often a coping mechanism that tries to protect us against suffering and pain. Rather than being seen as sick, a client with dysfunctional behaviour can be seen as an innovative survivalist who just needs to redirect his or her desire to survive into more effective strategies. Taking this view, survival defenses, no matter how bizarre or damaging, can be viewed as a sign of vitality because they represent a desire to make it through. One just needs to peel back the layers of the defense to arrive at the core desire to live.

Take me, for example: when I was little, my five-year-old self decided I needed to become the perfect girl as a way to hold my family together. I did this as a survival strategy at the time to keep my world from feeling like it was falling apart. Later in life, I faced complicated repercussions as a result of this strategy. My anorexia was an attempt to be perfect. My secret world of binging and purging became my release valve, expressing all the parts of me that didn't fit into my militant perfectionism. The end result seemed crazy until you peeled back the layers and found the five-year-old just trying to hold things together.

Is Allen unwell? He has named a stagnated state of being involving food addiction and depression. The food addiction may once have served a purpose, but now it interferes with his vitality. He has named his "disease" with his life. His presence in my art studio, after looking at the flyer hanging on his fridge for a year, represents his desire to find the road back towards wellness.

Allen feels unwell, but how did he get stuck in this state? Over time, patterns of flow within our actions, thoughts, emotions, inner body sensation, spirit, and even our blood and the body chemicals in our physiology can become ingrained, creating a tendency for repetition. Well-known psychoanalyst Carl Jung believed that throughout our life experience, "riverbeds" or grooves related to particular themes become etched in our psyche. When a theme arises, psychic energy tends to flow, like a river, into these well-etched grooves.[35] Discoveries in neuroscience have shown that something similar to these hypothetical grooves can be seen at a physical level. Brain scans show that neural pathways are created and become ingrained through the repetition of specific life experiences. For example, piano players who practice for many hours a day show increased neural pathways in the area of the brain devoted to finger dexterity when compared to non-piano players.[36, 37] A similar phenomenon can be seen in experienced taxi drivers, who have a larger number of neural pathways devoted to spatial representation and learning routes than their novice counterparts.[38]

I believe that through life experience, neurological riverbeds are traced in every aspect of our selves, resulting in patterns of flow or lack of flow in our movements, inner body reactions, physiologies, thoughts, emotions, and sense of spirit. We tend to fall into these riverbeds over and over again, which causes them to deepen further and increase the probability of repetition and rigidity.[39, 40] Pathways are created through experience that range from positive to dysfunctional. For instance, an often-neglected child may form a belief that life will forever be lonely. A child with close and vital human connections may develop the belief that her life will be full of friends and family. As each child grows, her internal view often prevails and affects the way she moves and holds her posture. In an effort to match their external world to their internal beliefs, these children may even make life choices that fulfill their perspectives and resist redirection towards alternative outcomes. The neglected child might also develop chronic physical symptoms such as persistent migraines or stomachaches as a result of stress or emotional trauma she has experienced.[41, 42]

Patterns of Dysfunction

My map of wellness and dysfunction includes the following dysfunctional patterns that people tend to favour.

1. Challenge in Connecting to the World
   a) Fragile Boundaries
   b) Rigid Boundaries
   c) Over- or Underextending one's Energy
2. Fragmentation
   a) Disconnect from the Body
   b) Disconnect from Other Aspects of the Self
3. Rejected Aspects of the Self Find Form and Expression
   a) Escalating Body Messages
   b) Projection
4. Self-Harming
   a) Matches that Hurt
   b) View of Self and the World
   c) Addiction

I will now describe each of these in detail.

1. Challenges in Connecting to the World

Our connection with the world is something we have to manage throughout our lives. How much energy do we put out into the world? How much will we receive back? What are our expectations? How vulnerable do we make ourselves? Every person answers these questions in a different manner, possibly developing patterns in dealing with the world that chronically interfere with wellbeing.

a) Challenges in Connecting to the World: Fragile Boundaries

Life overwhelms us if we can't create sufficient boundaries against the onslaught of the world's stimuli. Sensitive individuals who cannot dampen their ability to absorb the detailed nuances of life will be especially stressed by the inundating aspects of the modern world.

If the boundary between myself and others is not clear, I will have difficulty separating the emotions and thoughts of others from my own. The border between where I stop and another begins becomes blurred at this point, and I lose a sense of my unique identity. When I have felt the desire to find a partner and get married, I have had to ask myself if I really did want to get married or, as a woman in her thirties, if I was just succumbing to society's pressure to get married.

In cases of sexual abuse, where boundaries are repeatedly violated, sufferers often feel their body is no longer their own. They feel their body is almost an extension of the abuser, something that is used as a stage on which to act out the abuser's dysfunction. Recovery often involves reclamation of one's body and the right to create boundaries (both physical and emotional).

b) Challenges in Connecting to the World: Rigid Boundaries

Life experiences can sometimes feel so devoid of genuine beauty that we anaesthetize our senses in order to protect ourselves from intolerable realities.[43] As a defense against being hurt, a person may build a "wall" between him or herself and the world. This wall can be a combination of both physical barriers (controlling your surroundings so that no one can reach you) and psychological barriers (building emotional blocks to intimacy). When the wall between ourselves and the world becomes so rigid that we are unable to break through, we are protected, but truly alone in life, without connection to the world and those around us.

c) Challenges in Connecting to the World: Over- or Underextending Our Energy

If people fail to engage in the activity of living, they will stagnate. If we do not use our muscles, they will atrophy. If we do not flex our minds or our heart-feelings, they will atrophy, as well. Alternatively, some people suffer from the opposite affliction – they do too much. This can lead to burnout, a state of exhaustion caused by excessive and prolonged output of psychological or physical energy.

Each form of wisdom (action, inner body, physiology, thoughts, emotions, and spirit) is unique, and one can overextend in one area while underextending in others. A typical workaholic overextends his or her actions and thoughts and underextends in the area of emotional intimacy.

2. Fragmentation

A person may repress a threatening aspect of self to the point that he or she feels entirely disconnected from it. This harms vitality, because pieces of us that could offer wisdom and rich depth are not accessible.

a) Fragmentation: Disconnection from Our Bodies

As a society, we tend to estrange ourselves from embodied experience because we fear the body – its emotionality, its physical imperfections, and its potential for disease, suffering, and inevitable death. This estrangement makes us feel as if one's body and psyche function separately, which ironically accentuates our suffering, because we lose a sense of our vitality.[44]

In reaction to prolonged or severe trauma, a person may suffer extreme disassociation from bodily experience. This is often the case with victims of torture. Expressive arts therapist Melinda Ashley Meyer works with refugees who have survived torture. She explains that when individuals face extreme physical and psychological pain, they often breathe shallowly, tighten their muscles, and temporarily shut down one or more senses until their bodies become numb. This disassociated state can prevail long after the trauma. Melinda uses the analogy of a house:

> The individual will "flee from the house of the body" in order to survive . . . all networks are shut down. . . . The lack of energy makes the house cold and dark. Over time, this house breaks down – the body experiences pain through discomfort in muscles and joints. What the

soul cannot express, the body will express. Being in exile from the body as a method to avoid the pain of trauma will, over time, give an individual the experience of belonging to the "living dead," a state where one feels totally isolated from life.[45]

When we disconnect from our embodied experience, we are no longer at home, becoming orphaned from our own bodies.

b) Fragmentation: Disconnection from Other Aspects of the Self

I highlighted disconnection from bodily experience in the previous section because of its prevalence in our society and its relation to trauma, but we can become disconnected from any aspect of our selves. In fact, even the most psychologically fit person will not know and accept all of whom he or she is. We all have some aspects of the self that we continually turn away from because they make us uncomfortable. Various therapeutic methods have different names for this: your shadow side, your disowned parts, the submerged self, or the unconscious self.

We are all disconnected from various aspects of the self, but some people are more profoundly disconnected than others. Some people have such a narrow view of themselves that only a few chosen aspects are included. Any events, people, and feelings that remind them of their disowned parts will cause anxiety, because they fear that the illusion of the self they have created will be broken. The more profound someone's disconnection, the more risk they have in bumping up against who they really are. These people are likely to use all sorts of defenses to protect themselves from ever meeting their true selves. Profound disconnection from the self also makes people feel less whole because they are living only as part of themselves.

A teenage girl may dismiss her intellect and become an "airhead" because she thinks boys will like her better that way. Moments in which she proves herself to be smart will then cause anxiety because she fears losing her social network. A man who is always happy might disown sad emotions because he finds them disturbing. When he finds himself crying while watching a film, he will feel uncomfortable because it feels so unlike him. Alternatively, a woman might accept disturbing emotions while disconnecting from pleasant feelings because she does not think she deserves to feel joy. Feeling joy is scary for her because there is suddenly so much to lose. She will likely sabotage her happiness so that she can get back to the familiarity of feeling miserable.

3. Rejected Aspects of the Self Find Form and Expression

Aspects of the self will continue to function even if we don't consciously acknowledge their presence; they may strive to enter our consciousness through expressive symptoms. Our rejected aspects of the self are like disowned family members knocking at our door. If not let in, they will knock louder and louder.

a) Rejected Aspects of the Self: Escalating Body Messages

The energies of rejected aspects of the self send their messages quietly at first, often in the form of subtle body sensations like a tapping foot or a tense shoulder. If left unattended, however, they may eventually notify us of their presence more dramatically. For instance, a person under stress at work might experience irritability and fatigue that, if listened to, would suggest a lifestyle change. Something inside them is crying out, "Stop! Stop! I can't take this anymore!" If this cry goes unheard and the person continues to ignore these messages, the symptoms of stress may become extreme, finally resulting in a physical or mental breakdown.

b) Rejected Aspects of the Self: Projection

Rejected aspects of self may strive to enter our consciousness in disguised forms. For example, a child who receives messages about the importance of being nice to others may begin to repress his anger in order to please. This repressed anger may then surface as passive-aggressive behaviour, such as "accidentally" dropping mom's keys behind the radiator just before she is due to leave for an appointment. This is an indirect way of expressing anger at being abandoned. The child projects his anger onto an "accident" so he can maintain the belief that he is a 100% "good" child.

Rejected aspects of the self are not just projected onto supposed accidents: they can be projected towards any person, group, object, or event. The things that bother us about other people or groups are often projections of the things we have rejected or disowned in our selves. It is easier to blame someone else than to look too closely at our own shadows.

4. Self-Harming

There are many ways in which we act out against ourselves.

a) Self-Harming: Matches that Hurt Us

We all have an unconscious need to find physical matches for internal feelings. We find such matches when we discover or create something in the world outside ourselves that represents how we feel inside. This need is so powerful that it can overshadow all other considerations, even the need to take care of ourselves. This can result in matches that hurt, rather than support, our well-being. A heartbroken woman may bang her head against a wall or cut into her skin because the physical pain she creates matches her emotional pain. A person with low self-esteem may find a life partner who continually criticizes him because this provides a match for his lack of self-value.

b) Self-Harming: View of the Self and the World

How individuals tend to interpret themselves and their environment is influenced both by their life experiences and what they learn from those around them. This interpretation is like a lens through which they see life. A person may believe that she is a failure because her father always told her she was. Someone who has experienced hardship might believe his life will always be full of challenges. In both of these cases, their worldviews are like blinders that cause them to see only their hardships and failures while blocking other possible outcomes. When I was a ballet dancer, for instance, I had a very narrow worldview in which I believed I was only successful if I was extremely skinny. This caused me hardship because I hardly ever met my perfectionist standards and was continually relegating myself to the status of failure.

c) Self-Harming: Addiction

At a psychological level, addiction is a search for something: a utopic nirvana, a feeling of invincibility, or an escape from physical or emotional suffering, for example. Through addiction, we try to escape ourselves and our lives, to escape the human condition with its pains and imperfections and failures. We reach outside ourselves for something we need, but the answers we are searching for can only be found within. We need to come home to ourselves in order to find the sense of wholeness and love that provides resiliency and hope. With addiction, the keys to the soul-home are lost and the addict is without a map. She searches in the bar down the road or in a bag of donuts at her local bakery, even though the misplaced keys are somewhere deep inside her. The addiction holds the promise of success but brings no lasting relief, so the addictive action is repeated again and again. The addict is led further away from home; the further she goes, the more hollow she feels. This fuels the addiction, as higher doses of the addictive substance are needed to fill the ever-increasing emptiness. The addiction escalates into bigger spending, more intense drug use, or larger amounts of food. What at first was an attempt to find salvation becomes destructive.

Allen

Allen has just finished telling me what isn't working in his life; now he sits, awkwardly looking down at his hands. After a few seconds, he looks up and meets my eye. I feel as if he is measuring me to see if I am up for the challenge.

"So, you've come here to get help with your depression and binge eating?" I ask.

He nods.

"And you've been stuck in this place for a long time, feeling the same way and doing the same things over and over again?"

"Yes, that's right," he says. He exhales, his shoulders settling.

I settle comfortably into my chair. "There, you did it. You told me why you've come. And look . . . the walls of the studio are still standing and the sun is still shining. You're still sitting here on the couch. I am still here."

Allen smiles. From the mixture of relief and chagrin on his face, I can tell he is amused by the thought that admitting his problem wasn't so terrifying after all.

Chapter 3

HEALING THROUGH THE ARTS

When I tell people I am an expressive arts therapist, they frequently make the mistaken assumption that I only work with professional artists. When I tell them that expressive arts therapy can work for anyone regardless of artistic skill or talent, they become perplexed. "But how can art help someone who isn't an artist?" they ask me.

Our society draws a line between artist and non-artist, between those who are on stage and those who watch. I believe there is no such dividing line: the capacity for creativity lives within all of us. Every day we express rhythm, sound, and shape. Hearts beat and create the rhythm of a pulse. We walk and create footprints in the sand. We meet another and build a relationship. Destructive acts like war create scars on the landscape. Creation goes on every minute, both inside us and around us. Art taps into this innate human impulse by directing, amplifying, and framing natural expression. Traditionally, art is framed by the shape of the canvas or stage or by the length of a dance or play. The frame, however, need not be a professionally stretched canvas or an opera theatre. It can be as simple as the scrap of paper you doodle on, the three-minute morning shower that transports you into "operatic" song, or the plate on which you aesthetically arrange food. Not being trained as an artist can actually be an asset in the process of therapy because one's mind is not cluttered and restricted by the "shoulds" and "shouldn'ts" of formal art.

The untrained artist might feel nervous about his lack of skill, but once he gets past his nerves, he often has an easier time finding an "honest" flow of expression that both enlivens him and leads to self-insight. When an untrained dancer lifts her leg, her foot does not automatically arch, but simply moves in a way that feels right to her. The predetermined patterns of expression a trained artist perfects sometimes need to be dismantled in order to access honest expression.

You don't need to be a trained artist to benefit from expressive arts therapy, but entering the process as a novice is still a big step. It's my job as an expressive arts therapist to usher my clients towards their first steps into artistic expression.

Allen

"So what happens next?" Allen asks.

"I'm an expressive arts therapist, so we do art. In a way, you already began with the art of storytelling when you told me why you're here."

"Humph." Allen raises his eyebrow. "Well, before we do any more 'art'," he says, making air quotes with his fingers, "I'm curious how this can help me."

"Well, you see, we all tend to do the same things day after day. If we want change, we need to try something new. When you create art, unexpected images, sounds, and movements arrive that can help you see things in new ways and nudge you out of a rut. You may discover resources and strengths you didn't know you had. And not being an artist can actually help in this process, because expressing through the arts will be so new to you that it is more apt to nudge you out of stuck places. Artistic expression also acts like a mirror, but not a regular mirror that just shows what is on the outside. It's a mirror 'plus' that helps you see deeper into who you are and helps you understand why you do the things you do."

Allen looks at me with a glazed expression.

"Okay," I say, "my explanation probably doesn't mean much to you . . . just a bunch of words. I think the best way to answer your questions is to show you. Maybe try some stuff today and tell me what you think."

I know I need to start with something small and non-threatening to ease him into this unfamiliar world of art.

"How about exploring the space? You can peruse through my books or see what's in the art cupboard. Have a walk around the studio to get a feel for it."

He peruses the studio, looking at things and making comments. "It's nice you have a park out back. It feels cozy in here . . . sort of like a cottage." He stops in front of the art cupboard.

I get up and open the cupboard door. "I call it the magic cupboard. There are all sorts of things in here." I show him the paints and the pastels, the clay, the costumes, the musical instruments, and the poetry cards.

"I feel like a kid looking at all this," he says.

I nod and smile. "Yeah, some clients call my studio Kathleen's Adult Kindergarten." I pause, trying to get a sense of whether or not Allen can tolerate "feeling like a kid."

"Would you like to draw today? That might be a good place to start."

He frowns. "The last time I drew a picture, I was about ten."

"Not to worry," I say. "This type of drawing doesn't involve any skill. It's sort of like moving your arms around while you happen to be standing in front of a paper holding pastels. Why don't we do it together?"

A few minutes later, we each stand in front of a large sheet of white paper that has been taped to the wall, pastels in both hands. We draw, eyes closed, not trying to draw anything in particular. The sound of scribbling fills the studio. I feel relaxed and start to enjoy myself. It feels great to let go of thinking for a moment and just doodle. I take a quick peek at Allen. From his stance, I guess that he is feeling similar. *Ah*, I think as I return to my drawing, *a tolerable entry point*.

Allen finishes and steps back. "It's just a bunch of scribbles," he says.

"Yes, that's true," I say. "Now is there any part that wants to be filled in or shaped into something? Here, I'll show you. This part of my scribble looks a bit like a half moon, so I'm going to fill it in with yellow and make it look more moon-like."

We both start finding shapes within our drawings.

"I'm done," Allen announces after a few minutes.

"Okay, how about talking to the painting and telling it what you see? Here, I'll show you." I look at my drawing and say, "You have a moon and sky and lots of playful shapes. You are full of yellow and blue."

"Just speak to the drawing?" Allen asks. "That seems a bit silly, but I guess no one will see me except you!"

Allen looks at his drawing. "You are colourful," he says. "And . . . ah . . . you have lots of different shapes . . . and . . . at the center you have a dense blobby thing . . . and . . . lines shoot out from this blobby center."

He stops and looks at his picture with curiosity. He is lost for a moment, gazing at its colours and shapes.

"So Allen," I say gently, "that was expressive arts. What do you think?"

"Well, I still don't understand how it works."

"How do you feel right now?" I ask.

"Good, actually," Allen says. "It's like doing the picture made me forget to feel bad about myself. I'm not sure how long that will last. I'll probably go outside and start to think about all the things wrong with my life."

"Well, if this drawing helped you feel good even for just this moment, that's no small thing. Do you want to come back next week and see if the arts can help you forget to feel bad about yourself again?"

"Yeah, I think that would be alright," Allen responds while nodding his head.

We book a session for the following week.

A RECIPE FOR TRANSFORMATION FROM A NEUROLOGICAL PERSPECTIVE

I believe the arts can help Allen, but what substantiates my belief? I look to the field of neuroscience to understand the conditions that encourage transformation. Recent discoveries suggest that the brain is more malleable than we once thought. We now know that if we challenge people with new experiences, their brain pathways change to accommodate the new activity. This type of brain malleability was originally thought to be contained to childhood, but it is now understood to occur throughout our lifespan. The brain is not a static entity, predetermined only by genetic programming and childhood experience. Rather, it is an organ continually built and rebuilt by life experience.[46]

Although our brain can change according to our experiences, we have the tendency to run along the same neural pathways over and over again, causing a repetition in behaviour, thought, and feeling patterns. This repetition will occur even if it's detrimental to our well-being. These patterns can be seen as well-defined paths in the forest, which we defer to because they are so familiar. Any transformative process needs to include leaving the well-travelled path in order to forge new paths. The main ingredient needed to help this process along is "having a new experience." It's like the saying, "if you continue to do what you continue to do, you will continue to do what you continue to do."

Expressive arts therapy is an acting, feeling, sensing, thinking, and imagining form of therapy; as such, it offers a diverse range of possible new experiences. However, having a new experience is not the only ingredient in transformation. I once attended a lecture by Norman Doidge, an acknowledged expert in brain plasticity, in which he named several conditions that, when they occur alongside a new experience, help to enhance and solidify the process of neuroplasticity and corresponding personal transformation. From my own notes from his lecture, I compiled the following list of conditions:

1. *Reduced anxiety* helps people open up to new experiences.
2. *Sustained and concentrated attention* helps solidify newly formed pathways.
3. *Repetition of the new experience* is needed, especially when trying to unlearn old patterns so new ones can be established.
4. *Experiencing intense memories or emotions* has an effect akin to clicking "save" on the computer, saving whatever neural pathways have formed in that moment.
5. *Dopamine surges* are also believed to help save whatever neural pathways have formed in the moment of the surge. Dopamine is the brain chemical related to pleasurable and rewarding experiences and romantic love.
6. *Increases in Oxytocin* (a love hormone related to bonding) are believed to help dissolve old neural pathways so new ones can form.
7. *Sleep or periods of rest* are needed in order to solidify neural changes that have occurred.[47, 48]

Allow me to provide an example of how the arts can provide both the new experiences and all seven other conditions needed to encourage and help solidify transformation. For the past six years, I have worked with groups of youth who are challenged by gender identity issues. Many of these youths are bullied at school and face prejudice as part of their daily existence because they do not fit into gender norms. These youths tend to shy away from traditional psychotherapy. Instead of offering to "therapize" them, we (two other expressive arts therapists and I) invited them to create a play inspired by their life experiences.

The idea of theatre is **engaging and draws their attention**. This creation is an important type of fun, because it invites them into **new self-esteem and community-building experiences** they otherwise would not have had. Most of the youths involved in the project suffer from isolation and lack of community. Although they crave connection, many have had past experiences that make it hard for them to trust others. The gradual revealing of self that occurs through the arts allows the group to get to know and trust each other within the safety of the group and at a pace that is tolerable. The trust between group members builds over time and provides them with a place in which they feel **less anxious**. Through the project they **develop strong and caring bonds**. The sense of camaraderie and support allows the youths to take more risks in expressing **moving elements of their life stories** through the arts. The youths often **fall in love with the play** and the characters in it. They frequently tell us that working on the play is the best part of their week. The play tells their life stories through theatrical metaphor, so this "falling in love" with the play is an indirect way of **experiencing self-love**. For many, this type of self-appreciation is an entirely **new experience for them**. The youths rehearse the play week after week, which provides **repetition of positive new experiences**. The play is created over a period of eight months, which leaves plenty of time to **sleep** on the new experiences they are having. As opening night approaches, rehearsals are **intense and emotional**, with opening night jitters threatening. Finally, opening night arrives and provides a **powerful and rewarding experience**. Each year the youths receive a **heartfelt** standing ovation for their performance. As they stand with glowing faces, receiving their ovation, I know the youths will save this memory like a snapshot. In so doing, they will also save the confidence, interpersonal skills, and sense of community they have gained.

THERAPEUTIC ART-BASED EXPERIENCES

After Allen leaves, I exhale and relax my shoulders. As a therapist, I am always nervous the first time I meet a client. Ushering someone into his first expressive arts experience can be a delicate thing. The balance between helping a client feel safe enough to proceed and intrigued enough to come back needs to be just right. With Allen's first session, I think the balance was achieved. He made his first successful step into artistic expression. The door is open; now, many therapeutic possibilities lay ahead:

1. **Expressive arts can help Allen feel a sense of safety by:**
   a) giving him something to hold onto.
   b) holding his expression.
   c) providing him with a creative companion.
   d) providing a nonjudgmental place to create art.
   e) helping him assert his personal boundaries.

2. **Expressive arts can help Allen explore new territory by:**
   a) encouraging honest expression rather than artistic skill.
   b) encouraging him to follow the creative phenomenon.
   c) engaging his imagination.
   d) providing a multidisciplinary approach.
   e) encouraging him to move away from fixating on his problems.

3. **Expressive arts can help Allen build relationships when:**
   a) the art provides a connecting bridge between him and myself.
   b) I stay present with Allen as he engages in artistic expression.
   c) his expression is witnessed by me.
   d) I respond artistically to Allen or the artwork he creates.
   e) he connects with me by telling me elements of his life story through artistic expression.
   f) he uses artistic expression as a chance to try out new relationship patterns.

4. **Expressive arts can help Allen engage with the world by:**
   a) engaging his senses.
   b) helping him find outward expression that matches his internal world.
   c) offering him time to play.
   d) helping him reframe his view of himself in relation to the world.

5. **Expressive arts can help Allen get to know himself better when:**
   a) the art objects he creates give him the distance that allows him to see himself from afar.
   b) he dialogues with the art he creates.
   c) he interacts with the art he creates.

6. **Expressive arts can help Allen connect things together in new ways by:**
   a) fostering the healing properties of love.

b) fostering the healing properties of beauty.

c) ushering him into liminal space where change is possible.

I will spend the rest of this chapter explaining each of these in more detail and visiting Allen's story throughout.

1. How the Arts Provide a Sense of Safety

People need to feel "safe enough" in the therapeutic process to stay engaged and continue coming back to therapy. Expressive arts therapy employs the following to help people feel safe enough to proceed:

a) Having Something to Hold on To

People often feel anxiety when asked to talk about challenging issues or to express themselves artistically. Art projects with "to-do" tasks, especially those that involve objects (paintbrushes, clay, drums), help alleviate this anxiety because rather than focus on self-expression, the person is able to focus on completing a task.

To give my clients hands-on tasks, I will say, "How about we both hold this ball up in the air and let it float about?" or, "Take these pastels and fill the paper with as many colours as you can."

Rather than being overwhelmed by a sea of possibilities, the client now has something to hold on to. He can hold on to the ball or the pastel or the task at hand. His hands are busy doing, leaving less time for self-conscious angst. He is distracted from nervousness, which lets him try new things he might otherwise have shied away from.

b) The Frame of the Artwork Holds Expression

The frame of a piece of artwork provides a physical container that literally holds the client's expression. In visual arts, the frame is the size of the paper or picture frame. In performance arts, the frame is the limit of time (the start and end of the performance) and the limit of space (the end of the stage).[49] For example, performing a spontaneous theatrical piece that expresses a range of emotions can be terrifying for a shy or guarded person, so I will narrow the frame by suggesting increasingly smaller limits to expression until the person feels safe enough to proceed.

A client may start a session feeling sad. When I suggest that she create a dance to match her sadness, she may shake her head. Then I will say, "Okay, how about doing a dance of sadness lasting only a minute?" If she still says no, I may counter with, "How about a thirty-second dance using only your hands?" or, "How about a ten-second dance using only your pinkie finger?" Typically, at this point the client will laugh and think I'm joking, but I'm very serious. It doesn't matter to me whether the dance is ten seconds or an hour, or whether it's performed from head to toe or with just one finger. These small steps are the opening that leads towards bigger steps.

c) Artistic Companion

Expressive arts therapists will actively engage with clients in imaginative play and artistic creation. Yes, what I am saying is that we will paint, sing, and dance with our clients. Having an artistic companion helps people feel safe, because they don't feel like they're being watched and judged. They are also more likely to go into an "unknown cave" when they have company. I will often join my clients in their art making either at the beginning of our therapeutic relationship or when clients first approach a subject that is challenging for them. I do this to help give them the courage to proceed.

d) Artwork Treated with Unconditional Regard

Expressive arts therapists are taught to accept any image, sound, or movement without categorizing it as good or bad. This nonjudgmental treatment of artwork helps clients learn to avoid self-censorship. I once worked with a young child who drew a vivid picture of a madman stabbing a doctor with a large knife. She was a quiet child, almost too well behaved, who had a long medical history and was facing yet another surgery. In the face of a disempowering illness and possibly death, she may have drawn the picture as a way to re-enact her doctor's fight against her disease. She may have been angry at doctors for cutting her open so many times, even though she knew that they were trying to help. The girl's well-behaved persona probably left her uncertain as to how to express these confusing feelings. If I had judged or diagnosed her drawing in even the smallest way, shame may have caused her anger and fear to go into hiding. Instead I welcomed the image uncon-ditionally, letting her know that her "madness" was welcome in my stu-dio.

e) Invitation to Assert Boundaries through Artistic Creation

The ability to defend our personal boundaries helps us feel safe in the world. Through play and art making, a client can learn to build and practice defending their boundaries. They can build walls with cush-ions, draw protective fortresses or create imaginary bubbles. They can use theatrical play to practice saying "no" and physically pushing away.

I once asked one of my newer clients if she wanted to paint. She agreed without hesitation. I was just starting to get to know her, but I noticed that she always said yes to my suggestions.

"Okay," I said. "Maybe take a moment, close your eyes, and check in with yourself to see whether you really want to paint."

Upon reflection, she admitted that she was not sure if she felt like painting.

"Can you tell me directly?" I asked.

"It's hard to say 'no'. It sounds silly, but I feel like I'm disappointing you."

"Interesting," I said. "How about we turn this into a game? I will pester you to paint. No matter how persistent I get, your job will be to say NO."

This turned into a fun game. I kept making increasingly more an-noying suggestions, my client saying "NO" louder and louder each time. While this game was fun, it was also important practice. Although I played the role of the persistent "thera-pest" being rebuffed, I was ac-tually cheering for her newfound strength in defining and protecting her needs.

If a person has boundaries against outside influences, they can tune in to their inner guidance more readily. I have faith that inner wisdom leads people towards healing – it is a brilliance that just needs support and encouragement to shine. I say to my clients, "How about taking a moment to tune everything out until you can listen to only yourself? Listen to your heart, listen to the flow of your blood, listen to how you crave to move, listen to images that form in your head, listen to your thoughts."

Allen

When Allen first came to see me, the leaves were green. Now as I look across the park, they are flaming red and orange.

"I'm really pissed off," Allen says. "My boss blamed me for a programming error, but it was the graphics guys who messed up. It's totally not my fault."

Allen has said he's angry, but in contrast to his words, he looks defeated, as if he has been punched in the chest. Even though Allen is trying to aim his anger at his boss, I feel like his self-defeating view of life has directed his anger back at himself.

"You're angry at your boss, but it looks like your anger has boomeranged back and hit you in the chest," I say.

Allen looks up, surprised. "That is sorta how it feels . . . like I've taken a few punches."

"Hey, would you like to try an experiment?" I ask.

"Maybe. . . ." He squints. He knows about my experiments.

"Why don't you aim the anger out and not let it circle back. Maybe aim it at the studio wall. You could hit the wall with a pillow." I offer this suggestion because I know that being physically expressive takes Allen out of his comfort zone.

"Humph," Allen says. "I thought you were going in that direction."

"You know, I think it's great when people say 'no' to my suggestions. Sometimes it's good to practice saying 'no;' sometimes it's good to practice saying 'yes.' Both are equally important. So, if you want, you can tell your thera-pest to go away, and that would be a fine piece of therapy!" I smile reassuringly as I say this. I know I'm repeating myself. I've told Allen this before, and he has made good practice of saying "no" to all my suggestions that involve physical movement.

Allen closes his eyes and takes some time to get a sense of what he wants. This "going internal" is new for him. It's something I invited him to try in previous sessions.

He opens his eyes. "I'll say 'yes' today. I am really tired of the way I feel and I want to see if doing all this stuff can help me. But I'm not sure how to start."

"How about we do it together?" I suggest. "We could stand side by side with our pillows and hit the wall together." While I say this, I grab a big pillow from the couch and act the scene out in slow motion.

Allen is still, except for a barely perceptible shake of his head. He then stares at me with a raised eyebrow.

"Okay," I continue, "How about if we do it for only ten seconds?"

He's still glued to the couch. Marveling at my own persistence, I say, "How about we stand still for ten seconds, pillows raised, while we *imagine* we're hitting the wall?"

Allen brightens and says, "I think I can do that."

We get up and stand side by side, holding our pillows poised to hit. I signal the start with a nod, and then we both just stand there.

When the time is up, I say, "Well, how was that?"

Allen has a thoughtful look on his face. "Actually, it didn't seem as scary as I thought. I think I might be able to do the real version. But only if you do it, too."

"Are you sure?"

"Yes."

I take a big breath and look at Allen, saying, "Okay . . . one . . . two . . . three!"

I run at the wall with my pillow yelling, "I! Am! Frustrated!" With each word, I wallop the wall.

Allen runs at the wall and also starts to hit it with his pillow.

We're both going at the wall when I say to Allen, "See if there are sounds or words that match."

He surprises both of us by yelling out, "Fuck you! Fuck you! Fuck you!"

I join him in a chorus of "Fuck you's."

Allen stops. He's panting and his face is red. He takes time to slow his breath.

"Wow, I've never done anything like that before!"

Allen returns to the couch and takes time to reflect. He says, "When I feel angry, I never really express it. It just hangs around, building up in me. And then rarely, like maybe only a few times in my life, I lose control and really yell at someone. And when it happens, it's over the top and scary and I don't feel good about it."

I nod. "When anger gets pushed down and pressure builds up, that anger can explode destructively without control. Think of yourself as a water pipe that needs to flow to keep from bursting. Anger needs to flow so that it does not get pressurized. Anger can be a good thing, because it helps us know where our stopping point is. It helps us say when we've had enough. And here, today, the scoreboard reads Expression of Anger: 1, Destruction: 0. Look . . . the sky hasn't fallen, the walls still stand, I'm still here, you're still here, and no one is hurt. You've gone to a place inside yourself that you feared and learned you can survive through it intact."

I finish my speech, noting that I've given in to the temptation of "lecturing." Although lecturing makes me feel very smart, it usually does not help people much. I believe the best type of learning happens through experience, so I turn my attention back to Allen and ask, "This new feeling of letting your anger flow, how does it feel in your body?"

Allen looks perplexed by this question.

"Okay," I say. "Right now, in this moment, putting your attention to your chest, does it feel heavier than before, or lighter, or about the same?"

Allen takes a deep breath. "Actually, it feels a bit lighter . . . I can breathe easier."

Allen knew he could say no to the exercise, which gave him room to figure out whether or not he wanted to proceed. Physical expression terrified him, so I searched for a tolerable entry point by:

- narrowing the frame by limiting the length of the first take
- narrowing the frame even further by limiting the amount of movement until it was only imaginary
- offering to be his companion
- giving him something to hold onto (the pillow, the task)

The sense of safety that holding these things provided allowed him to trust and follow the actions of his body and see what happened. I accepted without judgment the "Fuck you" that arrived. He learned he could survive through expression of his anger and breathe easier afterward. It was only a ten-second exercise, but from my perspective it was a big deal. It was an opening to new experiences: the practice of following the wisdom of his actions and a new way for him to be with his anger.

Researcher Ernest Harburg has shown that learning to express anger productively is a good thing. Harburg recently completed a 17-year study involving 192 couples. He found that patterns of chronic anger suppression within relationships correlated to premature death. It seems that learning to express anger productively might not just help Allen breathe easier, but may actually be good for his health.[50]

I also bless that "Fuck you" for another reason. When I had bulimia, my binge eating was a way to create a stopping point against perfectionist ballet ideals. It was my boundary, a protective blanket of food that soothed my soul. Bulimia was my "Fuck you." When I learned to defend myself in less self-harming ways, the need to binge faded. At this point in the story, I'm still getting to know Allen, and thus do not yet know the reason for his binge eating. I wonder, however, if his compulsive eating may also be a way to create a boundary against the world and if learning how to express his anger might be part of the cure.

2. How the Arts Entice Exploration

As I stated previously, if we continue to do things exactly as we have in the past, we will likely continue to do exactly *what* we have done in the past. An integral ingredient for change is that we try new things. The arts engage us in an open array of possibilities that entice us past familiar ground in the following ways:

a) Low-Skill, Honest Expression Approach

In expressive arts, possessing high skill in the creation of art is not necessary. Focus is placed upon expression that honestly represents a person and is sensitive to emotional and energetic nuances. Though this comes as quite a surprise to many people, skill is not needed in this endeavour. We do not need to point our feet or draw a tree perfectly to express ourselves evocatively. We just need to move or draw from our internal cues. In my practice, I had a client who had no musical training. During an intensely emotional session one day, she picked up the guitar and began to play in a manner that moved me to tears. I was moved not because her playing was so skillful – it wasn't – but because it was an honest and heartfelt representation of how she felt.

The low-skill, honest-expression approach breaks down creative barriers caused by people's self-perceived lack of artistic skill and entices a free flow of expression.

b) *Following the Creative Phenomenon*

Expressive arts therapists often discourage preplanning in favour of following the lead of the art as it emerges. This encourages new and unexpected ideas, words, sounds, movements, and images to arrive. Instead of asking the client what they want to get out of a dance, the therapist will ask the client, "What does the dance need? For the feet to stamp louder or quieter?" or, "Which colour does the painting want?" In this way, the art is honoured as having a life of its own, a will that leads the creative process with its own momentum. Following the art also takes pressure off self-conscious clients, because rather than speak about themselves directly, their thoughts and feelings are communicated through the emerging art.

c) *Engaging the Imagination*

The creative process entices the imagination with a play of images, sounds, and movements, which connects people to the wisdom of playful thoughts. Without this ability, we live only in reality and experience only the surface appearance of the world. Imagination invites us past the surface and gives us access to that which is hidden.[51] Without imagination, when looking at a tree, I sense only the tree I can see. If I have a well-practiced imagination, I see not only the physical tree, but the tree in my mind's eye. This can lead to a series of playful thoughts that can be enriching and give me insight into myself. I can imagine what the roots look like. Even though I'm far away from the tree, I can imagine what the bark feels like. I can listen to the wind rustling through its leaves as if it is music. Eventually, this imagining may fill me with yearning to be at my cottage, where the trees grow tenaciously out of the craggy rocks and there is time to listen to the sounds of nature. Without this stream of playful thoughts, I might not have realized how much I needed a break from the daily grind of city life.

Imagination enriches our experience of the world, bringing us home to richness inside ourselves. In times of challenge, this depth of riches is especially needed.

d) *Multidisciplinary Approach*

Expressive arts therapy uses a multidisciplinary approach that provides an opportunity to choose or combine visual, auditory, written, and movement-based art forms. In Chapter 2, I describe six forms of body-based wisdom: action, inner body, physiology, thought/imagination, emotion, and spirit. One of the benefits of a multidisciplinary approach is that each art modality illuminates and focuses the voices of specific forms of wisdom. For instance, when performing a musical composition or a dance or theatre piece in a spontaneous manner, people tend to follow the wisdom of their actions and emotions. This playful spontaneity elicits new ideas and impulses. The result is usually an embodiment of someone's feelings.

The performing arts also provide opportunity to connect to inner body sensation. Often, the habitual nature of our internal sensations makes them hard to discern. For this reason, things like a tight feeling in one's heart or a sense of nervousness in one's belly might go unnoticed. When someone is swept up in performing a musical composition, dance, or theatrical improvisation, the intensity of embodied experiences stirs up internal sensations. Taking time for inward focus right after having finished a take can help people more clearly name and describe internal sensations. Finally, music, theatre, and dance arts are often group activities that unite people in a shared experience. They therefore have the power to enhance a sense of collective spirit and the wisdom that arrives from this.

Visual arts and writing also can tell the story of our emotions, but they tend to be less physical experiences. They are solitary activities that stand still through time. The end product is an art object that does not disappear into the air like the ephemeral dance. The benefit of this is that our feelings can be held in a solid physical object. This provides opportunity for client and therapist to interact with the art object, giving the client something they can take home or return to at another session.[52] Many clients have taken home a painting that represented a positive shift for them, often putting their works of art in a prominent location in their houses. This visual reminder of their therapeutic work helps to solidify transformation that occurred.

Another benefit of a multidisciplinary approach is that clients can deepen their artistic expression through layering, or moving between different arts modalities. A client may begin with painting, and then

embody the feeling of the painting in a song. They may improvise a
dance and then deepen their understanding of the experience by writing a story inspired by the dance. The experience is deepened for the
client because each new modality provides different insights. Also,
shifting or layering into a new modality provides a repetition that tends
to draw the experience into focus.[53]

I once worked with an elderly lady who used the arts to create a satisfying goodbye to her recently deceased cat. After her cat died, she explained, life just went on as usual. There was no ritual, such as a funeral, to help her deal with her grief.

"It just doesn't feel right," she said, "and I want to take time today to
say a proper goodbye."

She began by painting a picture of her cat. She then sat quietly and
wrote a poem that described her cat's personality and the way they
used to spend time together. When she finished, I read the poem out
loud while she moved in the studio, letting her actions be inspired by
the poem. During several takes of the dance, she played with different
movements, trying to find the just right physical expression of her grief.
In the final take, we danced together in silence. When we finished, I
suggested she stand still for a few moments and feel the internal sensations the dance stirred up. I could tell from her concentrated stance and
tearful eyes that she intensely felt the sensations of her grief. At the end
of the session, she said, "Now I feel like I've said a good and proper
goodbye."

My client found a satisfying goodbye to her old friend through poetry, dancing, and painting, with each art form enticing a different therapeutic result:

- through visual art she created an image that would stand still
  through time
- poetry helped to tell the story of her cat and her grief
- dance helped her to follow the wisdom of her actions and emotions; my act of dancing with her also gave her companionship
  within her grief.

e) Moving Away from the Center of the Problem

It can sometimes be helpful when a client places all his focus on an
issue or problem in his life. Sometimes, however, this focus can narrow

a client's view and make them feel like they're in a round-about in which there is no exit. When spontaneously creating art, the client is less focused on the center of the problem and can gain insight from new perspectives.

For example, a couple who always has the same argument about money may feel they're going around in circles with no hope of resolution. The therapist can draw the couple's focus away from their money issues by stopping their vocal debate and suggesting they paint a picture together in silence. This encourages the couple to engage in a new form of communication, which can help them see their money issues from new perspectives. While painting together, unexpected themes may emerge that help them realize that money is only the surface problem. Perhaps the wife is going on secret shopping binges as a way to distract herself from grieving the loss of a parent. With the habitual argument about money removed, there is the chance for these underlying emotional issues to surface, both in the couple's painting and in the way they interact. When the wife draws an image that stirs up her grief, the husband may feel compassion towards her instead of yelling at her for overspending. He is better able to support her grieving process in this way.

Sometimes, when we stop being preoccupied with the center, our sight actually becomes clearer. We see previously unnoticed things and gain a greater view of the whole.

3. How the Arts Build Relationships

Our ability to make meaningful and satisfying connections with others is fundamental to our well-being. Artistic expression is a connecting force that reaches out and touches both creator and witness in a shared experience in the following manners:

a) Art as a Connecting Bridge

Art strengthens the therapeutic relationship by forming a third entity between the therapist and the client that both can interact with. Imagine a client is deeply challenged by intimate relationships. If we, as therapist and client, sit on the floor and draw a picture together, we are no longer focusing directly on each other. We talk about and interact with the artwork. The focus becomes the shared artistic experience, rather than the intimacy of personal discussion. The art becomes a bridge that softens the awkwardness of revealing oneself to another.

b) Therapist "Stays-With" the Client's Artistic Expression

When a therapist interacts with clients by entering into their energetic space, they are making a statement of unconditional acceptance. The therapist is saying through their presence, "You do not need to change who you are for us to connect, because I am going to *stay-with* you wherever you are."

Steve Levine writes about the therapeutic benefit of *staying-with* in his essay *The Philosophy of Expressive Arts Therapy*:

> Usually clients enter therapy with a sense that their lives have already become chaotic; the experience of "falling apart" is often what motivates people to ask for help. . . . In this state of mind, the client tends to view the therapist as a potential savior, as one who will restore the lost self to its position of security. But what is most therapeutic, it seems to us, is not the attempt to "get someone together again." Rather the therapeutic effect comes from the ability to stay with the experience of nothingness and fragmentation without imposing a new structure. If the therapist can resist the impulse to help (a paradoxical task, since he or she works on the basis of this impulse), then there is the possibility that the client can find the way to a new sense of self. Creativity in the therapeutic process depends upon this ability to tolerate breakdown.[54]

I worked with a boy who was labeled a "bad kid" by the school system. At the start of a session, I asked, "Do you want to draw today?" The boy answered by defiantly throwing crayons at his paper. I joined him in a "game" of throwing crayons at the paper. This game became more and more vigorous until we collapsed in a puddle of giggles. Instead of reacting negatively to his crayon throwing, I "went with" his energy, giving him a companion rather than someone to fight against. As our session finished and we said goodbye, I felt a moment of sadness and loneliness build in my chest. I wondered whether this boy was lonely, and if through his aggression, he was crying out to be noticed. His behaviour did get him noticed, but also resulted in punishment and the label of "bad kid," which was not the best cure for his loneliness. Now, he had a new experience in which his cry for attention was met by a play companion. In this new "story," he stayed productively engaged with another. When I pointed out our unconventional artwork made from the marks of thrown crayons, he saw his resistance could be a source of creativity.

c) Being Witnessed

The therapist witnesses the client as well as the art they create, which gives the client a feeling of being seen. Being seen provides an important feedback loop that helps build our identities. We come to understand that we exist as distinct beings when our unique traits are noticed by another. For someone with a history of neglect, being witnessed can be an especially vital aspect of therapy.

I worked with a woman who told me that her parents had pressured her to follow in her father's footsteps and become a doctor, even though she clearly enjoyed artistic pursuits. Although she was loved, fed, and clothed, there was an aspect of neglect in her upbringing. Her parents, blinded by their own desires, failed to see who she was. For the first year of therapy, she played with stuffed animals and figurines, creating characters and building castles for them. I sensed that she did not want a playmate, but instead wanted to be seen for who she was. I sometimes joined her in her play, but the majority of the time I sat as a witness. At the end of each session, I gave her the gift of having seen her. I did this by making quickly-scribbled pictures of her castles, writing poems that told the story of her play, or by merely admiring the things she had built. I wondered many times if I was doing a good enough job as a therapist. The work was so simple, not involving deep psychological prodding on my part. Her therapy sessions involved activities you might imagine a six-year-old would enjoy, yet she was a thirty-year-old professional who was very successful in her field. I had to continually remind myself that watching her build castles was deeply vital work. She was going back into her childhood for the opportunity to be seen for who she really was.

d) Therapist Responds to the Client through the Arts

As an expressive arts therapist, I can respond to clients or the artwork they create through my own artistic expression. For example, I may sing a song or create a drawing as an offering in response to a client's story. Rather than respond through discussion, I enter into the expressive realm of action and feeling.

I do not, however, selfishly express whatever I want. If I had a rough day, I will not create drawings that express this. Instead, I create art that relates to and is inspired by the client. In doing so, I let the client see how their life experiences or artistic expression has moved me. As I make myself vulnerable through artistic expression, the hierarchy between therapist and client is lessened. In its place, a vital and connecting human relationship develops.

A client once told me the story of how she had been sexually abused when she was a child. She said that she never talked about it with her family or friends, and hardly anyone knew. I asked her if it was okay if I sang a song. I picked up my guitar and, making up the words as I went along, I sang about a young princess who had to find her way through a dark and scary forest. My song described how the princess had scratches from many thorns, but had bravely survived. I have no guitar training; I'm shy about my singing. I made myself vulnerable in that moment, letting my reaction to her story lead me. Visibly moved, she nodded her head and said, "Yes," indicating that my song had hit a chord with her. For years, the burden of her story had been held only by her. My song helped hold the burden of her experience. It let her know I understood her pain.

e) Connection through Storytelling

Clients tell their life stories to an expressive arts therapist not just through verbal description, but through artistic expression. Stories told through the arts often don't arrive cohesively, all at once, but in pieces over time. A client may sing a song that reminds her of her mother, which then leads her to describe a childhood memory. Then, a few weeks later, she may write a poem or create an abstract painting that expresses themes related to her childhood. As pieces of the client's story arrive through artistic expression, the therapist may not at first see how they connect. Different art pieces will seem to stand alone and not make much sense. Over time, the art pieces can start to connect together into a cohesive story – a story that would not have been told had the client verbally recited her life history while sitting on the couch.

A client once told me that when she was young, her mother was often sick and in the hospital. When I asked how this affected her, she brushed off my question with, "Well, we all just got on with life." I thought this response might represent a coping method that did not reveal how she really felt. Over time, the client surprised herself: paintings emerged that stirred up feelings of anxiety and loneliness. She did not intend to create these images, but they arrived when space was provided. The paintings disconcerted her because their abstract nature made it difficult for her to analytically explain them. The images seemed disconnected from the self-reliant person she saw herself as. Paradoxically, the feelings these paintings elicited felt like a coming home. Gradually, the accumulation of images, and her reactions to them, painted an unmistakable portrait of an anxious little girl. By painting and just letting things happen, an emotional element of her story had arrived. It became clear to her that although she was good at putting up a tough front, her childhood left her with a fear of being abandoned.

f) A Chance to Do Things Differently

The art created in therapy provides a play space where problems can be "worked out." The client can, consciously or unconsciously, start to see the therapist as representative of people from their past. In psychology, this is called transference. Transference occurs any time our past experiences cloud the current situation or add feelings beyond what the situation calls for. Suppose, for instance, I meet someone who reminds me of a teacher I did not like. Instead of seeing this person for who he is, I instantly dislike him due to that previous relationship. All of us experience transference to varying degrees throughout our lives. Transferences in therapy can provide an opportunity to go back and do things differently, to undo old relationship patterns that aren't working. For example, a client abused by his or her parents can learn to trust others when, over time, he or she is unconditionally accepted by a parent-like therapist.

For many years, my relationships with "dad-like" figures in my life – authority figures, male teachers, older men I dated – were clouded by anger that was uncalled for. Over time, I began to see this pattern and decided to work on my "man issues" because they were interfering with my relationships. I found an older male therapist with whom I had a strong rapport. He quickly became a father figure for me. When I was young, I censored my emotions in order to fit in with my dad's no-nonsense approach to life. Now I had the chance to do things differently;

the arts and my relationship with my male therapist were the playground for this exploration. I performed poems and songs and wrote stories that expressed anger and hurt. Every time I took these expressive risks, alarm bells sounded within me. In that moment, I was five years old again, paralyzed by the fear of being reprimanded for being emotional. My therapist stayed by my side as I learned to tolerate this anxiety. Over time, these internal alarm bells softened and it became easier to express who I was without self-censorship. Expressing these feelings through the arts with a "father-like" therapist as witness provided the chance to undo relationship patterns that were not serving my well-being, which left my relationships with men less encumbered by my past.

Allen

The park is about to burst with new life. I sense it even though the trees are still barren, through a smell in the air and the way my cat is pawing at the door.

"One second . . . I'll let her out."

I return to my spot, sitting on the floor across from Allen.

"Is it the beached whale again?" I ask.

Allen nods yes.

He is lying perfectly still on the floor. He whispers, "I want to disappear."

Allen has been exploring the beached whale in our sessions for the past two months. It began when he admitted to his self-loathing:

"I just don't like myself. This isn't who I'm supposed to be. This is not the way I imagined my life would turn out. And there's this . . . annihilating . . . thing in me that doesn't believe I deserve to be here. Sometimes I want to just disappear."

As he told me this, I worried that his wish to disappear would translate into a suicide risk.

He must have sensed this, because he paused and said, "No, no, I would never kill myself. It's not like that. It's just sort of like killing myself slowly with food."

When I asked Allen what the sensation of wanting to kill himself slowly feels like, he described a beached whale and an intense pull towards "nothingness."

Over the past few weeks, each time Allen took time to focus on internal body sensations, he named the image of the beached whale. This became his starting point for art making: poems about the nothingness that describe the freedom he has there, drawings of empty beaches, and embodiment of the beached whale through sound and movement. It was hard work, and at times I felt we might both be lost in the midst of his despair.

I wanted to rescue Allen and tell him how to escape from the barren beach. I wanted to tell him that everything would be okay. I wanted to tell him that he has so many good qualities; he doesn't need to feel this way. I wanted to help the beached whale back into the water so it could swim once again. I knew that by trying to rescue him in this manner, however, I would be sending the message that the beached whale was not welcome in my studio. I knew that staying with the beached whale was vitally important. It was probably the first time that someone had sat with Allen on this empty beach. Unconditionally accepting the beached whale *is* the rescue. It is the slow arrival of water. It is an act of unconditional love that I hope has the power to transform.

Today, as I sit with Allen, I imagine I can hear the tide arriving.

"Okay," I say, "how about following the motion of wanting to disappear?"

"There is no movement in it," Allen replies, "except wanting to get smaller and smaller."

"How about pulling your body in tighter and smaller and staying with that feeling?"

Allen curls up into a ball, and then is still again.

"What sounds might match this feeling of pulling in?" I ask.

"There is no sound. It's a nothing place," Allen answers.

In my experience, there is never "nothing." There is always something. The "nothing" is usually a cover up for the something. So I persist.

"What would nothing sound like if it had sound? Like the faintest wind or like TV static or like a snake? Which of these matches the best?"

He's silent.

"I'll make the sounds," I say, "and let me know which feels right." I whisper, "Whooooo . . . shhhhhh . . . zzzzzzz. . . ."

"The static sound," Allen answers.

"Can you make that sound?"

I see him really fighting to get the sound out, trying to push past the block he feels in his throat, the desire to become nothing, with no sound or movement to prove he exists. Then I hear the faintest "shhh-hhh," repeated with each exhale. He starts to rock ever so slightly.

Ah, I wonder, *is the tide arriving?*

I also begin to make the "shhhhhh" sound and rock gently.

Allen wants to disappear into the annihilating safety of nothingness. By amplifying the movement and sound of this energy, he begins to feel and hear signs of life. He is teetering between wanting to settle into oblivion and wanting to live. I sit with him in this dangerous, scary place, witnessing a battle I imagine has been going on for years.

I feel this battle in my own body as I witness him; it is a crushing still-ness and an unrealized desire to move that makes it hard for me to breathe. The tension is almost unbearable. I want to push against the stillness. For some reason, I feel the urge to sing. Not wanting to break the quiet, I hum a lullaby for the beached whale. As it comes to an end, Allen stops rocking and is perfectly still.

We sit in silence. It's not an easy silence for me. Staying with some-one in such a desolate place stretches me emotionally.

After a time, I ask, "What is happening to the whale now?"

"I just got such an odd sensation. It's like, all of a sudden, the way I feel right now reminds me . . . this sounds weird . . . I hardly remem-ber, but . . . I think I used to hide under the kitchen table when I was really little."

"How about imagining you're back underneath the table? What did the floor look like, the table cloth, the smell of the kitchen, the sounds in the house? Tell me what you notice."

"I'm underneath the kitchen table," Allen says, "trying to be really still and quiet. I don't want to disturb anyone. Everything in the house is so dark. I mean, not dark, but so . . . down. Everyone is pretending there's nothing wrong, but I can feel it. It's like everyone around me is sad. I think I hear people crying, but there's no sound. The quiet seems so loud, it overwhelms me. I just want to disappear into nothing and I have this immense desire to eat without stopping."

"It must have been very scary," I say, "for the little boy underneath the table to feel all that sadness, with no one to talk to about it. And food was the friend that helped him through."

Allen nods and says, "No one helped me. I mean, it's not normal for such a young boy to horde a week's worth of food under his bed. But everyone just looked the other way."

There are ten minutes left in the session. Allen has really gone somewhere today and it's my job to help bring him back to the present.

"Okay," I instruct, "how about putting your hands on the floor and pushing yourself up to sitting . . . Now, when you're ready, open your eyes and look around."

Allen does so.

"Are you back?" I ask.

"Yeah, I'm here."

As Allen gets ready to go, he says, "You know, it feels good to come here and not have to pretend everything is okay. For one hour a week I can just be exactly who I am, and that's such a relief. I'm not sure where we are going with all this. It doesn't quite make sense to me yet . . . but I trust you . . . I trust that we are making our way through to something good."

After this session, the image of the beached whale does not return. In my imagination, the tide arrived and carried the whale back into the sea.

Allen has not been working at the center of his problems (his depression and compulsive eating), where everything seems stuck. Instead, he has been doing art and just letting things happen. Allen and I follow the themes and images that arrive as if they have a life of their own. Thus, when the image of the beached whale appears, we treat it as a living, breathing entity. Allen listens to the beached whale and follows its desires. He gets to know the beached whale through many different art disciplines. The images, words, sounds, movements, and sensations that arrive during this time live in a world all of their own, not seeming to provide understanding that can help Allen heal from his compulsive eating.

For Allen, even though staying with the beached whale is challenging, a good feeling comes from it. He feels accepted and finds space to be himself without censorship. Allen embodies the beached whale for session after session; with each repetition, he gets to know the sensation of the whale and learns to tolerate my presence as witness. This is a chance for him to "try out" a new story, one in which he does not hide who he is. I communicate with the whale through a lullaby that reaches into the whale's deepest belly to find a key, a memory of a lonely boy sitting underneath a kitchen table, trying to survive the sadness of his family by disappearing into food. This is the key that I hope can unlock Allen's food compulsion.

After this key is found, the image of the beached whale does not return to our session work. It is common in expressive arts therapy for an image to arrive and stay for a period of months or weeks. When the image has had its say, it will recede, leaving room for new imagery and metaphors to take its place. Each image or metaphor is like a stone laid in the earth, each connecting together to form a path. This path does not always lead directly to analytical understanding of a person's issues, but I trust that although it may meander in a way we might not understand, it will lead Allen home.

Allen cannot quite make sense of the work he does in my studio, but he has an underlying sense that it feels right. What he can't make sense of in his head feels right in his heart.

4. How the Arts Engage People with the World

Our lives depend on our capacity to sense what is around us and navigate through it successfully. Creating art encourages exploration of one's interaction with the world in the following manners:

a) *The Senses*

To engage in life, we need to be able to hear, touch, taste, smell, and see ourselves and the world. People will often dampen their ability to sense as a result of trauma or intolerable conditions. By shutting out the world, they feel protected, but this can also leave them feeling disconnected from themselves and others. The arts are sense-enticing and draw people back towards a full-bodied experience of life. All forms of art entice our senses, but each differs from the others in that each leads with a specific sense. For instance, music focuses on hearing, painting focuses on seeing, and sculpting focuses on touch. Using a multidisciplinary therapeutic approach (using many art forms) encourages and exercises a full palette of sensory awareness.

b) Matching through the Arts

We create and search for things in the world that match our internal experience. When we see, hear, touch, smell, and taste things that match our inner world, a connection is made that brings us home to ourselves. It's like looking in a mirror and confirming that we exist. When we watch a play that we emotionally resonate with or meet a new friend with similar interests, we have found a match for something inside ourselves. We can find matches that contribute to our well-being, but we can also search out matches that are detrimental. For example, if I think I am worthless, then I may search out *bad* relationships, jobs, or circumstances that confirm this belief. This is especially true if someone carries with them unresolved emotional conflict or suffering. Our psychological energy needs a concrete place to land. This is such a fundamental need that whether our "matches" support or hurt our well-being is often secondary.

Artistic expression is a brilliant way to help create matches that support one's well-being, rather than harm. A self-harmer, instead of beating his head against a wall to match his rage and anguish, can beat a drum or cut into the canvas he paints on. An anorexic young girl wishing to disappear can draw wispy paintings that are almost invisible, expressing the dynamics of her disease through art rather than starvation.

c) Play

Play connects us to the world through the physical embodiment of the imagination and the relationship between the self and another. Play is a voluntary activity executed within certain limits of time and space and according to agreed-upon rules. Rules can be the set of rules for a hockey game, or the agreements kids arrive at before stating their play, i.e., "You play the storekeeper and I'll play the customer" or "You hide and I'll try to find you." Although rules are pre-set, no one involved in play knows exactly how things will unfold. This lack of knowing what will happen is so fundamental that the moment things become predictable, play ends. Can you imagine playing Monopoly if you already knew who would win? Winning often seems like the goal of play, but it is not the real goal. We are drawn to play by no other goal than play itself: the goal of play is to play.

Play creates a heightened state in which the senses are enlivened and feelings of tension, joy, and consciousness are intensified.[55] This intensity, as well as the unpredictability of play, leads to new discoveries. When someone is stuck on a problem and doesn't know how to proceed, the cure most often is to just "play with it" for a while until things become unstuck. The sense of discovery that play brings is revitalizing, whether it's a group of engineers playing with different construction ideas or children pretending to be lions.

Stuart Brown, the author of *Play: How it Shapes the Brain, Opens the Imagination, and Invigorates the Soul,* writes:

> Play lets animals [including humans] learn about their environment and the rules of engagement with friend and foe. Playful interaction allows a penalty-free rehearsal. . . . In play, most of the time we are able to try out things without threatening our physical or emotional well-being. We are safe precisely because we are just playing. For humans, creating such simulations of life may be play's most valuable benefit. In play we can imagine and experience situations we have never encountered before and learn from them. We can create possibilities that have never existed but may in the future. We can make new cognitive connections that find their way into our everyday lives.[56]

According to Stuart Brown, play provides valuable practice and exploration that is essential in successfully navigating life. In the field of child psychology, however, play is traditionally considered to be only vital to childhood development.[57] Expressive arts therapists believe that play is a vital component throughout our entire lifespan. Whether it's through sports, creating art, cooking a meal without a recipe, or goofing around with friends, play is an essential, connecting, and life-giving activity regardless of age.

As we mature into adulthood, we conform to social norms in which play is thought to be only for children. Exposure to the threat of emotional or physical abuse can also hinder our ability to play. Ever ready to engage in fight or flight, we have difficulty playing because we cannot let down our guard. We may also dampen our senses in response to intolerable living conditions and this creates a reduced sense of being alive that makes it difficult to be playful. When we lose the ability to play, we suffer because there is no physical connection between what we are and what we could be. We become stuck in sameness when we cannot playfully practice new possibilities.[58]

Expressive arts therapists encourage play both by helping clients follow the lead of the art without preplanning, and by joining clients as a willing play companion. Both therapist and client play with brush strokes, words, sounds, images, or dance steps. The expressive arts therapist also suggests, or helps the client create, therapeutic "games." The rules of the games can be set verbally such as, "How about I play your mom and you play with different ways of asserting your boundaries." These rules may also arise organically when, for instance, client and therapist mysteriously find themselves in an unspoken collective agreement to dance playfully in and out of a stream of sunshine that has arrived in the studio.[59]

I worked with a client who was not comfortable with spontaneous expression because he could not tolerate the unknown. He told me that as a young child, he had lived in the midst of a violent war. He responded by always being on guard. Living in persistent fear led him to excessively organize his life because it made him feel safer. This defense probably saved him from a psychological breakdown in his childhood, but now that he lived in a peaceful country, it was interfering with his enjoyment of life. He complained that he felt a lack of emotion, and felt that his life was numbingly predictable. I supported him in gradually using less and less preplanning in his expression. I encouraged many and varied takes of the same art project, giving him a chance to play with the images, sounds, and movements. I often joined him as a creative play companion. Over time, he expanded his ability to play. In allowing himself to be spontaneous, he began to feel less numb. He was also surprised to find safety in the "as if" world of play, because it allowed him to express, in a nondirect manner, things he found too painful to talk about.

d) Reframing One's View of the Self in Relationship with the World

How an individual views their connection with the world is often based on a set point of view that is created through past experiences. For example, I worked with a woman who thought she was a failure because she had dropped out of college. After failing the first year, she gave up and labeled herself stupid and lazy. She held this view for years without questioning it.

I wondered if this old story was working for her. Did it serve her? Was it even true? Was there another way she could understand her failure that would be more in keeping with who she is?

Through the dances and paintings she created in my studio, the image of a strong, independent woman emerged. Over time, she realized that failing school had been a way of saying no to her family's pressure to get a traditional job. She reframed her failure as a brave step away from traditional values. She came into my studio a "college dropout." Months later, she left as a "brave woman," ready to choose her own path. Essentially, she had not changed; the story she told about herself had.

In Chapter 1, I told the story of how I had "embarrassed" the nation of Canada with my thick thighs. For many years, I was deeply shamed by this story and wouldn't tell it to anyone. I internalized the judgments placed upon my body and felt ashamed of my ugliness. At the end of my third year in expressive arts training, I performed a clown routine in which I played an "out of shape" clown who was humiliated when she attended a militant exercise class. People were in tears with laughter. My concept of success and failure had been shifting since I left the National Ballet Company, but that performance was a defining moment, one in which I suddenly felt very proud to have challenged the status quo with my thick thighs. While I used to think that success was measured by body weight, I finally understood that I had achieved success just by surviving the rigors of a professional ballet career. I playfully reframed a once-shameful experience into a kind of *I Love Lucy* skit, in which I pranced around the stage in all my thick-legged glory.[60]

My chronic shame was beginning to recede, but I still suffered from bouts of low self-esteem and depression. During this time, I helped run a weekly support group with another expressive arts therapist. One evening, before the group members arrived, I felt particularly overwhelmed and hopeless. I decided to give myself some self-care through the arts and drew a picture of a figure with a gloomy funnel cloud overhead (Fig. 1). This image matched perfectly how I felt. My coworker, a seasoned expressive arts therapist, arrived and sat with me while looking at my drawing.

She responded to my drawing with, "The storm clouds can always be overhead. Or. . . ." She paused and turned the paper upside down. "The storm clouds can be the path that leads to an open sky."

I was stunned to see that my drawing, when turned upside down, did, in fact, look like a path to an open sky. I picked up a pastel and drew in a new skirt to hide the upside-down head. I then drew a new

Figure 1. Oppressive dark storm clouds forever overhead.

Figure 2. A challenging road led me to an open sky.

head and hands for the figure and made the sky more sky-like (Fig. 2). I was so struck with this image that I took it home with me and taped it to my bedroom wall. Each time I looked at it, I felt I could breathe easier. My old story that the dark storm clouds were always overhead was replaced with a new story: I had walked a stormy path, but had now arrived at open sky.

My experienced expressive arts colleague nudged me at a tipping point – the point at which enough positive therapeutic work had occurred that I just needed a little nudge to redirect me into a more positive view of life. In my life today, I am the woman looking up at the open sky. The path behind me is full of interesting tales that no longer wreak havoc with my sense of self. Now, I relish the moment when the topic at a party turns to divulging embarrassing moments, and I say with a twinkle in my eye, "I once embarrassed the nation of Canada on the international stage. . . ."

Although reframing is a vital aspect of expressive arts therapy, I would never pressure anyone to change their view of their life story before they are ready. This is often ineffective and can instigate a power struggle that may cause dissonance between the client and therapist. However, when reframing occurs at its own pace and through the exploratory nature of the arts, it can have powerful healing properties. A skilled therapist can also sense when someone is at their tipping point and ready for a nudge in a new direction.

5. How the Arts Increase Self-Knowledge and Interaction

Expressive arts connect us to others and the world, so it makes sense that its connecting properties can also help us connect to and interact with aspects of self. This happens in the following ways:

a) Creating Distance Allows Us to See Ourselves

Art objects created in expressive arts therapy represent aspects of the art maker, but they also have a physical presence all of their own. The "otherness" of the art objects enables the exploration of self with a feeling of distance. This distance allows people to step back and see aspects of themselves from afar. Expressive arts therapist Majken Jacoby states:

> They [the art objects] need space and so do we, a space large enough
> for us to be able to look away; [for] we can only see what is in front

of us if it is possible to look at something else. We need distance, spatially and emotionally, in order to come close and grasp it.[61]

I once worked with a woman who suppressed her anger in order to appear nice. She did this to such an extent that she did not recognize her anger when it did surface. One day, I recorded her performing a loud, chaotic drum solo and then played it back. I asked her to describe the music in the recording. After a minute of searching unsuccessfully for the right descriptive words, she tentatively said, "I guess it sounds a bit angry." Sometimes we can see things from afar that we cannot see up close.

b) Dialoguing with the Images One Creates

When an aspect of self is expressed through the arts, a dialogue can occur between the image and the creator. I will ask a client to write or speak from the point of view of the image he or she created. This is an imaginary game in which he or she pretends he or she is the image speaking.

Once I asked a client who painted something that looked like a star burst to speak as if she was the image. She said, "I am orange with yellow swirls that move outwards." From here, the doorway opened to descriptions that were beyond objective sight. She continued, "I have movement. I like to be quick and to explode out. I crave to feel alive." I then asked her if she had anything to say to the painting. Looking at her image, she said, "I know you crave to feel alive, but living with so much feeling scares me." This dialogue revealed a pull between her desire to experience life fully and her desire to back away from life's intensity.

We all have thoughts or feelings that we would rather push away and pretend as if they do not exist. When these aspects are expressed through artwork, they are invited to the table for a discussion.

c) Interacting Physically with the Art

We can also interact physically with artwork that represents aspects of self, which allows the wisdom of action to lead. I worked with a client who was feeling angry with his dad, but sad at the same time because he craved to be closer to him. In one session, he wrote an angry poem to his father. He scribbled furiously, making sure to cover up his writing so I could not read it. After he finished, he felt terrible for having expressed anger towards him. Even though his dad would never see this paper, my client felt anxious that his anger might result in the loss of his dad's affection. I suggested that he play with moving the paper around the studio at different distances from himself. When it was closer to him, he felt overwhelmed with anxiety; the further it was from him, the less anxious he felt. Finally, he decided to tear up the paper and put the pieces in a box, which he then hid in my art cupboard. He said, "That feels better; when I am ready, I can open up the box during another session."

Through action, he was getting to know and learning to tolerate his anger towards his father. Through action, he let the anger know that he needed to put it away for the moment so as not to be completely overwhelmed by the anxiety it caused him.

Allen

"I think I'm gonna try the Zone diet," Allen says. He squints as a single beam of sun makes its way through the canopy of trees outside and shines on his face.

I get up and pull the curtain closed.

"You know, Allen," I say, "Extreme diets like the Zone exasperate the desire to binge, because when you starve yourself, your body naturally craves big quantities of food. The best thing to do is just stop dieting and focus on eating healthy."

"I know, you keep telling me that. But it's really hard to let go of the dream of the perfect diet that will fix everything . . . and besides, I feel everyone is judging me and my size and looking at what I eat. I feel like they all think I should just eat a salad."

"Who are they?"

"Everyone."

"Who's everyone?"

"The whole world!"

"I'm part of the world and I don't think that."

"Yeah, well, people like you are very rare."

"Thank you. I take that as a big compliment. But tell me about these other people who aren't like me."

Allen looks down. "I remember kids laughing at me all the time when I was growing up. I was sent to fat camp every summer. You know, the camps where they put kids on diets and make them do sports. Anyways, I was always one of the bigger kids at the camp, so even the other fat kids made fun of me."

It's such a sadly pathetic story that I'm at a loss for words. After a while, the best I come up with is, "Wow, that must have really sucked."

My response is not my most brilliant therapeutic moment, but then I remember that even the most challenging things can be played with, so I say, "Well, how about going back to that memory of being teased and we'll see how we can play with it. Can you describe it to me?"

"Okay. I'm in the cafeteria and the kids at the other table are laughing at me."

"What does the cafeteria smell like?" I ask.

Allen closes his eyes. "There's that smell of the horrible salad dressing they forced us to eat."

"How does your chair feel?" I ask.

"It's wood, and I like to rub my fingers on the worn edges."

"What are the sounds?" I ask.

"Clinking utensils. And, of course, the kids laughing at me."

"And how do you feel in this cafeteria with the bad-smelling dressing, the worn chairs, and the kids laughing at you?"

"Like shit. Like I wish I was invisible."

"Let's see what we can do. How about imagining there are no longer any kids in the cafeteria? Just make them disappear. Imagine you're sitting in the same cafeteria all by yourself."

"Oh . . . okay. They're all gone."

"Does that feel better?"

"A bit, but not really, because I still have this stupid salad with the horrible dressing sitting in front of me."

"Okay . . . BING! The salad is gone. You're in the cafeteria and there's no one else, no stupid salad. How does that feel?"

"Well, I'm still at the weight-loss camp."

"BING! There's no camp. You're standing alone in a clearing with no laughing kids, no stupid salad, and no camp."

"Now, this is getting better. But I'm still worried because I know that when I get home, my mom will look to see if I've lost weight."

"Fine, no mom!"

"No mom?"

"Yes. You're in a clearing with no laughing kids, no salad, and no mom hiding behind a tree."

"Well, there are still people on the subway who look at me, and even if I'm in a clearing, I know I'll have to ride a subway sometime soon."

"All right, you're standing in a clearing on a world with absolutely no people. You are entirely alone."

"Oh, well, now that feels better! There's no one to laugh at me."

"Now follow what your body wants to do in this world all by yourself."

Allen, with his eyes still closed, unfolds his arms from their usual crossed position and lifts them wide into the air. He smiles.

"Wow, this feels good."

"Allen, you know my style. Let's put this image into the arts. Do you want to paint, sing, dance, sculpt, or write poems about Mr. Outstretched-Arms-Guy?"

Allen opens his eyes and sees my large blue exercise ball.

He walks to the art cupboard, takes out a piece of cardboard, and cuts out a very tiny figure with arms outstretched.

He tapes the figure's feet to the exercise ball and balances the ball on the studio floor so that the paper figure looks like it is standing on top of the world.

"There," he says. "That's it!"

"Okay, how about stretching your arms out again so it really gets in your body. Maybe do a few takes. And imagine you're on a world all alone."

As he does this, I grab a paper and start scribbling a poem.

"How does it feel, Allen?" I ask, looking up from my paper.

"It feels good, there are no judgments. But . . . it's also a bit lonely."

I scribble some more lines, and then ask if I can pick up the ball.

"Yeah, but make sure the man doesn't fall off. I'd hate to fall off the world today. That would really suck!"

I pick up the ball and, looking at the paper man perched on top, I recite my poem to him.

There was a paper man,
And he had a thousand judgments in his pocket from a thousand referees.
His head was so full of their words, there was no space for him to be.
And so he went away to a world where there was no one else to see,
Especially no referees telling him what to be!

And one by one, he took their judgments from his pocket, and he
threw each into the sea.
He laughed and whirled around, he did, his arms wide outstretched,
So full of glee, with his pockets as empty as can be.
When he finished laughing, he looked around to see his world was as
empty as can be.
He sighed wistfully, because from the mountain to the sea, as far as he
could see, there was only he.

Allen laughs. "Yes. That's it, isn't it? You hide out from the judgments
of the world and, at the end of the day, you end up all alone. Ah, I did
that for many years . . . so many years. But I'm not like that anymore.
Things are changing."

He takes the paper man off the ball and holds him in his hand.
Looking up at me, he says, "You know that woman I met this summer?
Well, we're getting along great, and she doesn't care what I weigh. She
just loves me. Can you believe it? I have a hard time believing it myself. I keep waiting for the bubble to burst. Meanwhile, she's talking
about us moving in together! I've had this secret world of binge eating
for so long it's hard to imagine letting someone in."

"What would you like to say to the paper man, Allen?"

He looks in his hand. "Hey, paper man, you cannot be on a world
by yourself forever. You need people."

I am speechless after Allen's camp story. For a moment I feel sorry
for Allen, which is never a very useful thing for a therapist to feel.
Worse, a story about being teased at fat camp for being too fat is so
extreme that it almost makes me want to laugh. How *should* I respond? A typical therapist statement like, "That must have been really
hard for you" seems too much like a canned phrase. Instead, Allen and
I play with the images from his camp story and he has the chance to
go back to camp and feel and respond differently. This play happens
with a "here-and-now" feeling. Allen stays attentive to the sensations
in his body and follows the actions his body craves. In this way, in addition to building new thought pathways, important shifts in action and
sensation occur. Free from judgments, he is able to take back his power, stretching out his arms without apology. He then creates the image
of the man alone on top of the world to represent this freedom. The
distance allowed by the art object enables Allen to see that a secret

world, kept to one's self, is lonely. I witness his creation and I respond artistically with the poem, which helps support Allen's realization that being in a world all alone is safe, but lonely. When Allen speaks to the man alone on top of the world, in an indirect way he is telling himself that it is time to leave his secret world and let others in.

Allen

The last hot days of summer still reign. My air-conditioning is broken, so it is hot and humid in my studio, despite the fan. Allen's face is red and sweaty.

"Allen," I say, "you told me in your last session that your doctor is concerned about your health, and that some of your blood levels are dangerously high and erratic."

Allen looks uneasy, but I continue.

"You've said yourself that you're feeling a lot better about life and you're binging less. You've met someone you really like and you're talking about moving in together. You're looking for a new job. You've stopped your extreme diets. Things are moving in a good direction; at this pace, you'll probably eventually feel even better and stop binge eating entirely. But you face some very real health risks as a result of years of yo-yo dieting and binge eating. I'm afraid you might not be around to finish your work here if we don't speed things up. I think you need additional support to get you physically healthy. For the past year I've suggested that you see a nutritionist, but you've been reluctant to go. Today, I'm giving you an ultimatum: you need to see a nutritionist, or you can't continue therapy with me. I think your health is at risk; I will not stand by and potentially see you die without intervening."

I take a big breath. This is hard for me to say. It is rare that I give a client an ultimatum that might turn them away from therapy, but I'm worried that if his blood sugar levels skyrocket during a binge, he could die from a heart attack or insulin shock.

"Hmm . . ." Allen says. "This isn't easy to hear. You know me. I like to pretend nothing's wrong."

"What's holding you back from calling the nutritionist?" I ask.

Allen gives me a blank stare.

"Okay, imagine you're holding the phone and giving her a call. How does that feel?"

Allen closes his eyes. "I feel panicked. Like my heart is racing."

"Panicked because . . . ?"

"Well, it's like finally facing things head-on instead of turning away. It's like this huge leap of faith."

"Faith in what?"

"Faith in myself."

"Allen, this is a decisive moment. I'm giving you a big push here: you can decide to move towards life or you can keep turning towards oblivion. I think you're worth it, and I think you're ready."

"And if I don't call?" he asks.

"Then you can't come back here for any more sessions," I repeat.

Allen looks stunned. He's never seen me like this before. My gentle pacing is gone; in its place, there's just this big kick in the ass to help get him moving.

"If you want, you can make the call from here."

"No," he says quickly. "I think I can manage this myself."

"Good," I say. "Next question: Will you give me permission to call the nutritionist and talk to her about you?"

"Really?" Allen looks surprised again.

"You've told me that you can't stay on a diet for long because all the restrictions make you feel like rebelling; then, when your diet fails, you feel like a big failure. I thought that instead of her giving you a list of good and bad foods, which will just be a big set-up for feeling bad about yourself, she could put you on a diet that works by addition, in which she would never tell you what you should not eat. Instead, week by week, she will tell you the nutritious things that she wants you to add into your diet. It's a 'more' diet rather than a 'less' diet."

Allen nods his head slowly.

I continue, "I bet seeing the nutritionist will also help with the binging. During my recovery from bulimia, there was a point when I had worked through the emotional reasons for binging. Because I wasn't eating well, I still had intense cravings to over-eat. My body was trying to recover from nutritional deficits."

In our next session, I find out that Allen has taken the leap of faith: he phoned the nutritionist and made appointments to see her regularly. Over the next weeks, he learns about healthy eating. He starts making sure that he eats protein in the morning and that he eats at regular intervals. He eats more fruits and vegetables and starts using healthier cooking techniques.

> Allen's health was giving him a message, but he was not acting on it. I took a risk by confronting him about this because I was worried for his life. No matter how effective I am in helping people sort out their psychological challenges, if their behaviour seriously risks their health, any work they accomplish in therapy may literally be short-lived.
>
> I also sensed that Allen was at his tipping point. Enough therapeutic work had occurred to make a push in a new direction effective.
>
> This session involved no art-making, but the connection we had built through the bridge of art enabled our therapeutic relationship to withstand my ultimatum.

6. How the Arts Encourage New Connections and Long-Lasting Change

Even though transformation is possible, we tend to experience the same thoughts and behaviours over and over again because we default towards ingrained pathways. There are, however, certain experiences that awaken the ability to let go of old patterns and build new pathways:

a) Love

Love sweeps over and through us, opening and building new pathways at all levels of self: hormones and body chemicals are released, we feel enlivened, we are open to new ideas, our bodies feel softer and less shielded, we become disarmed as our defensive patterns relax, our senses become more finely tuned, and we recapture the ability to sense things as if for the first time. Love creates receptivity to self, other people, and the world within every aspect of our being.

At a neurological level, love is related to the "love" brain chemicals dopamine and oxytocin. Dopamine is a neurotransmitter that triggers our brain's pleasure and reward centers. We experience dopamine surges both when we win a race and when we become intoxicated with the intensity and excitement of romantic love. Surges of dopamine are believed to increase neuroplasticity by helping to save any newly-formed neural pathways. Dopamine triggers an intense good feeling, which causes us to save in our memory, consciously or unconsciously, the method of getting back to that particular feeling state. This causes a likelihood that we will repeat the circumstances and behaviours that got us to this state.

Oxytocin is a hormone that is active in the bonding love between long-term partners or between parent and child. It is often referred to as the "snuggling" hormone. Oxytocin surges also trigger a "good" feeling that we want to get back to, although the experience is less intense than with dopamine. Neurologically, oxytocin is theorized to have the ability to wipe out learned behaviour by melting down existing neural connections so that new connections can be made. It can be seen as a solvent that dissolves old pathways, enabling us to experience new thoughts and behaviours. One theory is that the survival of the human race depends on our ability to bond so that we can procreate, care for our children, and pool our resources. This joining-together requires massive amounts of change. Old patterns need to be unlearned and new ones built if one is to successfully merge one's life with another. Oxytocin is thought to be the solvent that helps in this adaptive process. When dopamine or oxytocin are at their strongest, usually when we initially fall in love or bond with someone, they recreate the chance for a rapid restructuring of self.[62, 63]

While neurological theories speak of romantic and parental love, I believe there are similar effects when the energy of love enters the therapy room. In expressive arts therapy, we do not cultivate romantic love or snuggle with our clients. We instead support an "in the moment" opening of one's heart in combination with a sense of beauty and deep caring. This type of love in therapy helps us to be open to change in the same way romantic and bonding love do, but maintains professional boundaries appropriate for a client/therapist relationship. It's important to consider that the personal transformation that may be ushered in and solidified by love's powers may not always be for the better. When the energy of love arrives in the studio, it is the therapist's ethical duty to guide love's transformative qualities towards positive change.

Love enters into the therapeutic process in many ways. As clients are drawn into the intensity of the creative process, they can fall in love with an artistic modality, surprising themselves, for example, with a previously undiscovered love of dancing. Persons can also learn about love as they "fall in love" with specific art pieces they create. This happens especially when the creator feels compassion for characters that emerge in his or her artwork. For someone with very low self-esteem, feeling self-love is a huge leap. Direct self-care and love might be inaccessible, but standing back and seeing a painting he or she created may allow him or her to see beauty in aspects of "self" expressed within the art. This witnessing creates an opening towards seeing value in their existence. It is a seedling that, if given care, can grow and wipe out old patterns of self-critique and eventually blossom into a compassionate and caring attitude towards the self.

I have witnessed group members offer love in workshops as they are touched by a fellow member's brave and honest artistic expression. I was in one workshop in which we listened to a woman sing a song that told her story of being sexually assaulted. Before she sang, she told us that this was the first time she was going to share her story publicly. Her song, which was full of sadness and rage, moved us all. After she finished, we spontaneously formed a circle around her and linked arms. Rocking back and forth, many of us weeping, we hummed our own song in response. When she saw others respond to her artistic expression with such compassion, her existence as an individual who is worthy of love was validated. The rapist had damaged her faith in the world and in herself; together, we were helping her to rebuild it.

The therapist can also teach the fundamentals of love through example. Each time the therapist unconditionally accepts the images, sounds, and movements the client creates, he or she demonstrates open-heartedness. When the therapist lets him or herself be moved by the beauty of a client's expression, he or she is teaching vulnerability. An open heart, capable of love, is an intimate and delicate thing that requires bravery; a therapist can be a model of this bravery.

The care-bond between therapist and client can also fulfill a client's need for compassionate and unconditional love, which he or she may not have received growing up. This can help someone complete developmental stages passed over due to neglect or trauma. Artistic communication from the therapist to the client can be the "good-enough" parent that holds the client like a mother's arms.

Once, a client told me that she was invited to give a presentation to a large group of people interested in her unique way of working with people living on the street. She was proud of her work, but thought it strange that everyone was making such a fuss about it. She had not received acknowledgment for her accomplishments when she was young, so this type of recognition was not familiar to her. As she told me this story, I picked up a piece of paper and made her a quick drawing, which I then showed her while describing my scribbles. "This is you at the center. You're giving your speech, and these leaves growing around you are trees you have planted with your words." Pointing lower, I said, "See these people watching? They are learning from you how to plant trees even in the most devastated landscapes." She was moved by my scribbles and asked if she could take the drawing home. My drawing was like a mother's arms reaching out from the past, giving her the care and recognition she had not received as a child.

In both the story of the victim of sexual assault and the woman who couldn't acknowledge her accomplishments, compassion helped each of them take in and solidify new messages: "I can be vulnerable and let others in; I can trust; I am of value; I can be loved; and I can love."

In therapy, love is not something that can be forced. When it arrives, though, faith in life can radiate into the arts studio and open a chance for a clearing and rebuilding. In that moment, a client's face softens and I can see the energy of love rushing into his or her body. It is like watching a ship at sea, having trouble staying afloat, magically deconstruct and rebuild itself into a more seaworthy vessel. Love is essential to health. Therapy can teach people how to love and be loved.

b) Beauty

In traditional art forms, beauty is often thought to result from the perfection of form and technical skill – precisely executed violin notes and pirouettes, for example. From the expressive arts perspective, beauty is thought *not* to arise through perfected form, but through shaping our life experiences into honest expression. I believe that no matter how exact the violin note or pirouette, there is little beauty in these expressions unless they reveal human truth. When we see, touch, smell, taste, or hear something that we know is true, we are "touched" by the beauty of truth itself. We experience this beauty regardless of the skill or content of the artist's expression. Witnessing this beauty may not always be pleasant or easy, either. It can arrive through the honest expression of joy and harmony, but it can also cut into us with expressions of discord, chaos, and suffering.[64]

If beauty through artistic creation does not require technical skill, then it is accessible to all, from art novices to seasoned professionals. Thus, someone who has never lifted his or her arms in a dance or put a crayon to paper can, in my expressive arts practice, benefit from the therapeutic qualities that beauty offers.

Some people understand beauty through a disembodied intellectual process. They may understand that a painting is beautiful because it perfectly demonstrates the golden ratio.[65] However, in expressive arts, we value experiencing beauty through body sensation. When we allow beauty to strike us physically, we instantly become connected to our bodies through changes in sensation. We lean forward in our seats when moved by a performance. We feel goose bumps when stepping back and seeing an evocative painting. We have our breath taken away by the beauty of a dance. In these moments, a current of life force shoots through us, waking up our body, our heart, and our spirit.

Beauty is also therapeutic because of its communication and connecting properties. By forming life experiences into honest artistic expressions, a person can communicate his or her truths. People can find either the very simple or technically difficult arm movements that exquisitely express how they feel. They can create the "just-right" image, whether drawn crudely or with great technical finesse, that beautifully expresses their grief, happiness, or loneliness. They are no longer alone with their emotions, because they have shaped them into a work of art that can now be seen and held by others. Beauty connects people together as they are collectively moved by the beauty of a play, a concert, or a dance. In that moment of connection, all who are witness understand that although their lives differ, they share in life's fundamental challenges and joys. A sense of humanity's spirit is collectively felt.

The process of forming one's life experiences into moments of honest beauty is therapeutic because it helps draw forth clarity of thought and feeling. When talking about beauty, expressive arts therapist Paolo Knill likens the process of shaping one's art to the process of crystallization. He states that during the art-making process, a crystal clear image begins to form out of the blur of sounds, colours, or movements. He believes that if you continue to follow this crystallizing expression, you will reach an "ah-ha" moment, in which you are struck by the beauty or the "just right" feeling that your artwork elicits.[66, 67] This "ah-ha" is the moment in which your artistic expression has fully crystallized. It is the moment in which your artistic expression matches a truth living within you. It is the moment of coming home to oneself. Beauty in expressive arts is the path to self-understanding. Beauty in expressive arts is the path home.

Finally, and most importantly, when we form our truths into honest artistic expression, we can be moved by our own works of art. Seeing the beauty of our own creations helps us to see and recognize the beauty that lives inside us.

Honest beauty and love are two closely tied phenomena. Once our heart opens to love, our heart also opens to seeing the beauty in others and the world. Similarly, being touched by honest beauty opens our heart to love. Thus, love and beauty are doubly therapeutic, because with each comes the healing properties of the other.

Once, a client and I (both of us having no musical training) chose instruments and played an impromptu musical piece together. When we finished, I asked the client what he thought the musical piece wanted more of or less of.

"Maybe the music wants to be a bit louder," he suggested after some hesitation.

With each subsequent take, he asked, "Can we try even a bit louder?"

As we went from take to take, increasing our volume, he edged forward on his chair and I could see the start of a mischievous smile. With each take, he was guiding and shaping the music, much like a composer drawing his expression into focus.

Finally, he burst forth, saying, "Let's begin with quiet bells at the start. When we get to the middle, let's go crazy with as much sound as we can and build a huge crescendo!"

After this final take, which involved a huge and satisfying build, he announced, "Yes, that's it. That's exactly it!"

Upon reflection, he said, "I would describe myself as a quiet and reserved man, but the truth is that I really enjoyed making that loud music. I am surprised to discover that there's a part of me that wants to announce my presence on earth in such a big way!"

Although the final take sounded more like garbage cans rolling down an alleyway than music, it helped me to understand his desire to be seen and heard. I was moved by his bravery in creating such cacophonous music, as well as by the truth it represented. Based upon his reflection and enlivened stance, I could see that he was also touched by his music and the insight it gave him. Seeing beauty in his composition was a shift towards accepting the part of him that wished to be big in the world, which was an opening to self-love.

Expressive arts therapists believe so strongly in the healing power of beauty that we often work in an art-focused manner. Rather than focusing on "fixing" psychological issues, we focus on helping people create art that stirs the creator and their audience. In Chapter 2, I wrote about an annual project, in which I and two other expressive arts therapists support a group of youth in creating an interdisciplinary play inspired by their life stories. Rather than focusing on treating their "dysfunction" (isolation and low self-esteem related to identity issues), we help the youth make the best damn play they possibly can. We help each participant find the artistic expression that really gives them a satisfying "ah-ha" moment, a feeling that their performance really captures the truth of their life experience. Each year, the youth perform their play in front of an audience, who are moved to tears by the beautiful images, songs, dances, and dialogue. It is not an "easy" beauty to watch, as many of the youth's life stories are heartbreaking, but it is a beauty that deeply engages the viewers. As I look at each youth during his or her final bows, I see radiant and confident faces and bodies that are alive with energy. When I talk with audience members after the show, they are visibly moved. Through the beauty of the play, the audience falls in love with the group of youth and their brave performances. It's a life-invigorating type of therapy not just for the youth, but for the audience, as well.

If expressive arts therapists help clients experience beauty through artistic expression, then one might assume we are beauty chasers. In a sense, we are. Beauty and its therapeutic attributes are the goal. We also know that if we chase after beauty too directly, we hinder its arrival. Beauty is not something that can be forced into existence. It tends to surface unexpectedly when we are not looking for it. If beauty becomes the direct aim of expressive arts therapists, they get stuck aestheticizing – chasing beauty to the point of losing connection to their clients and themselves. Chasing beauty too closely also narrows the playing field and opportunities for honest expression fade.[68]

Instead, expressive arts therapists create conditions that allow beauty to arrive unexpectedly. We secretly usher beauty through the back door when no one is looking, allowing it to be a surprise gift. There is an interesting correlation between the surprise gift of beauty and dopamine, whose transformative attributes I discussed in the previous section. Studies show that we do not experience a dopamine surge just by receiving a reward. It has to be a reward that surprises us with its arrival or magnitude.[69, 70] I am suggesting that beauty is the unexpected reward in expressive arts therapy that causes a dopamine surge, which helps "save" the new feeling, doing, and thinking pathways that are forming.

How do expressive arts therapists create conditions that allow for beauty to sneak in through the back door? Primarily, we encourage a phenomenological process in which clients are so closely chasing after the phenomena of the emerging art that when beauty arrives, it is a surprise. For example, I will encourage someone to paint so quickly on a huge piece of paper that he or she hardly has time to think about or see what he or she is painting. I will ask people to paint with their eyes closed or to write fast, just letting the words flow out. I will suggest that someone pick up an instrument and spontaneously create music without any preplanning. In all these cases, rather than analyze and try too hard to create something beautiful, the person follows and forms his or her expression as it unfolds. They follow the blur of colours, sounds, and movement so intently that they lose sight of where their expression is leading them from one moment to the next. They lose sight of their predetermined sense of self. They lose sight of their predetermined sense of the world. This leaves room for the person they truly are in that moment to flow into their artistic expression.

I earlier described how chasing after beauty can blind us from seeing truth, making honest beauty inaccessible, and I just now explained how getting lost in emerging art can also blind us. However, the end results are very different. Chasing beauty too directly blinds us from our truths. Letting ourselves get lost in the art-making process blinds us from our untruths. When we lose ourselves in the task of following emerging shapes, colours, and movements, we lose sight of the tightly-held untruths that have made us so unhappy. We can lose sight of feeling unlovable, or a belief that we are ugly. With these untruths out of the way, the truth can emerge – that somewhere underneath our layers of defenses, we are all lovable and beautiful.

Beauty flourishes when we let go of what we think we know and who we think we are. Expressive arts therapists help people clear the space inside and outside of themselves so that the enlivening and truthful nature of beauty has the chance to grace the moment. These beautiful moments of truth take clients home – not to whom they think they are, but to whom they truly are.

Ephemeral in nature, the moment of experiencing beauty inevitably passes, leaving the art-maker feeling alive. The art-maker is left with a sense of connection to those who bore witness and with an increased sense of knowing and appreciation for who he or she is.[71]

c) *Liminal Space*

Liminal space is a state of consciousness that invites transformation and is characterized by ambiguity, openness, uncertainty, and a sense of the infinite. In this state, one's sense of identity dissolves to some extent, which can bring about a sense of disorientation. Normal limits, thoughts, self-understanding, and behaviour are relaxed, opening the way to something new.[72]

Liminal space exists in-between known territories. In rite-of-passage rituals, liminal space is the time spent between two societal roles. In many aboriginal cultures, young lads are sent into the wilderness alone. They enter as boys, spend time in the "liminal" wilderness and, hopefully, survive their walkabout to finish as men. In theatre, both performer and audience enter liminal space when they are so deeply engaged and moved that they are carried away into the world of the play – allowing them to forget the trivialities of their everyday lives.

Expressive arts therapist Ellen Levine writes about her experiences performing as a clown:

> For the clown performer, the experience can be described as a "free fall" or "riding a wave." When the clown experiences the connection to the audience and to his or her play partners, there is a feeling of excitement and a wish to go on forever. Playing with the audience, as well as playing against the audience, allows the clown to forget about literal reality and enter an alternative reality. This is the same kind of transitional experience that one achieves in the play-space of therapy with the arts.[73]

In expressive arts, clients enter liminal space whenever they lose sight of everything except their emerging art. At this moment, a whole new world opens up. They play, paint, write, sculpt, sing, dance or leap in wonder and awe, not knowing what will come next. There is chaos and disorder, old rules dissolve, and images hurtle upon them unbidden.[74] Everything that makes us who we are is put into a bag and given a good shake. As the pieces settle, there is the chance for a reforming of self. The liminal space in expressive arts is not a place of safe knowing; it is a place where change is possible. Expressive arts therapists are experts in helping people enter liminal spaces through the arts, where beauty and truth roam free. In doing so, we hope that when someone completes an artistic walkabout, he or she will come back into his or her everyday life transformed.

I teach dance in a professional training program, in which my boss graciously lets me use my "freestyle" methods. During one class, about halfway through the first term, I noticed my students settle into the music. They were so involved in the movements that they seemed to forget themselves, the studio, and the dance technique they usually held onto so tightly. Perched on a ballet bar, I watched as an uncontrolled beauty emerged. After finishing, one student looked up at me, shocked, and said, "It was like I was not even in the room, I was somewhere else. All these images of flying came to me. I was aware of you in the corner, sitting on the ballet bar . . . but you were not like you. You were this bird watching over us. It was like I went somewhere and you flew with me. I didn't even realize I was in the studio anymore. When I came to class today, I was all down, but now I feel different. It's hard to describe. I never knew dancing could be like that."

She suddenly stopped talking and looked confused and slightly embarrassed by her verbal outburst. I saw a look in her eyes that I recognized. It was an understanding that something had changed and would never be the same. *Ah, my young one*, I thought, *this is your first time in liminal space. The door is open to you now, and you will enter again. Play well in this wild kingdom.*

Liminal space is the wild landscape that we risk entering in order to leave our ingrained pathways behind. We may get lost at first, but if we stay true to our task, we will stumble upon the honest beauty and love that roam free in the wild kingdom.

Allen

It has been a winter full of snowstorms. I just spent half an hour clearing off the walk and knocking down icicles. Allen is my only client today. I wonder if my work is for naught. He didn't confirm our appointment; I don't know if he's going to show up.

Half an hour later, Allen walks in, late for his appointment. "We do have a session today, right?"

I draw a deep breath as I feel tension build in my shoulders. I'm irritated with Allen's cavalier attitude.

"Actually, I wanted to talk with you about something," I say. "It's been hard making appointments with you lately. We often have tentative times booked, which makes it difficult for me to work out my surrounding appointments. I need you to be more definite."

"Yeah," he answers with a wince. "I thought maybe I was playing things a bit too loose."

Allen told me a month ago that he felt he would be ready to finish therapy soon. He isn't binge eating anymore. He is getting married in a few months. He's just started a new job he really likes. Even though he says his therapy is pretty much finished, I wonder whether something big is brewing therapeutically. He's cancelling frequently, changing dates, and not confirming sessions, which is making it almost impossible for me to schedule our last few appointments. Does this represent a fear of what might emerge in the final sessions? Sometimes, with an end point in sight, the work that needs to get done arrives at a quick pace.

Allen sits down and starts to tell me about his week and the details of his new job. After he settles in, I ask him what he wants to do today.

He closes his eyes for a moment, then opens them wide and says, "I just need to say something before we start. I'm having a big reaction to what you said about me messing up your scheduling . . . I feel really bad about it. Like I've disappointed you."

"How does it feel to disappoint me?" I ask.

He pauses. "It makes me feel really young."

"And this feeling of being young and disappointing someone, what does it feel like in your body?"

He closes his eyes again. After a moment, he responds.

"I feel a tension right here," he says, pointing to his sternum.

"What shape is the tension?" I ask. "Is it flat, long, short, or round . . . like a fist? Like hands pressing down?" As I say this, I sense a palpable sadness overwhelm my heart. This feeling lasts only for a brief moment, like a window opening, and then closing, quickly.

Suddenly he blurts out, "I'm angry at myself for disappointing you!"

I know that getting angry with himself is a familiar pattern, while letting his sadness flow is not. In past sessions, Allen has told me that he never cries. Even when his mom died, tears were inaccessible. I make a guess that he flips to anger as a default to protect himself from a flood of tears.

"Being angry at yourself is very familiar, isn't it?" I gently ask. "Like a reflex?"

He nods in agreement.

"How about taking a step back to the thing you were feeling right before the anger came?"

He takes a breath and closes his eyes again, still holding his hand on his sternum.

I feel tightness build in my chest that draws my focus inward. I feel like my well-being and my life force are being pushed down. This sensation reminds me of something: an image flashes into my head of four-year-old Allen sitting underneath the kitchen table, hiding from the sadness in his family.

Looking back up at Allen, I say, "I'm remembering right now the story you told me about hiding underneath your kitchen table when you were young."

"Yes," Allen says, "I remember. I felt so sad because my mother was so sad. There was nothing I could do to fix it, and no one talked about it. Everyone acted like all this sadness wasn't there."

I think of the beached whale that Allen worked on more than a year ago, and how it came to its conclusion with the image of the boy under the table. At the time, I wondered whether the boy was the key to Allen's addiction to food. Here we are again, now, with the boy under the table. This time, however, Allen is on much sturdier ground. It is time to turn the key and unfold the mystery of Allen's addiction with food.

"It was so overwhelming for the boy under the table, wasn't it?"

Allen is silent. I continue, "What sensations are you noticing now?"

His eyes are still closed as his hand moves lower, to just below his sternum. "I'm feeling the overwhelming urge to eat and never stop. I want to get as big as I can," he says.

I'm not sure whether he is talking as the boy under the table, or as adult Allen, but I suspect that it may be both — that these two are somehow fused.

He opens his eyes and looks surprised by what he has just said.

"I've talked with a few people about my overeating, but I've always had this understanding that I really wanted to stop so I could lose weight. I've never admitted to anyone, or even to myself, that I actually wanted to be really big – that my weight gain was intentional. Like a buffer of protection between me and the world. I remember when I was young. Whenever I stepped on the scale at the doctor's office, I could feel the doctor's judgment. But there was always this secret part of me that wanted to yell out, 'No, I'm not big enough! I need an even bigger layer of flesh between me and the world!'"

"That makes sense," I say. "You needed protection against the overwhelming sadness. How about staying with the feeling of wanting to eat without stopping? Move in towards the sensation to get to know it better."

His hand moves lower, to his belly. He is quiet for a while. He then describes a hollow feeling in his belly that just wants to be full, and how food is the only thing in his life that has ever filled this hollow place. He spends the remainder of the session staying with this sensation.

Allen has told me over the past few months that he is pleased with the improvement in his eating habits, especially that the urge to eat compulsively has almost completely disappeared. His life used to revolve around food, but now different things have taken food's place: self-expression, relationships, and putting himself out into the world. Today, though, he leaves the session overwhelmed by his old ghost: the single-minded desire to eat without stopping.

I worry about him as he leaves. I want to tell him that there are other ways to be full, to be big. He does not have to use food. I worry that, after months of not binging, he will endanger his health with a massive food binge. I think to myself that being a therapist takes faith – faith that clients know what they need to do to heal. I just need to trust.

Over the past year, Allen has achieved the therapeutic goals he set out in our initial session: he has stopped binge eating and he is no longer chronically depressed. He achieved this without unravelling the exact reason for his depression and binge eating. His session work has provided many clues about the origins of his troubles, but I hold back from offering him my thoughts. Allen is the expert on himself. He is in charge of his own pacing, and I know from experience that concrete answers are not always needed. Giving clients and their artwork unconditional acceptance can be a healing balm that works regardless of whether one knows how the wound happened in the first place.

As Allen approaches our final sessions, it seems that something is brewing. His behaviour involving scheduling and showing up for appointments has radically changed. He has gone from being very dependable to completely undependable. I wonder if Allen is close to taking a big leap in self-awareness; maybe his behaviour is hesitation and avoidance of this. Maybe Allen has filled his cup of self-understanding with each piece of art he has created. Maybe a flood of answers will arrive.

These were my background thoughts, because mostly I was focused on how irritated I was with Allen's behaviour regarding scheduling appointments. I accept that the range of feelings I will have as a therapist includes irritation. Rather than hiding this feeling, I modeled self-expression by naming my irritation. This honesty provided an opportunity for Allen to explore the feeling of having disappointed someone.

In this session, I stayed attentive to my body sensations. In the moment right before Allen expressed his anger with himself, I noticed a crushing heaviness in my heart, which I named sadness. Rather than helping Allen aim his anger out through the arts — something we had done in previous sessions — I decided to explore a hunch that Allen becomes angry at himself as a way to avoid his sadness. This pattern is like a switch that Allen had been flicking over and over again throughout his life. When I said, "Go back a step and explore that thing that came before the anger," I stopped the switch from flipping in its usual manner. Allen had a chance to stay with his sadness and the body sensations that accompanied it.

As he did this, I received a flash of the image of young Allen under the kitchen table. I named this image, tying the beached whale session work from a year ago back to this moment. The threads of different sessions were starting to weave together into a clear picture.

When Allen described how sad his mom was when he was young, and how he was unable to rescue her, I realized that my annoyance had taken him back to feeling inadequate in his role as mommy-rescuer. This reaction was a transference in which I became the mommy figure, giving him the chance to go back to childhood and try out new solutions. Remembering his mom's overwhelming sadness stirred up his desire to binge. Instead of going on auto-pilot and eating without awareness, Allen stayed with the sensation of wanting to binge. For most of his life, he has been switching quickly from feeling sadness, to feeling anger at himself, to eating compulsively without being aware of this pattern. By helping Allen stop and experience each step, I have slowed down the pattern so that Allen can really get to know it. New learning arrived from this, as Allen discovered that he purposely became big as protection against being overwhelmed.

However, by drawing Allen back to a childhood memory, I also helped him dive deep into his food compulsion. As he left, I feared he might endanger his life by succumbing to the overwhelming urge to binge.

Allen

The following week, Allen tells me a remarkable story: after our last session, he walked straight to an all-you-can-eat buffet and filled his plate, planning to have many more plates after that. As he ate, he became full. He couldn't eat more than an average-sized meal. He describes seeing a lady, one table over, binging on a huge pile of sweets. After watching her for a while, he thought to himself that food just didn't work for him anymore. It was no longer the answer for him.

I reflect on my own experiences.

"Yeah, I know what you mean. When I was recovering from bulimia, there came a time when I realized that food was not the rescuer I thought it was. It was like buying an infomercial product and getting it in the mail after weeks of anticipation, only to realize it didn't do what they said it would do. When food lost its power over me, I remember feeling ripped off, like I had lost this great promise of a ready-to-order lover that was supposed to soothe me."

"Yes, it is like a relationship, isn't it?" he remarks. "Realizing that food does not have the power I thought it did is like giving up a relationship . . . like breaking up."

"Yes!" I say. "That moment when you realize that your relationship with your addictive substance is not all it's cracked up to be, that it doesn't do the job it promised . . . that's a really big thing. It's like growing out of your addiction. Some people think addiction is cured just through abstaining, but I believe that addiction heals when the power relationship with the addictive substance is broken."

"Even if my food addiction is passing . . ." Allen starts. He pauses, sighs, and looks down at his body. "I still have to live with the repercussions of it."

He talks about his weight, how he wants to be more active, but because of his size, he is too shy to do so. He talks about wanting to swim, or dance, or play hockey, but he worries about being ridiculed.

"Being more active," he says, "is the last piece in getting my life back on track. Everything else is falling into place."

"Well," I ask, "how about practicing being more active today?"

He knows that my style is to head straight into the discomfort in order to become more comfortable, so he moves into the center of the studio. He knows the drill, and he's game for it.

I put a fun, up-tempo jazz CD in the player and say, "How about you pretend you're at a club dancing?"

The music starts to play, but Allen remains frozen. I ask him, "Do you dance at clubs?" He laughs and says, "Once every five years or so, and only after many drinks."

I laugh and suggest, "Maybe today is the day to try it sober."

I think for a moment. "How about if I sit facing the corner so I can't see you? Then, you turn on the music and give it a try."

I sit facing my corner and Allen turns on the music. I imagine him grooving to the music, as if my imagination will help him dance. He stops the music and I turn around.

"I moved a bit," he explains, "but it felt so awkward, like my legs were really heavy and all these thoughts were going through my head – like judgments and stuff that I looked ridiculous. I couldn't get my head to be quiet so that I could move my legs."

After a pause, he reflects. "You know, though, what is interesting? Two years ago, when I first came here, I felt totally disconnected from my body. Like it was a separate thing I had to take places. Today, when I danced, I felt like my body was mine. Sure, it felt really awkward . . . but at least it's a part of me now."

"Wow," I say. I'm moved by the impact of what he says, but I don't want to stop the momentum of the session by talking about it. "How about trying the dance again, this time exaggerating the heavy awkward feeling in your legs?"

I again face my corner. Behind me, he does a second take. He tells me that it felt better this time, but he still couldn't get his critical thoughts to be quiet.

I remember an exercise I once learned in a dance improvisation workshop, in which one lies on the floor and moves, but never lets any movement complete itself. For instance, one would reach halfway and then stop, then start to roll, but stop, and so on. Watching it, the exercise looks like a fussy baby trying to get comfortable. The "fussy baby dance" seems to soften people's self-judgments. Participants are so focused on never letting the movements complete that they do not have time to think.[75] I wonder whether the dance might both match and amplify the awkwardness Allen describes and help to calm his mind.

Allen is willing, so we both do the "fussy dance." After five minutes, he finishes on his back with his arms outstretched and a relaxed expression on his face.

As I thought about Allen's therapy process this past week, I felt that I should teach him ways to create a buffer between himself and the world that does not involve food.

I decide to do something I don't normally do. I become very directive. Without asking Allen whether he wants to, I say, "Start to make vocal sounds. With each sound, I want you to imagine that you're pressing out an 'Allen bubble.' Using sound, you can make this Allen bubble as big as you want. This bubble is your magical space; no one can cross into it."

He starts to sing in long, loud tones. As I listen to him, I remember that a year ago, he had such a block in vocal expression that he could barely sing louder than a whisper. Now he's making big bellowing noises.

After a few minutes, he stops singing, and lets me know he has finished making his bubble.

I ask him how big his bubble is. He tells me that it is one foot outside his left arm, five feet above him, and squished up against the bookshelf on his right side.

An image flashes in my mind of Allen lying on his back within a bright blue circle that indicates the edges of his bubble. The image is so captivating that I feel a rush of excitement. I run to the art cupboard and grab a blue pastel. I pause for a brief moment, wondering if pastel can be cleaned off a hardwood floor, but then I decide to go for it – this moment is the culmination of almost two years of work; I'm not going to let it pass, even if it makes a mess.

"Okay, Allen, I'm going to draw the edges of your bubble on the floor."

He nods and says through laughter, "It's your floor!"

"It might sound crazy to draw all over the floor, but this bubble is really important."

I start to trace the edge of Allen's bubble while making sure to not cross into his space. I keep checking with him to make sure that I'm getting it right. I have to squeeze by the bookshelf on my tiptoes and climb over the art supply trunk to complete the outline.

After I finish, I spontaneously pick up the guitar and ask Allen if I can play a song for his bubble. He nods.

I strum while singing in high wavering tones:

> Allen has a bubble.
> Allen's bubble is five feet above his head.
> Allen's bubble reaches past his arm,
> and it squishes up against the bookshelf.
> It is Allen's bubble,
> It is all his and no one else's.
> Allen can do whatever he wants in his bubble, because it is his bubble.
> Allen's bubble is so great,
> because it is all his.
> Allen has a bubble.

As the song ends, Allen turns his head towards me, and says softly and slowly, "I really liked that song." Lying in his circle of blue, he's relaxed. His eyes are soft, blissful. His arms are still outstretched, which is a big change from his usual closed posture. He continues, "I feel so young right now, and your voice reminds me of my grandmother's voice. She used to sing to me."

I think to myself that little Allen learned that the only way he could protect himself from his mother's overwhelming depression was to eat lots of food. I know that Allen feels much better about life lately, but the message he learned long ago still haunts him. Here in front of me, I have four-year-old Allen. I now have the chance to give him a new message, closing off the pathways of the old message.

This is a decisive moment that takes a lot of bravery on my part. I dive in. Strumming the guitar, I sing.

> I am Allen's grandma,
> and I am here to tell him what a lovely bubble he has.
> I am so glad Allen has his bubble because it protects him.
> We all deserve to have our bubbles,
> and we all need space to be.
> That is why I am so happy to see Allen in his bubble.
> I am Allen's grandma,

and I am here to tell him that he can make his bubble anytime he needs.

Look at Allen's bubble, it is all his.

It is his space.

I am happy Allen has his bubble.

Allen is silent for a moment, and then says, "It's great to have so much space and not to have to do anything."

"You can do whatever you like in your bubble," I reply, "because it is your space."

We sit in silence.

Twenty minutes pass since the song ended. It is almost time to finish the session. Allen gets up and heads towards the couch.

He sits down and says, "I've never felt as safe in my life as I did lying in my bubble . . . not ever before. I mean never before. Not as an adult, or as a child."

"You can make that bubble anywhere you go," I explain. "It is an energetic thing, defining your space. You can do it on the subway, at work. . . ." Allen is lost in thought and not listening. I smile at my own persistence in trying to solidify the new message. I let go of my lecture and we just sit for the last few minutes of the session.

Allen has been dipping deeper and deeper into liminal space through art-making over the past two years. With this session, he surrendered fully into liminal space, beginning an artistic walkabout that will continue over the next two sessions. This walkabout is an altered state where time seems to stand still and different periods in his life collide. The past and the present exist together, merged in the here and now. For much of it, he is like a four-year-old boy, but he is also adult Allen, as well. New sensations and connections emerge, while old patterns loosen their hold.

Surrender into liminal space was achieved through a movement experience that enabled Allen to find freedom from judgment. In this new space, his body relaxed, as if floating on a cloud. I saw an opportunity, an opening, so I took bold steps to give Allen a new message: he can make space for himself in other ways, ways that don't involve food. I did not explain this message verbally; instead, I presented the image of a protective bubble that he could create with his voice. Drawing the outline of Allen's bubble on the floor made this image concrete. I then delivered the message via a heartfelt song, as well. As I pretended to be Allen's grandmother singing to him, I felt, in a very real way, love for the four-year-old boy I sang to. Allen received my message not just analytically, but through "here and now" sensations and feelings. He experienced the message through the wisdom of his thoughts (imagining a protective bubble), the wisdom of his heart (a feeling of safety), and the wisdom of his body sensation (the outstretched arms, an easy sense of breath).

Allen

Allen comes in the next week and describes how he felt heavy in his heart all week. I am surprised. I had assumed that after the last session, he would come in feeling good and we would spend the time getting ready to say our goodbyes. Looking at Allen's intense expression today, I realized that he is still deeply engaged in his "walkabout."

When I ask him to describe the feeling of heaviness, he says that he kept thinking of his mom the whole week. He starts to tell me her story. I've heard it before in separate pieces, but this time, all the pieces arrive and fit together, like puzzle pieces organizing into a cohesive picture.

"My dad died when I was very little. My mom woke up, and he was just lying next to her, not breathing. When I was older, someone told me that she'd run out of the house and sat on the front lawn frantically crying and pulling at her hair. That is such a hard thing for me to imagine, because I never remember her having any outward expressions of sadness. She never faced her grief, instead burying herself in the work of being a single mom to my brother and me. She worked so hard and gave up everything for us. It was a raw deal. There was always such sadness in our house; it was like an extra person no one ever talked about. It lived in the walls. It was so intense, I felt like it would swallow me up.

I wanted to fix it, to fix everything for her. I tried so hard to be really good and strong all the time. I didn't want to disappoint her or give her any extra worries – she had enough already. But I had a secret: I hoarded food, hid it under my bed, and ate it when I was alone. It helped me feel better. It made me feel strong, so I wouldn't get swallowed up by it all. Then I ate so much, and got so big. This stressed my mom, because she started to worry about my weight. I didn't want her to worry, but then again I did want her to see what a hard time I was having and how much I missed my dad.

I've held this sadness inside me my whole life. It is always there; it never leaves. Even after my mom died and the house was sold, the sadness never let up."

Even though Allen's story describes deep emotional challenges, there is an excited energy in the room as we both lean forward in our seats. A shift of understanding is happening for both of us that beckons us forward.

"Yes," I say. "The sadness never lets up, because even if the house was torn down, the sadness still lives inside you."

He walks to the art cupboard and grabs paper and a pencil. He sits down on the floor and hunches over the paper, writing and crossing things out until he is satisfied.

He reads,

> The Sadness was a circle.
> Sadness without sound is zero.
> Zero is nothing.
> In the absence of something zero takes its place.
> Zero was the sound the white house made,
> Zero is the amount of times I heard the house cry.
> Zero is all I heard.
> The absence of something,
> The absence of sound,
> The hollow place.

"Since I started coming here, I have learned how to give myself the things I need. I have so much to live for now, but there is still this sadness that haunts me." He places his hand on his upper belly. "I feel it right here."

"Do you think it might be time to give the sadness you've carried all these years back to the house so that you don't have to carry it anymore?" I ask. "What might be the best way to do this?"

"I want to draw," he responds.

We set up the art supplies and he begins to draw a big scary monster with a house in the background. As he fills in the drawing with paint, the big scary monster starts to look more and more like a little boy. Allen paints polka-dot pajamas on him and draws black rain drops falling around the boy and the house. The monster/boy holds a small person in his large hands. His teeth are bared, as if he is trying to look strong and fierce, but behind this show of strength, I sense the monster/boy is vulnerable and scared.

Figure 3. Monster/boy painting.

A flash of knowledge impacts me. I reflexively sit upright and gasp as I feel a wave of energy snake up my spine. I finally get it:

- This is the "sadness monster" living in Allen's family house that no one ever talked about.
- This is the scared young boy under the table wanting to disappear into food.
- This is the hungry monster who wants to eat everything in sight without stopping.
- This is the little boy who wants to get so big and impenetrable that nothing will hurt him.
- This is the lonely monster whose roar is a cry for help.
- This is the boy who feels inadequate because he cannot rescue his mom from her sadness.
- This is the monster with nowhere to put his anger. Arms outstretched, he becomes his own target.

- This is the boy trying to roar like an angry monster in the hope that this will hide his sadness.
- This is the monster that Allen sees himself as.
- This is the monster that Allen has been running from most of his life.

This image is all of these things, jumbled together all at once. In this moment of knowing, I feel love and compassion for this monster/boy who is trying to use a show of strength to hide his sadness: teeth bared, fists clenched, and eyes so sad.

Allen finishes the painting and returns to the couch. We both sit in silence, looking at the image.

Allen looks at me and says, "That's the little boy."

I nod. "You mean the little boy underneath the kitchen table?"

"Yes."

More silence.

"When you first started drawing," I say, "I thought it was an angry monster. Then, slowly, I realized it was a little boy."

"It's both," he says.

"And growing up, the sadness in your house was like an invisible monster that lived in the walls, wasn't it?" I say. "This monster has been chasing you your whole life."

"Yeah, that's right," he says. "And the only thing I could do was to try to become bigger than that monster so it couldn't hurt me."

I nod and continue. "By waving his arms and grabbing a person in his fist, this monster/boy seems to be trying so hard to be big and scary," I continue. "But when I look in his eyes, I see that he is not really a monster. Inside, he is a scared and sad boy."

"Yes, very sad," Allen agrees. "The black rain is all the sadness falling on him; he can't make it stop. He gets so angry with the rain, but there is no place for the anger to go. It was all up to him. He had to try to fix everything on his own. Everyone was in shock after my dad's death. There was no one to help me figure it all out . . . I mean, it's not normal for a four-year-old boy to hoard piles of food under his bed. And some days, I would look under my bed and see that someone had taken away all the food, but no one in my family ever said anything about it."

"Could you become the monster/boy right now?" I ask.

He closes his eyes and says, "I feel so scared."

"It must be overwhelming," I respond.

"My mom is so sad all the time."

"It must be hard that no one talks about all this sadness," I say. "It must be hard not to be able to fix it all."

Tears start to fall down Allen's cheeks. This is the first time I have seen him cry.

"Allen, this is your chance to talk to your mom and tell her what that little boy never got to say."

"I'm sorry you're so sad," Allen says.

Pretending to be Allen, I prompt, "Mom, it's been hard all these years, holding your sadness for you."

"It makes me feel so heavy," says Allen. "I want to let it go, but I can't. It's always here . . . Mom, I need to let it go."

I pretend to be Allen's mom, saying very softly and slowly, "Allen, thank you for doing such a great job taking care of me and trying to fix my sadness. I see that it has been a really hard job for you over all these years. I am here to tell you that I can hold my own sadness now. You can give it back to me. I can carry it. It is not your job anymore."

"Mom . . . I give it back to you."

"Allen . . . I accept it," I answer.

After a long moment, Allen opens his eyes. "I really needed to let that go," he says.

We sit looking at his painting.

"I care deeply about the monster/boy in the picture," I say.

Then the thing I have been hoping and waiting for happens.

"I do, too," whispers Allen. "He is doing such a valiant job of fixing, saving, protecting, fighting, trying to escape, and crying for help, all at the same time."

As he says this, I sense love build in Allen's heart. His eyes become alive with compassion and care. Those elusive tears shine just behind his eyes. We sit together like this, letting time pass.

Allen finally breaks the silence.

"Now I'm ready to finish therapy."

We schedule our last appointment for the following week.

Over the past two years, Allen has come to know himself more completely by creating art that illuminated his truths. At first, the images, sounds, movements, and poetic words that emerged were like paving stones that seemed to be randomly laid in the earth, not connecting or leading anywhere. For instance, the beached whale image provided only a vague inkling as to how it related to Allen's food compulsion. Over time, as Allen continued to create art that revealed his truths, the disparate pieces began to form a path.

During the past two years, Allen accessed many forms of wisdom. Artistic expression enticed connection to different types of experience: action, sensation, physiology, thought, emotion, and spirit. Each provided a different type of understanding. Over time, this understanding converged into a knowing that he felt at all levels throughout his being. Let's go through some of his previous sessions and see how action, sensation, physiology, thought, emotion, and spirit played their roles:

- Allen's first scribble-drawing, with its fascinating colours and shapes, gave a hint of his rich **emotional** landscape. It created enough good feelings and curiosity to entice Allen back for more sessions. The shared experience of creating our scribble drawings, and the way each drawing gave a glimpse of who we were, was also an opening towards collective **spirit**.
- Allen learned to aim his **anger** outward through the **action** of hitting the wall with a pillow.
- Allen created poems and drawings that were inspired by the beached whale theme. **Communicating his despair** to me through the arts was an act of sharing that helped Allen feel understood. He **embodied** this despair when he curled himself into the beached whale as he **imagined** lying on the barren beach. Staying with the **inner body sensations** of this experience brought him to the memory of hiding under the kitchen table when he was young.
- Through playing with his camp story, Allen **imagined** a world of his own where he felt safe. He then **created** a paper man that was standing on a ball as a representation of his imaginings. Allen **embodied** this art piece by taking on the stance of the paper man. How he **felt** when he embodied this image led him to **realize** that separating one's self from others was safe, but also lonely.
- When Allen first started therapy, he felt that his body didn't belong to him. Through **following action** and **sensation**, he started to **feel** that his body was his home. With some prodding on my part, the new feeling of **owning his body** enabled him to listen to the physiological (health) messages that his body was giving him and go see a nutritionist.
- When I expressed irritation with his scheduling, Allen stayed attentive to his **inner body** sensation and noticed a crushing feel-

ing in his chest. This drew him to the memory of trying to rescue his mom from her sadness. He **understood** that his binge eating was a way to feel big and strong in order to protect him and his mom from the troubles of the world.

- As the sense of being a caretaker of his own body grew, Allen wanted to be more active, but feared being ridiculed. He faced this fear by experiencing the **sensation** of "club" **dancing**, and then **realized** that even though he felt awkward in his body, it now felt like home to him.
- He created an **imaginary** bubble through the **action** of singing. He learned that he could feel safe and be completely himself within this protected space. As this happened, the **spirit** of "just being" settled upon the studio.

The result of this process was that the stones previously laid in the earth had come together to form a discernible path that Allen could follow. A childhood story once obscured from sight had come into view.

When Allen was young, his sadness over his dad's death merged with his mom's sadness, the house's sadness, and his family's sadness. It was all fused together in an overwhelming muddle. Allen had no one to talk with about all this sadness. There were no role models to show him how to cope successfully with grief. Everyone just pretended it did not exist. It is possible that his family thought kids did not feel grief, so the best thing to do was to just not talk about it. Maybe, due to shock that later evolved into depression, his mom did not have the emotional capacity to help him. Without expressions of grief for Allen to see and take part in, the sadness in his house became the absence of something, a hollow feeling he tried to fill with food. This hollow feeling was an overwhelming force that had no name and took on the qualities of a scary monster that he feared would devour him and his mom.

Allen was driven to tell me the story of his mother, driven to write the "Zero" poem, and driven to paint the monster/boy. I had never seen Allen create art with such intensity before. He was deeply engaged in a walkabout in the wild kingdom of liminal space. In this place of transformation, honest beauty flowed into his artwork. Allen's monster/boy painting expressed many contradictory truths in one image, evoking in both of us a sense of awe and wonder. It was the perfect match for Allen's story. It was the fully crystallized "ah-ha" moment that Paolo Knill speaks of.

How is it that the monster/boy's seemingly contradictory truths could exist together? How could overeating be a way to disappear, while at the same time being a way to make him larger as protection from an overwhelming world? How could food both fill a void and be used to help him feel numb? How could food be a way to self-soothe while being a self-punishment? How could over-eating be a cry for help and an expression of anger? If viewed from the standpoint of our adult thinking brains, these truths do not match up analytically. To really understand how this could be, we need to see through the heart of a scared, lonely, and sad four-year-old boy. We need to see through the heart of the monster/boy who chose food as the answer to every question he had.

It is possible that an addiction can be all these contradictory things bound together. We are fascinating creatures; the way we organize ourselves in order to survive is often layered and complex. We want, yet we fear what we want. We want love, for instance, yet we fear the sorrow it can bring. We run in two directions at once, leading us to come to a standstill that, if not unfrozen, can last a lifetime. Pervasive addictions are most often held together by seemingly divergent forces that press in upon each other, making the addiction hard to unravel.

The compulsive eating pattern that started when Allen was four was one such addiction. It was so tightly pressed in upon itself by contradictions that it became frozen in time. Even after his mom passed away and the house was sold, the pattern still prevailed. In our sessions, however, the warmth of honest beauty and unconditional acceptance softened Allen. In this more yielding state, aspects of Allen's compulsive eating became unstuck, leaving room for him to play in their midst and allowing him to discover new ways to establish and defend his personal boundaries that did not involve food. This freedom and discovery came with a price, however. In leaving old patterns behind, he felt like he was abandoning his mom. Young Allen made himself the caretaker and holder of his mom's sadness, a role that still lived in him after she died. In his final session, he separated himself from this role so that he could move forward with his life, leaving the past in the past.

Allen was moved by the beautiful truths in his monster/boy painting. This opening towards loving himself was the final stone in the path that led Allen home. The monster/boy was no longer at the helm of the ship, unconsciously driving Allen's life with his defenses. The monster/boy was now on Allen's ship, with Allen as his caretaker. Adult Allen was now steering his ship. He had many paths to choose from in an ocean that was now unfrozen by insight, love, and beauty.

THE SUM EFFECT OF EXPRESSIVE ARTS METHODS

Expressive arts methods bring us home to our body, which puts us in connection with the wisdom that lives in us. Awareness of our senses deepens. We feel both our sorrows and joys more deeply. Both emotional and physical pain can be incredibly challenging, but connecting with these sensations offers many gifts. When we know our pain, we are better able to not only express the story of our suffering to others, but to find understanding within it. When the joys and pains of life are shared through the arts, they transform into a collective expression of what it is to be human.

Steve Levine writes, "The therapeutic power of the arts lies in its capacity to render life valuable by showing both its horror and its pity. If we hold fast to this task, we may be blessed with the presence of joy."[76] Any movement towards life – by which I mean the urge to feel alive despite the range and intensity of feeling that our liveliness brings – is an act of unconditional acceptance. At the core of unconditional acceptance is the energy of love, which opens a sky wide enough to hold the entire rainbow of self.[77]

Allen

Allen pauses at the door after our final session. "I want to thank you for something," he says. "You never once talked with me about losing weight. You accepted me and my size one hundred percent. You saw me as who I was, not who I should be. I think that if you had made this process about my size, it would have crushed me. I would've been a number on a scale, and I don't think I would've stayed with therapy."

He reaches out to shake my hand and adds, "I just wanted to say thank you for that."

He takes one last look around the studio, turns, and walks down the path towards the park. I sit down and look at the pile of paintings and sculptures left in the studio. We spent the last hour looking at the art he created over the past two years. We assembled it in chronological order and relived his journey through the images. As we finished our reminiscing, I asked Allen if he wanted to take his art home.

"You can throw it all out," he answered. "I don't need it. It represents who I used to be, not who I am now."

As I sit looking at the pile, I realize that I'm hesitant to dump it all in the trash. I shake my head and smile. Allen let go of the past so that he could move into the future. It seems fitting that the student teach the teacher a lesson in letting go as he walks out the door.

I have half an hour before my next client, so I sit quietly, letting the day settle. I glance at the pile of artwork on the floor every once in a while. I finally get up and put Allen's clay sculptures in a large bowl of water. After they soften, I'll squish them back into the clay bag. I start to sort his visual art pieces between the garbage and the recycling box depending on how much paint they have on them. The last piece to go in is the painting of the monster/boy.

I hesitate for a moment, then whisper to the picture, "Don't worry, monster/boy, you're in good hands. Allen will take care of you."

When I look up, I see my next client rounding the corner towards my studio.[78]

Chapter 4

THE ART OF GRIEF

A teacher of mine once said that all therapy is grief work. She explained that we all grieve all the time for something or someone. We grieve the loss of loved ones, the loss of innocence, the loss of youth, the loss of health, the loss of power, and the loss of the things we never had. Even when good things happen, like a wedding or baby, we still grieve the loss of our old selves as we step into a new existence. Life is one long grieving process that ebbs and flows like a river.

We try to run from this truth. We try to stop the flow of grief because we fear it, and besides, it doesn't exactly fit well into our busy lives. So we brace our muscles, hold our collective breath, and busy ourselves with stuff. We turn our attention towards catching the latest television show, checking our Blackberry every five minutes, or going on a special diet. We choose any one of a myriad distractions to stop the tears, to protect ourselves from the intensity of feeling, to protect ourselves from pain.

We may think we have escaped grief, but we haven't. Through sensation, it reminds us of its presence in a sore muscle, a twitching eye, or a feeling of heaviness. Grief pushes against the walls we built to keep it out, so we fortify our walls. We tense our muscles even more, which causes a chronic spasm. We go on a TV binge and start to feel that sitcom characters are more important to us than real relationships. We check our Blackberry so often for messages that we are no longer able to listen to a friend. The healthy diet steps up a notch and veers towards an eating disorder. The pressure builds; with it comes the threat of a "flood." This flood will be massive, because once the wall crumbles, that buildup of held-back grief will hit at the same time. The constant

131

danger of this devastating flood leaves us with an underlying sense of anxiety, forcing us to fortify our dams even further in an effort to make it virtually impenetrable. We become chronically numb, unable to feel both grief and joy.

"Why would we lose our ability to feel joy?" you ask. "I thought we were talking about grief." My answer is that joy and grief are linked. If our grief gets all dammed up, then so does our joy. We only know how to build a dam that blocks everything. We either feel, or we don't feel.

It's my job as an expressive arts therapist to help grief flow into a poem, a song, a dance, or a painting. Feeling and expressing our pain opens our ears, eyes, and heart so that we can experience the beauty in our lives that we had stopped noticing. Grief flows from us into the art we create, leaving behind room inside our bodies for us to feel joy again. Our stories are shared; we are no longer alone in our loss. We return to our body-home because we no longer fear the grief that lives there. Even if this coming home is painful, it is a relief to arrive home after having been away.

So, tell me the story of what you have lost.

*****

Bang.

Crash.

Metal bangs against metal as my dad adjusts the food warming trays. He is sweaty and pale. A spot of blood seeps through the bandage that covers the cancerous tumor on his neck. He leans on the table, winces, and crumples into a chair.

"Okay," he says between shallow breaths, "the caterer is coming at four and we need to get the burners on the food trays working. The furniture in the hallway needs to be moved to the garage, and I need someone to make flower decorations using a mix of the fake flowers and the real ones we just bought."

He sits up taller, looking like a general giving final attack orders. I exhale slowly. Today is not his day to die.

A few hours later, I stand with my dad's arm linked in mine. Well, it's less of a "link," and more of a steel grip, as if he thinks there is a chance I might run. A silly grin covers his face. His status as a dying man got me from proposal to wedding in four weeks. It also gave him the last say on all wedding plans: the flowers a mix of real and fake, a wedding cake from Save-On Foods, an evening playlist that includes mostly ABBA, and the food a mix of Thai, Indian, and Swiss Chalet. These details do not matter to me, because I am about to marry my love, and against steep odds, my dad is standing by my side, about to walk me down the aisle.

But I'm sure my dad thinks the greatest miracle happening today is the fact that his almost-forty, free-spirited daughter is finally getting married. There were so many "almost-the-ones" that I think my dad gave up hope. There was the one who wanted me to quit my "crazy artsy job" and get a job at FedEx, the one who wanted me to move to suburbia, the one who wanted me to convert to his strict religion, the one who wanted me to move to a remote part of Finland, the one who wanted me to wash dishes more efficiently, the one who wanted me to help out with the family pot cookie business, the one who . . . But now I have found the one who loves me exactly the way I am.

Later that evening, ABBA blares, moving people of all ages onto the dance floor. My dad grabs my stepmom Gerri's hand, and they perform a "Saturday Night Fever" style dance. Everyone stops to watch and cheer. The collar of my dad's shirt hides his bandage. With his devilish grin and rosy cheeks, it's as if he is no longer sick.

My new father-in-law, who sits beside me, says, "If I knew I was about to die, I think I would be sitting at home, depressed. But look at him. He really knows how to live."

*****

Nine months earlier . . .

I stand in the dance studio wondering if something of beauty can be created in such drab surroundings. It's a fair size for a Toronto studio, but there are no windows, the walls and ceiling are made of concrete, and the few pieces of furniture strewn about are dull and worn. Brown-tinged leaves emanating from large planters reach up towards fluorescent lights. I have worked here for ten years, and in all that time, these dusty plants never died and never seem to grow. A solitary glass Christmas ball hangs off one of the leaves – someone's attempt at Christmas cheer. Eight dancers look at me, waiting to follow my lead. I adjust my yoga pants and pick a piece of lint off my T-shirt. It is the first day, the first hour, the first minute of rehearsal for my new ballet, which is set to premiere in seven months. I have no idea what I want to do. The first words out of my mouth will be as much a surprise to me as they are to the dancers. I go into these situations having no idea or purpose, because the work I create in the moment is much better than the work I create when I start with a plan. With preplanning, I create art that represents who I *think* I am. Without a plan, there is space to just let stuff happen, and then I create art that tells the story of who I *really* am. This real person is more nuanced, interesting, and full of surprises than the other. Just letting things happen is very "expressive arts" and, in theory, sounds liberating.

I adjust my yoga pants and T-shirt again. I take a calming breath, but the air gets stuck in the back of my throat. My dance company, which is basically just me, is poised to produce a show that has yet to be created. The theatre is booked, contracts are signed, and my grant money is half spent on publicity and marketing. All this hangs on the hope that I will create something meaningful.

Just start . . . start somewhere, I think . . . *anywhere.* It doesn't matter where I start; the important thing is to start.

"Okay, how about doing the helium breath exercise . . ."

After I finish rehearsal, I head to my job as an expressive arts therapist. I have a private practice, in which I see about ten clients a week in my home studio. It's no mystical happening that my choreographic process parallels my work with my clients. These processes both follow the same progression: create in the moment, search until one finds that "just right" expression, follow the creative phenomena, be surprised and illuminated by what emerges, and, through this process, arrive a bit closer to the truth of who you are. The difference is that as a therapist, my aim is therapeutic, and as an artist, my aim is to create damn good art.

After my client's weekly update, I ask her what she wants to do today.

"I don't know," she says.

"How about just walking over to the art supply cupboard? Whatever you pick up first, that's where you'll start. It doesn't even need to be exactly the right starting place. It'll just be the point from which stuff can happen."

She looks terrified at the prospect.

Yes, I think to myself, *it's terrifying entering the unknown, especially in my case, with reviewers ready to pounce and money and reputation to be quickly gained or lost.* I have been skinned by reviewers in the past. Pen and paper in hand, they usually watch from an intellectual standpoint, missing the emotional nature of my work. I know that my client's fear is just as great as mine, even if she is in the safety of my therapy studio. It is the unknown that is terrifying, not the studio, or the audience, or the reviewers.

After several sessions with different clients, my workday comes to an end. My body feels heavy and my shoulders ache. Having my own pains and fears, and helping to hold the pains and fears of my clients as well, is a burden that sometimes threatens to overwhelm me. I escape the pressure of my day by watching mindless television until I fall asleep.

After two weeks of rehearsals, I fly to Vancouver for Christmas with my dad. He was diagnosed with lymphoma cancer four months ago. It's Christmas Eve and my sister, brother, and I arrive for what we fear will be the last of such holidays with our dad. We sit on the stairs, forming an impromptu audience for him.

He explains, "They really don't know how long I have left. With a tumor on my neck, so close to the arteries, a piece could break off and go into the blood stream, and then it would be a matter of minutes. But the tumor could also grow slowly and gradually suffocate me over the next year. You guys should know, there might not be time for good-byes."

We sit dry eyed. Our dad hates tears.

My sister asks him, "Is it hard for you?"

"Life is terminal for all of us," he says. "I just have a shorter schedule and know what will get me. I don't think too much about it. I just get on with life with Gerri and you guys, walking the dog, skiing, my Coast Guard duties. I'm busy living . . . It's just at night, sometimes, when I can't sleep; I feel the weight of the tumor pressing down on me . . ." He falls silent. His shoulders slump, his eyes watering.

For a moment, it's as if a door opens. I get a glimpse of my dad's suffocating pain, his fear of dying, and his worry for those he'll leave behind. Then the door slams shut as he jumps to his feet and says, "We're wasting this sunny day sitting around. Let's head out to the Canyon."

I have been sitting on my hands and hardly breathing in order to make sure I don't cry. I am an emotional anomaly in a family of people who "do" rather than feel. I hold back my emotions in order to fit in. I do it well, but it's never easy. My eyes are dry, but my body is numb and heavy. Somewhere, floating above my unmoving body, my mind is active with an odd feeling of objectivity. I see clearly the beauty of my dad's human weaknesses. The glimpse of his inner working is so rich and beautifully mortal that it could be the makings of an entire ballet. Shocked that I even had this thought, I shake the idea out of my head.

Climbing back into my body, I force myself to stand. Switching into hiking mode makes me feel disoriented and nauseous.

"I just need to find my hiking boots," I mumble to no one in particular.

*****

I am back in Toronto early in the new year, choreographing. Suzanne, one of my dancers, walks to the subway with me after a long day of rehearsal. I hired her because of the emotional presence she brings to the stage. She has what I call "old eyes," which look as if they have seen many things.

Today's rehearsal was uneventful. It was simply another day spent distracting myself from my creative void. I generated random steps that were meaningless, except for the possibility that they might lead me somewhere. I have been lost in my creative process longer than usual this time. Expensive weeks of nothing consume my grant money. Privately, a sense of foreboding builds – maybe my direction won't arrive. Maybe my creative spark is all used up, and it's time to get that FedEx job.

Suzanne pulls me back from my musing. "How was your trip?"

"It was good to see my dad, but his health is so precarious. Each time I talk with him, I think that this conversation could be our last and the words I choose become so weighted with importance."

Suzanne nods. Her dad died of cancer twelve years ago, when she was twenty. She understands. As we walk, Suzanne tells me about her dad's death. Her final story is about her mom.

"After my dad died," she explains, "my mom sat in his favourite chair for three days. She couldn't bear to go on with life. It was like everything stood still. I don't think she even changed clothes or showered. Then, one day while she was napping in his chair, he came to her in a dream and told her she had to keep going."

An image hits me with such force that I cannot see or hear anything else. I see a man playing the role of a father sitting in his favourite old chair. Suzanne, in the role of his daughter, walks around the chair. As she does, the father slips behind, hidden from view. She completes her circle to stare at an empty chair. The sense of loss she feels causes her body to tremble.

I gasp. A shiver runs up my spine as if I have been plunged into a freezing lake. I am no longer lost; I have things to do. I have to find a tacky, worn-out arm chair. I have to put wheels on it so it can be pushed around the stage. Can I get all this done for rehearsal tomorrow?

Later that evening, I sit facing a client. My mind is still racing, and it takes a few calming breaths to bring my undivided attention to the woman in front of me.

"How is your body letting you know you've had a tough day?" I ask.

"Well, I feel tightness here." Her hand moves to her throat.

"Can you show me with your hand the shape of the tightness?"

"I'm not sure."

"How about just trying some movements? Is it pulling in, or pushing out, or like something being flattened?"

"Hmmm . . ." Her brow furrows.

I continue, "Finding the right movement is like shopping for the perfect coat. You try on many coats. Some may feel closer to being the right coat and others less so, but eventually you put on a coat that suddenly just feels right. Try out shapes and movements with your hands until you feel an '*ah-ha!*' — a feeling that rushes in and tells you it's the movement or shape that matches how you feel."

She experiments with hand movements until she settles on flat hands pushing in on each other.

"That's it," she says. "I feel flattened."

She spends the rest of the session exploring movements and shapes that express this flattened feeling. From her focus and intensity, I see that embodying this feeling invigorates her.

The following day is a Saturday. It's supposed to be my day off, but now that I have had my "ah-ha" moment, I spend every moment chasing it. I dream of choreography while doing the dishes, riding the subway, and even sleeping. My current project is to "imagine up" the just-right prop chair by Monday.

My designated helper in this endeavour is a guy named Jeff. We have been dating for the past year, seeing each other once or twice a week. He is an engineer with a haircut to match. And, unlike my long list of previous boyfriends, most of whom I fell in love with almost instantaneously, our relationship has been slow to gain momentum. I am not sure if it's going anywhere. Friends and family keep telling me that he is a great guy, and that I should give him a chance. When my dad met Jeff, he kept saying what a perfect match we were, and something about puzzle pieces that fit together well. I took my dad's comment as criticism. I was sure he meant that Jeff was practical, dependable, and financially stable and, apparently, I was not – or rather, I was an artist.

I stand next to Jeff in a large department store on a busy Saturday afternoon, marvelling at how clean cut his hair looks. I sigh, tucking my bangs behind my ear. *Today's not the day to decide on whether he's The One; today's the day to find a chair.*

Jeff and I have sat in nearly every chair in the store. Each one is missing something or just doesn't feel right. Jeff flops into yet another chair and says, "How about this one? It feels nice and deep like a real man's chair. It's got a sturdy back, easy to push around the stage. And look! It's fifty-percent off."

He knows what I'm looking for, because I've been telling him all day long.

Jeff gets up and turns the chair upside down to see if the frame will allow us to attach wheels, at which point a store clerk comes rushing over and says, "Ahhhh . . . can I help you?"

"Just checking the frame," Jeff says. "It looks good and sturdy. I think this is the one."

I spend the rest of the weekend distressing the chair. I rub it with sandpaper until it looks threadbare. I stain it with red wine and create a dent in the pillows so it looks well sat in. Jeff puts wheels on the bottom.

As we drive the prop to the studio, Jeff says, "This is supposed to represent your dad's favourite chair, right?"

"No," I say, laughing at the naive simplicity of his assumption, "my creative process is not as obvious as that. Everything is a mysterious metaphor that even I hardly understand. And besides, my dad doesn't have a favourite chair. He is too busy to have time to sit."

The following Monday, I stand facing the beaten-up prop chair that sits in the middle of the studio floor. It looks at me as if to say, "now what?"

Stretching on the floor behind the chair, my four principal dancers, Suzanne, Tom, Karen, and Robert, also give me a "now what" look.

"Hmmm . . . let's see what we can do," I say. "Tom, how about you sit on the arm of the chair and pretend to hold a steering wheel."

Tom is a rare combination of dancer and retired boilermaker. When I say boilermaker, I mean he used to repair three- to four-story-high boilers built for massive factories. His body is still nimble, but one can see the years of metal work in his gnarled hands. His eyes are his most extraordinary feature. They seem to dance even when he is not moving.

Tom holds his imaginary steering wheel and Robert pushes the chair around the studio.

"That's good, but try it again. This time, use proper hand-over-hand steering."

Tom repeats his "drive" with exaggerated precision, looking pleased with himself.

"Okay," I say, "do it again. This time, play up the man enjoying his car-kingdom even more."

He does the second take. His eyes start to shine with pride and he begins to look like a man out for a ride just to show off his car. All of a sudden, it's perfect; all of us watching start to laugh.

"Now, let's dismantle this icon of manhood with some sticky-fingered kids. Robert and Suzanne, sit on the back of the chair and fight like a brother and sister would after spending all day in the car."

Robert is lanky and statuesque, but in his eyes one can see the little boy he used to be. He strides towards the chair, poking Suzanne incessantly and instigating a full-blown child's fight by the time they take their places.

"Karen, I want you to sit beside Tom and pretend to be the harried mom on a family trip."

Karen takes care of two teenage daughters and her own dance company. I suspect she enjoys working with me because she gets to be not in charge.

Karen places a finger on her head and says, "Hmmm . . . yes, I remember what that was like!"

"Tom," I say, "continue driving, but now you're at your wits' end. Your car-kingdom has become a whiney-kid-wagon."

Tom's shoulders droop, and his eyebrows lift in exasperation.

"Oh, it's so perfect," I say, laughing. "This reminds me of my dad's crazy trips in his VW van. We would drive for hours, and with all the kids in the back, it was mayhem! He always took us on rigorous hikes, and made us feel like babies if we complained. We mostly camped in gravel quarries and fields. These "economy" camp sites meant that my sisters and I had to suffer through the angst of not being able to use our curling irons! An adventure in my dad's eyes was not worth it unless it involved a lot of suffering."

I sit on the subway on the way home from rehearsal, thinking about my day. After finishing the family vacation scene, I asked Tom and Suzanne to stay and work on the father-daughter chair scene. We created it just as I had imagined when I had my "ah-ha" moment. Its simplicity and grace mesmerized me – Suzanne repeatedly circling the chair and Tom fading from her view like a ghost. As I watched, I felt my heart stretching, growing bigger to accommodate the grief that would soon come my way. This sensation was oddly soothing, in the same way that a deep-muscle stretch hurts, but also feels good because it leaves one feeling freer. I wish I could spend tomorrow working on this scene, just to be able to watch it again and again, but I must create the rest of the show. *What will the rest of the show be?* I wonder. Then it dawns on me that the vacation and father-daughter scenes could be pieces of a larger story about a family and the grief they face. It's been many years since my National Ballet Company days, in which I danced all the classic story ballets, but with this piece, I am returning to my roots.

I shake my head. The National Ballet Company has a million-dollar budget and a huge staff. My company is just me and the dancers I hire. This piece will be a huge risk both artistically and financially, but it feels like this story is pushing itself into existence, and I have no choice but to follow.

As I walk home from the subway to my small basement apartment, my shoulders slump. I'm crazy to think I can do this.

*****

A couple of weeks later, as I get ready for rehearsal, I think about a crazy idea I have for the young family scene. I worry that my dancers might jump ship when I tell them about it. I found two vintage Oopsie Daisy dolls on eBay. They are the size of real babies and have battery-operated moving arms and legs. They crawl, fall over, cry for their mama, and then get back up. Now they're sitting in a bag, ready to go. Yes, today's the day I'm going to ask Karen and Tom, two highly esteemed veteran performers, to dance with battery-operated baby dolls!

Once in the studio, I take the babies out of the bag by the scruff of their PJs and show my find to my dancers.

Karen says, laughing, "You're kidding . . . right? You really want me to dance with those?"

A few minutes later, Karen is holding the two crying babies and doing a harried-mom dance in which she keeps trying to hand a baby over to her husband.

I turn to Tom and tell him, "The father doesn't really get the whole baby thing. To him, babies are blobs that poo. Smell the baby's diaper, and then hand it back to Karen. Grab your briefcase and make your escape. Run as quickly as you can to the car-chair and 'drive' away."

Tom says, "My kids are going to tease me when they see the show. This 'dad' will be all too familiar to them!"

A memory flashes into my head: I am about three years old, and my dad is so grossed out by my diaper that he puts me in the bathtub and hoses me down from afar while I wail.

A few hours later, we've moved past the crawling babies. Suzanne and Robert now play the growing kids.

I explain the next scene to them, "When you see your dad arrive home, I want you to run to him and give him a big hug, but then run right back to your mom. And Tom, you watch the three of them from a distance, longing for the closeness the kids have with their mom. Your kids have grown up, and you realize you missed so much of it. Being an emotionally distant dad is not who your character *is* but who he *became*. His father taught him through example and strict discipline that men were supposed to be tough and show no weakness. He became the dad society expected him to be."

I did not plan this character description. It arrived spontaneously. I am surprised by how much empathy it demonstrates for the dad character, and an alarming series of thoughts strikes me: What if the audience assumes the show is autobiographical? What if they think *my* dad is pathetic? How could I do that to him when he is dying? Am I being fair to him? Certainly, my dad was not very good with babies, but once I was older, he took me swimming and hiking and taught me how to ride a bike and play chess. He was never much of a nurturer, but what he lacked in nurturing, he made up by doing.

I soothe my guilt by telling myself that the dad character is not an exact copy of my dad, but a mix of many dads: my dad, Suzanne's dad, Tom as a dad, and also the archetype of the traditional North American Dad. I have also exaggerated and highlighted certain qualities to draw out the humour and pathos in the dad hero. Because I am not sticking to an exact biography, I feel freedom to play with the archetype of "Dad" in whatever way I like.

Besides, I know for certain that my dad will never see this piece performed. He has managed to miss all my premieres, and has never seen my choreography. The truth is that I've always been too scared to invite him. I wanted space to be creative and be free from his judgments. Even though I am almost forty, I find that there is still a "little girl" in me that wishes he cared enough to come – whether he was invited or not.

I spend my trip home that evening imagining the things I will have the dad character get up to next. It's a playful sort of revenge for being hosed down in the bathtub all those years ago.

I arrive home to multiple messages. Most of them have something to do with my dad having chemotherapy and then having a heart attack on a boat during a coast guard rescue.

I have no idea if he is alive or dead. I try to reach someone to find out what has happened.

My sister finally answers her phone.

"Don't worry. Dad's alright, but he has quite a story to tell. After his chemotherapy, he told Gerri he was going for a drink with his coast guard buddies. Instead, he snuck out of the house wearing his foul-weather gear to participate in a mock rescue. Well, it turned into a real rescue, because he had a heart attack on the boat. The hovercraft took him right up the beach to the door of the ambulance. When they got to the hospital, four men in his coast guard unit ran his gurney into the emergency room, all still in their foul-weather gear. Because he got to the hospital so quickly, the doctors were able to give him medication that prevented the damage that usually occurs with a heart attack. So, he's fine. They already sent him home. He is walking around telling everyone about his adventure. He keeps saying it was like something out of a movie. You should call him and give him the joy of telling his story all over again."

"What a rascal he is," I reply. "Do you know, last week, after his first chemotherapy, I called him because I was thinking he might be feeling depressed and sick? He answered his phone from the top of a ski slope!"

A few weeks later, I sit in the dance studio holding a letter. I look at it one more time to confirm that I have been denied my grant. I shudder. Going ahead with the show as planned will take my budget ten thousand dollars into the red. That might not seem like a lot for a big dance company, but my company is run solely by me. I take the hit for any losses. There is really no choice to be made, though, because the project has a life of its own. It's speeding into existence. The only thing I can do is follow, regardless of what sacrifice it requires. I have lost all subjectivity, so I make this choice from my heart. I need this piece. It gives me something to hold onto in the face of my dad's illness. I need to see it onstage, to make something beautiful out of the horror of my dad's cancer.

If my dad ever found out the cost of this production, he would tell me I am a complete idiot. He would never understand taking such a financial loss for a dance piece that will only run for a week. Yet I am following in his footsteps. He is a risk-taker of great audacity. He has climbed sheer ice cliffs, and slept in cocoons attached to the side of mountains. Is the purpose of these adventures any more tangible than the art I create? The line between stupidity and courage is very fine.

I look up, and see Suzanne and Tom ready to start rehearsal. I do not tell them my news; this is my burden to carry. If this ballet is going to cost me ten thousand dollars, I best get busy making it the best damn ballet I've ever made.

"Okay," I say to Suzanne, "your character has come to visit her dad, and you expect to see him as you know him — a strong, proud man. Instead, what you see is a vulnerable old man sitting in his worn-out chair. There are empty soup cans around his feet. You realize that's all he's been eating. You see that he is reading a newspaper upside-down, so you gently turn it the right way up."

I turn to Tom and say, "Give her a loving and grateful look, then continue to read the paper as if nothing is wrong."

My throat tightens. Working on this scene reminds me of how precarious my dad's health is, as well as how he tries to hide his vulnerability by pretending everything is okay.

The air in the studio suddenly feels heavy. The room seems darker. I feel as if everything is moving slowly.

I know these sensations. As a therapist, I feel them when a client enters emotionally heavy terrain. They are early warning signs that often precede a flood of tears from my clients.

"Okay, let's give it a try," I say, as I scurry to the safety of my chair at the front of the studio.

They act out the scene. When they get to the newspaper part, Suzanne bursts into tears. In between sobs, she says, "I remember my dad like that when it came close to the end. He was so fragile."

"It's okay to cry," I say.

As I move to her side, my own tears start.

Suzanne and I stand together in a shared moment of grief.

Tom jumps up and starts doing cartwheels and headstands in front of us, performing like a circus clown.

Suzanne and I watch him, dumbfounded. It's hard to concentrate on our tears with all his antics.

"Tom!" Suzanne says. "We're trying to have a moment."

"Girls," he says "No crying today. You promised!"

His manner is amicable, but I always feel angry when someone refers to me as a girl when I'm thirty-eight.

"Tom, can't you just let us cry for a few minutes? Does it really make you that uncomfortable?"

He does another handstand, a big grin on his face.

It's hard to stay mad at Tom. He might not be able to handle tears, but his method of avoidance is captivating.

My dad and Tom both sidestep vulnerability with such flare that they've made an art form out of it. I have to admit that their mastery of avoiding emotions is oddly delightful. Mastering an art form is something I respect and understand.

After taking some time to recover, we move to the next scene.

"Tom, I want you to take Suzanne's hand and gently twirl her around. As you lift her, whisper in her ear that you love her."

Turning to Suzanne, I say "This is the first time your dad has told you he loves you so directly. His illness and old age have weakened him. In this state, his emotions are more accessible. This openness is something you have craved from him your whole life. It's like drinking water after having been forever thirsty."

I lift Tom onto my back a few moments later, demonstrating to Suzanne how I want it done. I explain, "He cannot take care of himself anymore. He has become like a child. As he once carried you, you now carry him."

It is late in the evening, and we are the only people in the studio. Tom and Suzanne perform the sequence. It's a simple dance, but the result is powerful and so full of love. I realize that the piece I am creating is not just about grief, but the ways we fumble through loving each other and how beautiful these fumbles are.

The following day, I see a client before heading to rehearsal.

During the session, I ask her to draw a picture of the things she wants in her life. This terrifies her, because if she draws this picture, she risks believing that she can be happy, which could potentially bring her disappointment.

"This type of imagining is a rehearsal for making choices that lead to a more satisfying life," I tell her. "It's similar to how we tend to steer a car in the direction we look. By drawing this picture, you are giving attention to the things you want in your life. This will help you steer towards them."

She approaches the paper and starts to draw.

After this client leaves, my dad phones to give me an update on his spring skiing in the Rockies. Just as we are saying good-bye, he adds, "Oh, by the way, I'm going to come for opening night of your new ballet."

"That's really . . . great," I lie.

I shake my head. *Oh shit, I'm in trouble.* A rift has opened up in the space-time continuum and a dad from a different existence, one who is actually interested in my life's work, is coming to see my show. In a million years, I would never have thought that my dad's Bucket List would involve this. What will he think when he finds out my ballet involves the story of a daughter saying good-bye to her dying father!

My dad spends the rest of the phone conversation giving me a list of about twenty extended family members I also need to reserve tickets for. They have never seen my work before, either, and are mostly coming to see my dad for the last time. I can't help but think that they will be in for a shock once the curtain rises.

*****

The premiere is a few days away, so I spend today's rehearsal helping the dancers drop deeper into their roles.

Suzanne is practicing a scene that takes place after the dad's death. Her character sits in his old chair, experiencing the type of depression that makes doing simple things like showering completely overwhelming.

Lee, a dancer whose haunted eyes contrast his boyish physique, kneels by her feet, holding her hand. He plays the role of an angel helping Suzanne's character through her grief.

Lee's presence is as soothing as Suzanne's grief is deep.

I wonder if Jeff will be my angel when my dad dies. Will I let him hold my hand? Will I let him in?

Later in the day, I work with Suzanne on one of her solos.

She flails her arms in a haphazard, almost violent way, then stops and is totally still, a blank expression on her face. Then she starts the flurry all over again.

"Yes, that's it," I say. "Your character has no mastery over the flow of her grief. It flows all at once, threatening to completely overwhelm her. The only coping method available is to go numb. It's all or nothing."

Suzanne performs the scene. It's not easy to watch, but I am drawn to it. Her frenzied grief is the physical representation of what I feel building inside me when I think of my dad dying. It's a relief to see it acted out on stage. It relieves the burden of having to carry all these feelings on my own.

That evening, I see my last client before taking a week off to oversee the run of my new ballet, which I have named *Long Live*.

During the session, I mostly just sit and watch her paint, staying attentive to how the image emerges. As she concentrates on the center black area, I notice my chest tightening, as if something is pressing down upon it. When she starts to draw tentacles emerging from the black center, my chest lightens. I still feel sadness, but now it has more flow.

She stops painting and stands back from the image. "I feel so heavy in my mood today, but having a place to put it feels good. Strange to experience these two different feelings, all at the same time."

I nod. I understand this well.

*****

After seven months of rehearsing, it's opening night. Jeff, who is running the box office, is taking his role very seriously. He wears a suit and sits behind a table in the theatre lobby, looking very official.

"Are we sold out?" I ask.

"We are at 247. So, if the theatre seats 300, then you are about eighty percent sold out. If you wait a minute, I'll figure out the exact percentage."

"No, that's alright," I say as I run past him.

Damn. I spent many sleepless nights working on a marketing blitz aimed at minimizing my financial losses. Eighty percent full is not enough to pull me out of the red, but at least it's enough of an audience to make for a good show.

I run backstage and open the dressing room door. "Merde!" I yell.

Suzanne and I lock eyes. There is a determined, yet calm look about her. I see that she has already entered "the zone." *May your "walkabout" be a good one*, I think as I give her a slow nod.

I pass by Jeff, who has moved from the box office to his other job as the cameraman, filming tonight's show. "Remember to get lots of close-ups, and don't worry about making it perfect. We're filming every night, so I'll edit the best takes together."

The stage manager gives me his trademark grin and thumbs up, and ushers me to my seat with a wave of his hand.

I look over my shoulder in time to see my dad arrive with a huge bouquet of roses. My sister warned him about the subject of *Long Live*, and he still came. He sits many rows behind me, surrounded by family.

I am sweaty. I sit on my hands. I can hardly breathe.

The lights fade.

Near the end of Act One, Suzanne circles the chair and Tom slips behind it, out of sight. The theatre is silent. I hold my breath. Suzanne slowly walks forward, sits in the chair, and begins to cross her arms like knitting needles. I hear sniffles. I realize that many in the audience are crying, while my eyes are dry. My dad sits less than a hundred feet away from me, but I dare not look at him. I dare not even move.

In the middle of Act Two, Tom stands in a pool of light. His eyes pierce the blackness. His voice wavers as he sings, "Genius death, your art is done. Lover death, your body's gone. Father death, I'm coming home. . . . Father breath, once more, farewell."[79]

Every time I watch this scene, it's like getting a kick to the stomach. I brace for impact. He finishes the song and the lights fade, signifying the father's death.

Near the end of the show, fake snow covers the stage – remnants of the snowstorm from the previous scene. Angels pull the dad's chair gently away from Suzanne, who pulls it back. They take the chair from her again. Realizing it's time to live in the present, Suzanne lets the angels sail the chair into the wings.

The curtain closes, and the audience bursts into a standing ovation.

*****

I knew *Long Live* was going to be an emotional experience for me, but I did not prepare for how it would affect others. In the lobby after the show, I'm overwhelmed by people's responses. I don't know what to say. I find that I keep apologizing over and over again for making people cry. I know this is an odd thing to say, because helping people feel their emotions is my life's work, but my work has never made so many people cry all at the same time. I am not sure the audience knew what they were in for when they bought their tickets.

At the reception, my dad is all smiles and laughter, like he usually is. When I ask if he liked the show, his smile fades and he is silent.

Finally, he says, "I liked when the snow fell. That part was really pretty, Kath." He then turns away from me to talk with someone else, leaving me to wonder if any of the *Long Live* story got through my dad's emotional wall.

A few days later, I receive an e-mail from a man who saw the show:

> The father/daughter movement sequences were outstanding – the way they shifted and carried each other's weight. It was the Father that scared me the most. He was so isolated and helpless. So ineffectual and unable to reach out and really help, as if he didn't know how. It reminded me to never stop taking time to relate to my daughters even if I don't always do it in the right way.

My dad might not have been moved by *Long Live*, but at least this dad understood its message.

*****

Long Live has finished its week-long run. I sit in the dad's chair on the street outside the theatre with all the costumes, props, and crawling babies piled up beside me as I wait for my "Jeff chariot." Strangers stop to take pictures – they think all the peculiar props are some sort of art installation! I am too tired to dissuade them. My weight settles in the chair. I did it, even though it seemed impossible, and now it's time to rest.

Jeff arrives, and we load everything into the back of his car. He looks exhausted; I worry that my creative drive has taken its toll on him. We arrive at my place and sit in the car, too tired to unload.

"We did it!" Jeff says.

The word "we" turns around inside me, trying to find its place.

As we sit in silence, I ponder this "we." My mom told me about seeing Jeff dealing with a difficult customer at the box office, and asking him if he was okay. She described how tired he looked, but that his eyes were so alive as he answered, "I have never had more fun in my life."

I look at Jeff. Behind the weariness, I see what my mom saw. Jeff built the props, stayed up all night sending out promotional e-mails, drove me around while I put posters up, ran the box office, and watched the performance night after night. I realize that the *Long Live* adventure satisfied him as much as it satisfied me.

I have always strived to be self-sufficient, as there is no risk of being disappointed that way. For this reason, becoming a "we" has always scared me. For the first time in my life, however, this "we" feels like it just might be okay.

Two weeks after *Long Live* ended its run, I arrive home to find Jeff waiting for me. I'm a bit surprised, since we didn't have anything planned for tonight. He looks nervous.

He sits me down on the couch and asks, "Will you marry me?"

I am shocked. I further shock myself with the "yes" that comes quickly and calmly out of my mouth.

My "yes" does not sound like the me that I know. My old self, who chose ill-matched partners and was stubbornly self-sufficient, says, *Hey wait . . . what just happened? I thought we had agreed to never completely commit to anyone so we wouldn't risk being disappointed.* But with one word, I become a new person who carries the confidence of a woman able to choose happiness. I don't mean momentary bliss, but a deep contentment.

Jeff and I announce to our families that we are getting married. Three days later, we get an e-mail from my dad asking us to RSVP for our own wedding! Apparently he has the whole thing already planned; we just need to confirm our availability four weeks from today.

Jeff and I agree to the short time frame because I want my dad to walk me down the aisle before he dies. With the rapid progression of his cancer, we know there isn't much time left.

Over the next four weeks, I feel like I'm on a speeding train whizzing past racks of wedding dresses and catering menus and seating plans. When the train finally comes to a stop, I find myself standing at the back door of my dad's house in Vancouver, gazing out at the lush backyard garden, where my immediate family and a few close friends wait for me to walk down the aisle. I'm minutes away from marrying Jeff, and underneath my Audrey Hepburn hair-do and my graceful white dress, my heart is in a state of panic. I've been single for so many years; I'm not sure if I can do this marriage thing well. I'm about to take a leap, which terrifies me. My dad's steel grip on my arm really is the thing that's keeping me from running. I step into the garden and see Jeff waiting for me under the canopy. His eyes are full of love. He looks beautiful, honest, and full of heart. My panic fades, and joy to know such a man replaces it. My dad walks me down the aisle, and then I take my place by Jeff's side.

*****

A few weeks after the wedding, my dad and stepmom flew to the south of France. Granted, it was a stupid thing to do when one's health is so precarious, but they did it. The trip went well until my dad's kidneys failed. The French doctors stabilized him, but said the long flight to Vancouver was not advised, so he scheduled a layover in Toronto. Now, my sister and I sit with him in a yellow-curtained hospital cubicle at Toronto General Emergency, waiting for a doctor.

"If my kidneys hadn't failed," my dad says, "I would have flown straight home and not had the chance to see you guys."

"Well, dad, that's certainly putting a bright spin on kidney failure!" I say.

To pass the time, I tell stories of my new domestic bliss.

"Our toilet seat broke," I explain, "and we bought a new one, only to discover that toilet seats come in two different sizes. Unbeknownst to us, one is supposed to measure their toilet before making their purchase, because, for obvious reasons, they are not returnable."

My dad and my sister burst into laughter.

"What's so funny?" I ask.

My dad says, "My head-in-the-clouds daughter is talking about practical things like toilet seats. You're finally nesting in the real world!" He is laughing so much that he can hardly speak. "And yes . . . being able to take a comfortable shit . . . is really one of the most important things in life!"

A young doctor walks in. "So, Mr. . . ." He looks at the chart in his hand. "Mr. Rea. Your kidneys failed while you were in France, and I see they gave you dialysis?"

"Yeah, that's right," my dad says. "I always wanted to see the south of France. They've got some great castles, but did you know the beaches are quite rocky?"

My sister pipes in, "It's his Bucket List trip."

The doctor continues. "And now you're experiencing heart arrhythmia and you're. . . ."

"Did you know that they have great hospital food?" my dad interrupts. "They actually served me croissants with real butter!"

My sister and I can't stop giggling. Our laughter, which began over the toilet seat story, is now uncontainable.

The doctor pauses. The look of seriousness that you'd expect when a doctor is talking to a dying man yields to a smile. He lowers his chart, sits on the side of the bed, and says, "So, tell me more about those beaches. Are they really that rocky?"

Over the next few hours, a stream of increasingly experienced doctors comes by to see my dad. Between his tumor, his kidney failure, and his heart problems, his case is so complicated that none of them know quite what to do. To complicate matters further, rather than discuss his current condition, all my dad wants to do is talk about French castles and croissants, and why our Canadian government can't use our tax dollars to make decent hospital food like they do in France.

A doctor walks in and introduces himself as the head of the department. He then says, "People have been telling me about you all night. I hear you have a fascinating medical history. Start at the beginning, and take your time."

My dad tells him about his twenty-year history with kidney disease, a nearly fatal heart attack related to his kidney medication, a transplant with a kidney donated by my stepmom, three different types of cancer related to the antirejection drugs, and now transplant rejection. He tells the story not as a victim, but as a triumphant survivor who cleverly dodged death. The doctor listens avidly.

In finishing, my dad says, "My family tells me I am a cat who has nine lives . . . but I think, according to my count, that I'm on my second cat now."

The doctor nods. "That's quite a story. Now, in order to figure out the right thing to do, I need to ask what your long-term goal is here."

My dad lets out a big roar of laughter. "Well, that's a great question for a man in my state."

His laughter subsides. He takes a deep breath and says, "I want to live as long as I possibly can, and to enjoy my family while doing so. I don't want to lie around in a hospital bed waiting for the end to come."

"Usually, a man as sick as you would never be discharged. But I think I understand you. Go spend the night with your daughters. Go live your life."

A few hours later, we are all at my sister's house. My dad is hiding in the hall closet, waiting to burst out and scare my nephews. Instead, the kids burst in and surprise my dad. For the next half hour, squeals of laughter emanate from the closet.

My dad makes it back to Vancouver. He tells us that he does not want any of us to uproot our lives to take care of him. And so I wait for the right moment to go be with him. My life continues, but on edge. Every time the phone rings, I expect to be summoned to his death bed.

The call finally arrives one evening as Jeff and I are having a late dinner.

"He's dying," my brother says. "You have to come tonight if you want to say good-bye to him."

The plan is for me to fly out tonight; Jeff will join me as soon as he can. He is in the middle of closing the sale of his townhouse in the suburbs, and making an offer for our dream house in the city. I fire off a quick e-mail cancelling sessions with all my clients for the next two weeks and arranging substitutes for my dance classes. Jeff rushes me to the airport. There is no traffic at this time of night, so we drive well above the speed limit.

We arrive at 11:00 pm and see that the last flight to Vancouver departs at 11:45 pm. There is a huge line of people buying tickets, and only one ticket agent.

"Excuse me," I yell, "my dad is dying and I need to get on a plane boarding in fifteen minutes. Can I jump the line?"

Everyone lets me through, and I buy my ticket. As I pick up my bag and start running to my gate, I hear the voice of a person in line say, "God be with you."

I am the first person off the plane when the flight lands. I run to the taxi stand and make it to Vancouver General Hospital ten minutes later. After a frantic search, I find the elevator that takes me up to the Palliative Care Ward. The night nurse tells me the number of the room my dad's in. Before entering, I pause and brace myself for what lies behind the door.

I open the door and see my dad asleep, wearing a satisfied smile and holding an almost-empty bag of black licorice in his hands.

Confused, I turn to my brother, who is standing by my dad's bed.

"He's rallying," my brother explains sheepishly. "They said he would go for sure tonight, and I was so afraid that none of you would get here on time. And then, a few minutes ago, he woke up and asked if there was any black licorice. He's almost finished off a whole bag."

I sit down. This is so like my dad. He has frightened me so many times before with the threat of dying. Despite the smile and the half-eaten bag of candy, I can hear his laboured breath and I know he is coming to the end of his cat lives.

An hour later, he wakes up. The first thing he says to me is, "So, are you pregnant yet?"

"Dad!" I say.

He continues, "You know, you're old, so you guys shouldn't waste any time. I don't need to explain how it works, do I?" He grins.

"No! We're trying. It just hasn't happened yet."

I am disappointed not to be pregnant. I want so badly to be a mom, and for my dad to know I'm on my way to realizing this dream before he dies.

The next morning, a doctor stops by while making his daily rounds. He is a young redhead who has a smile that lets the world know that working in the Palliative Care Ward was his life's calling.

"How are you doing today, Craig?"

My dad stutters, "I f . . . f . . . f . . . feel q . . . q . . . q . . . quite f . . . f . . . fine. C . . . C . . . Considering."

My dad's right arm hangs limp by his side, paralyzed by the growing tumor. He waves his good hand in the air as he speaks, as if this will help him get the words out.

My dad has always stuttered when speaking in public without a chance to prepare. When I was a child, he would stutter when we went out for burgers, and he had to speak into the microphone while trying to get all our orders right. I always experienced a strange feeling of disequilibrium in those moments when my dad tumbled off his Hero Dad Pedestal, and became merely human. Watching my dad now, I feel that familiar disequilibrium. He looks so small in the big hospital bed. He reminds me of a vulnerable boy trying hard to show how strong he is.

Like all children, I never knew my dad when he was a boy, but I know his childhood was not easy. His father, who used corporal punishment, died when my dad was fourteen. His mother was a heavy drinker who became an alcoholic at some point. My dad was sent to boarding school at the age of ten, because they could not handle his hyperactivity. Somewhere in the midst of all this, he developed a stutter.

I want to hug that little boy and tell him that it'll be alright, but I don't, because I know that my dad hates any affection that makes him feel vulnerable.

An hour later, a nurse drops by and shoots meds into my dad's PICC line.

"What did you just give me?" my dad asks.

"Just topping up your morphine," she says cheerfully as she heads out the door.

My dad turns to me and asks, "Kath, do you know what the dose was?"

"You don't need to keep track of your medications anymore," I say. "The nurses are doing that for you now."

"But what's left for me to do?"

"I don't know, Dad. This is new for all of us."

After a pause, he responds in a voice that sounds like depressed Eeyore from the *Winnie the Pooh* books he used to read to us. "Well, I guess all that's left is for me just to learn to 'go with the flow.' I've never been good at that, have I?"

He settles back in his bed and exhales. He smiles weakly to show he is putting his best effort into this "going with the flow" stuff – all two seconds of it that he's had to endure!

I laugh. "Well, Dad, it's never too late to learn."

He looks around the room glumly. I imagine he is asking himself, *how did I end up here, having to go with the flow?*

My dad always said that if he got terminal cancer, he would climb a mountain and never return. This made my stepmom, Gerri, furious.

"Craig," she would say, "don't you dare ever do that. Cutting your time with your family short just so you can die some big hero is just about the most selfish and inconsiderate way to die."

It dawns on me that my dad is in this boring, yellow hospital room for us, his family. He loves us more than the mountains and the sea.

That afternoon, my dad struggles through four hours of kidney dialysis. It cleans toxins from his body and, unfortunately, also removes his morphine, leaving him in excruciating pain. The treatment will keep him alive for another few days, at which point he'll need it again. My dad drifts in and out of sleep. I sit by his side, listening to his breath and waiting for him to wake up and say, "Kath." Each time he does, I am up and massaging his back as if I never left his side. I repeat this strange dance all day long, jumping up when he calls and flopping back down when he drifts off.

I massage my dad's back for what feels like the hundredth time as he grimaces in pain.

"Do you want me to put the pillow under your arm?" I ask.

He nods, so I reach my hands behind his back and pull him forward onto my shoulder, lifting him higher on the bed. This action feels familiar, giving me such a strange feeling of déjà vu. Then, I remember the scene in *Long Live*, in which the daughter takes care of her ailing father. I remember showing Suzanne how I wanted her to lift Tom onto her back. I have done this before; I have practiced this moment.

The next morning, my dad feels better: the dialysis has cleaned his blood, and he is now topped back up on morphine. He sits in his hospital bed with a furrowed brow.

"Kath," he says, "I am confused about how successful you are. I know your brother and sister are doing well because they earn lots of money, but you hardly earn anything from your dance stuff, even though you've been doing it for twenty years. I worry about you. I want to know that you're going to be all right."

My dad may be free-spirited in his adventures, but he measures the success of his kids by how much money we make. As an artist, making money is something I do not excel in.

"Oh, Dad," I say, shaking my head, "we have different ways of measuring success. I measure the success of my job by how much it enriches my life, not by whether it makes me rich. And using my criteria, I am very successful."

"Hmph," my dad responds, clearly not that impressed with my "success."

Later in the day, Jeff phones and tells me that the offer on our dream house was accepted. I tell my dad the news. For the next hour, he pores over pictures of the new house that I brought with me from Toronto. He asks me all sorts of questions: Is it brick? What type of foundation is it on? What type of mortgage did you guys get? How many rooms? What is the kitchen like?

Finally, he pats me on the back and says, "Kath, I'm real proud of you. You did good."

I laugh and nudge him. "Was the house the tipping point? Am I now a success in your eyes?"

"Well, I think things are going to be alright for you," he says. With this pronouncement, his brow eases and his body relaxes into the bed.

My dad's room fills with more and more family caregivers as the day progresses. By late afternoon, the room is brimming with well-meaning helpfulness. My brother leans over my dad, trying to get him to eat. My stepmom adjusts his pillow, so that his arm will be more comfortable. My older sister tries to find out what my dad wants her to bring from home. Everyone is fussing about and speaking to him in subdued and caring tones, almost as if they are talking to a child. I tried to warn them earlier that they should ease off their helpfulness, but no one listened to me. I now sit in a hospital chair positioned as far away from my dad as possible, watching and waiting for the explosion.

My dad's face gets redder and redder, until he suddenly yells, "STOP. STOP. EVERYBODY JUST STOP IT!"

Everyone freezes.

"I can't stand all this emotional boo-hoo stuff. I want everybody to treat me like normal. You know I'm not an emotional guy; just because I'm dying, I'm not going to suddenly change and become all gooey for you!"

My stepmom fluffs his pillow with two brisk hits. "Well, I am sorry that we're sad that you're dying and want to care for you. Would you rather be the man in the room next to yours, who is dying and hasn't had any visitors all week? We are not inhuman, you know, and you're just going to have to put up with us."

My dad sits in silence. We all stay frozen, waiting to see what will happen next.

My dad's quick ignition to anger is a familiar thing. He has always been a happy guy, but he's also quick to combust when irritated. I've only seen him demonstrate rare and fleeting glimpses of what he refers to as the "emotional boo-hoo stuff." This way of being is not showing any signs of yielding now that he's dying. It seems that there will be no *Long Live* version of his death. This dad will not be softening emotionally as he approaches death. *Good for you, Dad,* I think, *for not letting go of who you are, even as death humbles you.*

Then, almost as if my dad heard me thinking about *Long Live*, he says, "It's like that dance piece you created, Kathy. Sitting in the audience and watching all that emotional stuff. It was so awful. I hated it."

The impact of his words hits me hard. I hardly breathe, because if I do, I will cry.

My family goes back to their caring activities, but at a reduced intensity. My dad starts drifting off to sleep. Then he lifts up his head and, so quietly that I barely hear him, murmurs, "But that's okay, Kath. I know you needed to create that piece. It was your way of dealing with all of this."

He exhales and drifts off to sleep.

The next morning, my dad refuses pain killers. He wants to be lucid for the afternoon meeting with his doctors. As the hours go by, he is in more and more pain.

The meeting finally starts. Three doctors and immediate family surround my dad's bed. The doctors describe the different ways that my dad's illness might proceed. They explain that going off dialysis will not involve the pain of kidney failure, and will likely be a calm death. If he remains on dialysis, his tumor will suffocate him, which is known by the Palliative Ward staff to be one of the more frightening deaths, although they say that antianxiety drugs can be given to help with that.

It's clear to all watching that the doctors want my dad to choose between treatment choices that will each result in a different type of death. Essentially, they're asking him to choose the way he will die. My dad doesn't understand this, though, because he is focused on another agenda – to prove to everyone that he is still all there intellectually. He tries to do this by answering the doctor's questions with complicated words and clever reasoning. His speech is slurred; each sentence takes him a long time to say. He senses there is something he is not getting, and this makes him more and more frustrated.

Finally, he pauses. His eyes brighten, and he lets out a big roar of laughter. Slapping his thigh with his good hand, he says, "Ah ha! I finally get it! You want me to choose which way I'll kick the bucket!" He is so happy to finally understand what's going on.

"Okay," one of the doctors says, "What is your biggest fear? Is it the pain?"

My dad's smile fades. "It's true that I can't bear the pain any longer, but pain isn't my biggest fear. My biggest fear is losing control of my mind. I want to be lucid right up until the end."

My dad drifts off before the doctors can get any more out of him. He figured out the doctor's riddle; now, it is time to rest.

I have my dad all to myself the next morning. He brings up the subject of his funeral.

"Well," he says, "there are a few things I know I want. All you kids need to stand up and say something. And Kath, I want you to make sure there's no emotional stuff. I just hate to think of everyone getting all sappy."

"Okay," I say, knowing it is a promise I will never keep. Getting emotional at his funeral, especially for me, is inevitable.

He is about to tell me more when three young men from the Coast Guard walk in. They are young and fit, with military-issue haircuts.

"Hey! Great of you guys to stop by," my dad says. His tone is casual, but I can see from the way he sits up taller in his bed that he is really grateful to see them.

They tell my dad about their recent coast guard adventures. Their expressions are jovial and their voices are conversational, but I can see that their bodies are tense, as if bracing against the inevitability of my dad's death. One particularly earnest fellow tells us that he is a few days away from becoming a father. This dad-to-be seems to be having a difficult time keeping the mood jovial. He is all smiles, but his hands shake and his face is red. He looks as if he might burst into tears. I realize that he loves my dad like a father; in turn, I see how my dad cares about and respects this young man because they share the values of adventure and courage.

When I was little, my dad used to take us up Grouse Mountain on the cable car. I was scared of heights, so he always dragged me on as I cried. I was convinced that the line would break and our whole family would die in a cable car accident. I am an adventurer of a different sort. I take my risks in the make-believe world of theatre, rather than on the mountains and the sea.

All of a sudden, I want to yell at these boy-men to get out. I hate them because they are close to my dad in ways that I never was. My chest tightens. I can't go back and show my dad that I can ride the cable car without crying. There is no time left for me to prove my bravery.

That evening, my dad decides that he wants to sit in the hospital observation deck and watch both the Vancouver city lights and his beloved ocean. The full entourage of immediate family waits just outside his room, while an orderly readies him for his adventure. As I open the door a crack to see if he is ready, I see my dad emerge from the bathroom while grabbing the large orderly's arm like it's a lifeboat in a stormy ocean. Looking up, he says, "thank you." Tears of gratitude well in his eyes for this man who helped him hold onto the dignity of getting out of bed to go to the washroom.

My dad is too proud to let any family member help him with such things. He wants us to remember him as a healthy man, not be haunted by images of his illness. This orderly, a complete stranger, is allowed to witnesses my dad's vulnerability, and we are not. I feel a rush of conflicting emotions: I am jealous of the orderly, angry at my dad for hiding his vulnerability from me, and sad that my dad has never thanked me in such a way. I also feel the urge to run, terrified, out of the hospital. I have never seen a glimpse of him so completely vulnerable and full of emotion. This is a dad I do not know.

My dad sees me and angrily shoos me out of the room, so I retreat to the hallway and wait with the rest of my family. Two minutes later, he bursts out of his room with a triumphant grin. He lifts his limp hand onto the handle of the walker, where it stays for a few moments before it falls off again. He teeters back and forth, but he keeps making his way towards us with a look of glee in his eyes. He looks like a man just let out of prison.

We rush towards him all at once to help steady his step. Our entourage slowly makes its way to the 360-degree viewing lounge. We dim the lights and the city sparkles, making the black expanse of the ocean even darker. My dad drops into a comfy armchair and drinks in the view. The beauty is soothing for all of us after staring at hospital walls for the past week. Lucidness settles upon him, and he starts pointing to different areas of the ocean and telling us stories of his coast guard adventures. I exhale. This is the dad I know.

I walk into my dad's room the next evening to find him sitting on the side of the bed with his face in his hands, my brother and sister on either side of him.

He shakes his head back and forth. "I can't even go to the bathroom without help anymore. How is life worth living if I can't do that?"

I realize that his hands are covering his face to hide the fact that he is crying.

The moment has arrived. This is my dad's vulnerability. I do not know what to do. None of us know what to do. There is nothing we can say to make this better. As a therapist, I should know that just being there with him is the most important thing I can offer, but I am too stunned by the depth of his sorrow to remember this.

The night nurse walks in and sees my dad in his inconsolable state. She kneels by his bed and grabs his hand. "Craig," she says, "is it still worth it?"

She knows my dad is trying to decide whether or not to continue dialysis and the agonizing pain it brings. It's the consensus of the family to support him in letting go, but none of us can bear to tell him this.

"It's not about whether it's worth it," he says, "it's about not wanting to disappoint my kids. I always taught them to be fighters. I don't want to let them down by giving up."

The veteran Palliative Care nurse says, "Craig, sometimes there is great valour in knowing when the fight is over. It's like a knight laying down his sword. Through example, you taught your kids how to be brave and to fight for what they want. Now you can teach them the valour and grace of letting go."

This nurse says what none of us have been able to say to him, that it's time to let go, and she says it in his language – the language of an adventurer.

My brother then suggests my dad postpone the next dialysis indefinitely. My dad agrees.

We sit in silence, feeling the weight of my dad's decision. The countdown has begun. He will not live for more than a few days without dialysis.

"Where is Gerri?" my dad asks.

"We sent her home for a night of sleep," my brother says.

"I miss her."

"But, she's always here," my sister says.

"Yeah, but I never see her alone. There are always so many people around."

"Dad," my sister asks, "do you want a date night, just you and her alone for the evening? We could even sneak in some champagne."

"Yes," my dad says.

I sneak out of the room, find a quiet place, and begin to weep.

We all have something that breaks us. For my dad, it was loss of his dignity, worry about disappointing his kids, and missing the great love of his life. For me, it's finally seeing my dad's vulnerability.

The following day, my dad's room is once again full. Jeff has arrived and joined the ranks. My dad is back to being the jovial, in-control dad I have known my whole life.

"Kathy," my dad says, "did you bring my credit cards?"

He did, in fact, ask for them a few days ago, but his recent requests are strange and I have learned to ignore the ones that make no sense. The other night he kept asking for his coast guard uniform, and so I made sure my stepmom brought it to the hospital. The next morning, when he was lucid, he said, "What idiot brought my coast guard stuff to the hospital?"

Now, though, he is coherent and demanding to know why I forgot to bring his credit cards. There is no mistaking his tone. He wants them now.

"I need to cancel them," my dad says. "A lot of fraud happens when people die because thieves take advantage of the families, who are distracted by grief."

I cover up a smile. Won't that be a funny phone conversation? *Okay Mr. Rea. Can you please tell me the reason you are cancelling your cards today? Well, I expect to be dead in the next day, so, you see, I don't need them anymore.* Then my dad would probably lecture that clerk about the importance of avoiding fraud in these instances.

Jeff drives me back to the house so that we can search my dad's office. Dad also wants his bank statements and a copy of his last insurance payment. As we are looking, we find a binder on his desk labeled "Gerri's Book." It is a sixty-something page booklet that gives details on everything my stepmom may need to know once my dad is gone – everything from how to download pictures from the camera, to how to fertilize the gardenias. There is even a detailed to-do list for the week after his death. This is a practical man's final love poem to his wife.

On the way out, I walk past the kitchen. I see my dad's breakfast chair in the shadows. I can almost see him sitting there in his beaten-up robe and dilapidated slippers, eating his crumpet smothered in peanut butter. I can almost see him reading the newspaper and hear him spewing conservative rhetoric in such a smart way that I dare not debate the issue with him. But today, the chair is empty, and he will never again sit in it. I feel Jeff's arms wrap around me from behind. As in my ballet, I am the girl saying good-bye to her father's chair; Jeff is my angel, holding me steady.

We arrive back at the hospital with all the requested documents. I show my dad his final life insurance payment. He makes us promise to cancel his credit cards. He settles back into his bed, knowing his affairs are in order.

My brother and sister and I prepare the room for date night: we move the vinyl fold-down chair close to my dad's hospital bed, which we lower to give the illusion of a double bed, and place a champagne bottle and two glasses on the side table.

As I leave, my dad mumbles something. He is less alert than he was earlier in the evening. His speech is now slurred and almost incomprehensible.

"Dad, I can't make out what you're saying."

I lean in closer to him and he mumbles a bit louder, "Kath . . . I w . . . to give sfa."

"I still don't understand."

He takes his good hand and yanks me into towards him, saying, "Kath, I want to give you a kiss."

His eyes are dazed, his lips dry and cracked, and his mouth drips with drool. The smell of death emanates from his body. He plants a big sloppy kiss on my cheek.

I give him a hug and say, "I love you, too."

*****

At five in the morning, the phone rings, and I jump out of bed. I know what a call so early means.

"He's hemorrhaging, come quick," the nurse says.

Jeff and I speed through the empty streets in the predawn light. I arrive at the hospital hoping my dad will still recognize me, but he is completely disoriented. His breathing has entered the death-rattle stage, so I realize that it's time to gather the family. It's my job to pull the "cast" together. I grab my phone.

"Hop in a cab," I say to my sister.

"Drive quickly," I urge my brother.

I organize the room. I pull my dad's bed away from the wall and place chairs in a full circle around his bed. I count to make sure there are enough chairs so that no one will be left out.

Setting the stage calms me.

This moment is familiar to me. I am filled with images of *Long Live.* I remember the physical sensations I experienced when creating the piece. I remember what it felt like to show Suzanne how to carry the father character once he became sick and how to circle the father's chair to discover that it is empty. I remember the physical sensation that always hit me when Tom sang the father's death song, signifying his character's death. I have practiced taking the hit of grief that is about to come my way.

A few hours later, we are all holding my dad and telling him we love him. I lean over and whisper in my dad's ear, "It's okay. You can let go now."

I watch the pulse on my dad's neck as it slows, and then finally stops.

*****

I sit at my dad's funeral surrounded by Jeff and my family. My eyes are red from crying. My heart is pulled wide open, past its stretching point. I shake from the tremor of the pull. But there is also a steadiness present. I know I can get through this.

My dad's coffin is draped with the Vancouver Auxiliary Coast Guard flag. The lid is closed, but I imagine what he looks like in there, his body pale and motionless. In life, my dad hardly ever stopped moving. Even while taking a nap, he always looked as if he was ready to jump up at any moment and run out to rescue someone. Now, inside his coffin, I know he is peacefully still.

My stepmom is standing on a podium behind his casket, telling stories of their life together. She is dressed all in black except for red dancing shoes.

"Kathy," she told me before the funeral, "I think I'm going to wear my red tango shoes. Your dad loved dancing so much. Ballroom, tango, disco, cha-cha . . . we did it all. I never told him, but he actually wasn't that good at it. But what he lacked in skill, he made up for with how much he loved to dance."

I was so busy with my dance career that I hadn't thought much about my dad's amateur dance lessons. As I sit there looking at my stepmom's red shoes, I now realize something that is rather obvious, but had eluded me before this moment. My dad and I shared a great love of dancing.

*****

The alarm rings and I hit the snooze button. My heart feels compressed and my legs and arms feel heavy and tight. I've been back at work teaching and being a therapist for a month. Each morning, it feels harder and harder to drag myself out of bed. Jeff pokes his head into the bedroom, then enters the room. He's holding a seaweed-green coloured drink.

"Getting up, love?" he asks. "I made you a smoothie."

I groan and roll out of bed, trying not to disturb the numbness that keeps me intact. Numbing-out is my only choice, since there is no space for grief in my busy winter days, with so many students to teach and clients to help. I brush my teeth and wash my face. At least these daily rituals get me moving.

Later that day, I sit in a circle with twelve youth and two other facilitators. It's check-in time, the time when each member of the theatre group, including us leaders, tells the group how they're doing. As I sit waiting for my turn, I feel grief threaten to breach my numbness. My heart skips a beat and my eye twitches. I have the urge to run out of the room before the check-in round reaches me. I sit immobile, telling myself that this is not the appropriate time or place to fall apart. As one of this project's leaders, I need to make it through this three-hour rehearsal. These young people have faced many challenges in their lives. They are considered by many to be "troubled." Today, however, they are fine and I am the one who is troubled.

I work to control my body in order to appear calm. Gradually, the check-in makes its way to me. Everyone looks at me, waiting for me to speak. With little air in my lungs, I say, "I had a good week, and I'm excited to start choreographing."

The first part is a lie, but one with good intentions; I want the focus to be on the youth rather than on my challenges. The second part is true. I can't wait to start making art with them and to forget my pain for a moment.

Over the next few months, friends and colleagues comment on how well I am coping with my dad's death. They have no idea how exhausting it is to keep my grief at bay. I hide well the panic that frequently surfaces. I plod through my endless to-do lists. I go to the dentist, send letters, mark papers, and call clients. The list changes constantly, but there is one item that never gets done. It is transferred to each new list I make: edit the *Long Live* video footage.

Spring arrives. With it, my busy schedule subsides. There is time now to grieve, but my numbness is a habit I can't let go of. *Long Live* starts to call me home. It's been almost eight months since the performance. I miss it, like a friend that's been away for a long time. I want to see its beauty once again, but I am scared to watch it. I know it will break me; I do not know if I'm ready for that.

I watch the *Long Live* footage on a quiet Sunday afternoon. From the first notes of music, I feel my heart opening. By the father/daughter scenes, I am weeping. The muscles I have braced to keep my emotions at bay soften and my chest feels lighter.

I spend the next month editing the *Long Live* movie, watching the different scenes over and over again in order to pick out the best shots. It feels liberating to bathe in the sadness of the piece. In the darkness of the editing suite, I return to myself. Each frame of film holds an image of my grief. I go backward and forward, cut parts out, create transitions, slow things down, or speed them up. This process allows me to control the flow of grief incrementally. Frame by frame, I sew my sadness into something that I can hold without falling apart.

I add a director's commentary. I don't expect that many people will ever listen to it, but I don't care. I do it for myself. On the monitor, I watch Tom run onto the stage. The fake snow is falling from the rafters, covering the stage. Tom has changed into his angel costume – white pajamas and a billowing white overcoat. His arms dance playfully with the snowflakes. He grins his mercurial grin.

I say into the microphone, "I love this moment. All of the dad's pains are gone. He is free. All that ailed him was healed by the act of dying."

*****

My client sits still, her body braced.

"How about taking a big breath in?" I ask.

"I can't," she says.

"I think you can do this. I think that you're strong enough to feel whatever comes. How about starting to move just your fingers?"

She wiggles her fingers, and then starts rocking back and forth.

"Okay, now how about letting out the tiniest sound?"

She takes a breath in, and on the exhale lets out a faint sigh. This opens the floodgates and she starts to weep.

The sound of her weeping flows through my body like a current. Being with her in this place of sorrow is effortless, because I can now access a similar place in myself without fear.

Time passes and her body relaxes.

As she gets ready to leave, she says, "It's funny; I always feared going to that place. And . . . sure, it was painful, but it also felt strangely. . . . What's the right word? Comfortable – no, comfortable is not exactly right. . . . It's like a sense of ease. I know that must sound weird."

"I don't think it sounds weird at all. You've just felt your emotions deeply without running away. This is a coming home to yourself, and coming home is a great comfort. Especially when you've been away for a long time."

She nods slowly. "I'm beginning to understand that."

*****

I have a dream one night, in which my dad visited me as a ghost. He came to tell me that it was time to plant the gardenias. He then gave me a list of pros and cons about being a ghost. He said it was frustrating that people couldn't see him, but one of the good things about it was walking through walls. He explained that it defied the laws of physics, and that he was determined to figure out the science behind how it worked.

My dream makes me laugh. My dad would not believe anything unless it was proven by a double-blind study.

I remember him once spending a whole day trying to read my expressive arts master's thesis. Finally, in exasperation, he said to me, "Kath, your premise is just not scientific enough."

"Dad," I returned, "It's not supposed to be scientific. It's about expressive arts, which is a hard thing to measure empirically! It's about experiencing life through one's heart."

"Hmmm . . . well, maybe you could put in a disclaimer saying that you're not intending to be scientific," he said hopefully.

At the time, I was so hurt by the miles of difference that divided us. Looking back now, I realize how amazing it was that he sat for hours reading my thesis, which was a document whose emotional and artistic content must have been like listening to nails scratching a chalk board for him.

*****

As we eat dinner one evening, Jeff is giving me an account of his workday.

He explains, "We're doing this reverse-osmosis pilot study for a cooling tower blow-down application, but we are having trouble maintaining flux in the ultra-filter membrane pre-treatment. We're going to try to. . . ."

My attention drifts. Jeff's detailed description of his day suddenly makes me think of that annoying puzzle-piece analogy my dad always used when he talked about relationships.

I remember him talking about it a few years ago, when I was moping about my latest failed relationship.

"You see, Kath," my dad had said, "a good relationship is like two puzzle pieces. The other person fits into the places where you are weak, and vice versa. Take Gerri and I, for instance. One could say that I am sort of an emotional moron, but that's okay, because Gerri has emotional smarts, so she fills in this area."

My dad paused, looked as if he was doing mental arithmetic, and then shook his head. "No, your last relationship would never have worked out. The puzzle pieces didn't fit together. He wanted everything all perfect and tidy, and we both know that you could never give that to him. Better it end now, before it got too serious."

"Gee, Dad, thanks. I feel a lot . . . better, now that you've basically told me I'm a slob."

My dad stood up quickly. "Well, I'm not going to sit around here all day long while you mope. I'm going for a walk along the sea wall! Do you want to come?"

At the time, his description of a co-dependent forever-after, in which I would fill in for someone else's weaknesses terrified me. I thought it seemed like using someone as a crutch when you could walk perfectly well on your own. Looking at Jeff over the dinner table, I see now what my dad was talking about. I see how the practical weaving together of different skill sets to form a sturdy bond can be a thing of beauty.

Jeff notices that I wasn't paying attention and asks, "Hey, where are you? You look so far away."

"I was just remembering something my dad said to me."

"What was it?"

"Let's just say that I love you, my detail-orientated, practical hubby."

I sit on the subway the next day after an intense evening of working with the youth group. The stories they tell through their art give me a clearer sense of who they are. I also imagine that it helps the youth know themselves better.

My dad was a great storyteller, but he never told stories about me. This was especially troubling for me, because he had many stories to tell about how clever my brother and sister were, which made me feel invisible.

I once asked him, "Didn't I ever do anything worthy of a story when I was growing up?"

"Hmmm. Kath, I'm not sure. I need to think about that one," my dad said.

He approached me three days later and said, "I spent some time thinking about your question, and this is what I've come up with: from a young age, the thing you were good at was emotions. You always sensed what other people were feeling. Emotions are something I'm not good at, and so it's been hard for me to pay attention to your abilities in this respect. Now you're an artist and a therapist, and have made emotions your life's work."

I was mad that it took him three days to come up with one thing I was good at, so I didn't hear what he was telling me. Now, I realize that he was saying that he did see who I was, even if he didn't completely understand it. I was not invisible.

As I sit on the subway, I look at my fellow passengers and a question comes to me: Did I really ever see my dad? I never thought to ask myself this. I was always so busy either looking up to him as a Dad Hero or feeling the pain of our difference. Then I see it – my dad and I are those puzzle pieces that he never stopped telling me about, the ones that fit together so well. We are the opposites that filled in each other's differences. Our differences gave balance to our family, our world. If the earth was populated by people only like me or only like my dad, it would simply be filled with too much of one way of being. I realize that the differences that existed between my dad and I can be, for me, a thing of beauty rather than a source of pain.

The train jolts. I look up and see that I am at my stop. As I exit, my mind is scurrying to recalculate my life from this new perspective. If we were puzzle pieces, then I was wrong to think that there was something wrong with my dad. For most of my adult life, I was critical of my dad for the way he dealt with emotions. I had a secret fantasy that he would go to therapy and learn to face his emotions; as a result, we would be more alike and better able to relate to each other.

I also wondered whether it was more than mere coincidence that a man who avoided emotional vulnerabilities suffered from a tumor that grew around his neck, which is often the very place that people tend to clamp down when they suppress feelings. If he had learned to express his vulnerabilities, he may not have had the illnesses he did. But is the aim of life only to live a long life? Is the aim of life only to become an improved and balanced version of yourself? My dad was stuck in many ways, but he also had flow in other ways. He was a passionate "doer" who experienced life with joy and excitement. He was a man who loved deeply. He was a unique person without apology. Yes, it's true that he was known for angry outbursts, for his lack of nurturing qualities, and for being, as he put it, "an emotional moron." And I say, "good for him." Maybe we aren't all meant to be nurturing weepers like I am. My dad was one of the funniest, most interesting men I have ever known. Part of what made him such a character was his no-nonsense, non-emotional approach to life. He performed his denial of the weaker emotions with such humour and style that I can't imagine him any other way. He was passionately engaged in life, just in a different way than I was. I realize now that different doesn't mean wrong.

I pause to cross the street. As my foot hits the curb on the other side, I have another ah-ha moment. Growing up as an emotional anomaly in a family that "did" rather than "felt," I had always thought that there was something wrong with me, but if there was nothing wrong with my dad, and my dad and I were puzzle pieces that fit together so beautifully, then this also meant there was nothing wrong with me.

I look up and realize that I am at my front door.

*****

Jeff and I are at the pre-party for the Toronto Performing Arts Awards. I found out a few weeks ago that *Long Live* had been nominated for three awards. It's the first time my work has been nominated. I am up against my former employer, the National Ballet Company of Canada, though, and they are a sure bet to win.

Karen arrives, and I yell over the crowd, "Hey Karen, did you ever think you would get nominated for dancing with Oopsie Daisy dolls?"

She laughs and says, "Did you bring them? If you win, maybe the babies can go up and give your acceptance speech!"

Jeff turns to me and says, "Speech! You have to write your acceptance speech."

"But I'm sure *Long Live* won't win," I insist.

Jeff puts a napkin on the table, takes a pen out of his pocket, and says, "Write a few things . . . just in case."

I write *I am touched that a dance piece about family, love, and loss that was so personal to me touched so many others. I dedicate this award to my dad for the inspiration his life gave me.*

Suzanne arrives and we chat. I ask how her latest rehearsals are going.

"Damn you for *Long Live*," she says. "I don't know if I'll ever have an experience like that again. Nothing I work on since fulfills me in the same way. I crave to be back there. You know, it was hard revisiting all those feelings about my dad, but it was also good. When my dad died, I was so young and with *Long Live*, I was able to revisit my grief as a more mature person."

Our moment of intimate discussion is broken by the arrival of more cast members.

As the evening progresses, I start to feel more and more nauseous. By the time the awards are announced, I don't care that I lost to the National Ballet Company of Canada. All I want to do is go home as quickly as possible so I can remove my dress, which pulls at my secret baby bump, and collapse into bed.

As my belly grows bigger, I start to write about *Long Live* and my dad's death. It is another step in sifting through the experience. As the words of the story get shaken up through many rewrites, my grief, which was close to the surface, starts to settle and become part of my life story rather than an open wound.

Through the writing process, I contemplated how creating *Long Live* helped me through my dad's death. Granted, it was no easy miracle cure (I still had a hard time making my way through my grief), but it enriched the process in many ways. The following is for you, dad. You always loved both concrete answers and bullet lists.

Long Live:

- allowed me to practice what lay ahead – it was a stretching and strengthening of my grief muscles so that when the time came, I was more prepared.
- held the story of my grief so that I did not have to carry the burden all on my own.
- enticed my grief to flow so it did not get chronically stuck in me.
- provided an opportunity to explore feelings about my dad under the protective guise of theatrical metaphors.
- encouraged me to explore the "dad's" point of view. While choreographing, I acted out the part of both the dad and the daughter as I showed the steps. To do so, I had to consider what made them who they were. Alternating between both points of view both physically and mentally was like a drama therapy exercise, in which I play-acted the different roles in a conflict in order to understand and feel more compassion for an adversary.

• helped me to step back. Although the father and daughter in my ballet were not me and my dad, there were many similarities. Watching *Long Live* from my theatre seat allowed me to see the dad character from afar. From this vantage point, I could see what made him who he was and forgive and have compassion for his failings. This helped me do the same with my dad.

• moved others with its story. People's reactions connected me with a collective spirit of grief, allowing me to no longer feel alone in my sorrow.

• taught me how to master my grief. The creative tinkering involved in the *Long Live* project gave me the chance to master the pace of my grief on my own terms, as if I had volume, fast-forward, repeat, and slow-down buttons to enhance my experience.

• gave me the opportunity to process my dad's death through various art forms (dance, film, and writing), with each art form offering a different type of wisdom.

There is one more thing *Long Live* gave me. I wished many times that I could have magically changed my dad into an emotionally sensitive father. I think my attraction to ill-fitting jobs and relationships was an attempt to reach a cathartic emotional connection with a person or thing that was diametrically different from me. In the dances between the father and daughter characters in *Long Live*, I gave myself the emotional connection and communication that I have always craved to have with my dad. Sure, it happened onstage in a fictional setting between a fictional daughter and a fictional dad. Sure, real life did not quite work out like my make-believe version. My dad did not gradually soften into a more nurturing father as he came closer to death. Sure, my dad saw *Long Live* and hated it. But these things made *Long Live* no less satisfying. By creating *Long Live*, I gave my heart what it wanted, which allowed the wound of our differences to heal. My anger and resentment softened, leaving room for me to love my dad more fully, leaving room for me to love everything and everyone more fully, including Jeff. Including myself.

*****

My client hesitates, pen in hand. "But I'm pretty sure that I'll never dare show this letter to anyone, so how can it change anything?"

"You can't go back and change the past. What you can do, in the here and now, is say or do the things you did not get to say or do back then. You can find a sense of completion or peace within yourself in regard to this person. It does not matter if they will ever read this letter. Even if this person ever does read it, it doesn't matter whether she understands it or not, because this letter is not about her. It's about a change that can happen in you."

*****

I stand in the dark of the kitchen holding the freezer door open. The door light shines on my huge beach-ball-like belly. Tears run down my face.

Jeff walks into the kitchen and asks, "What's wrong, love?"

"If someone were standing between me and a Popsicle, I'd kill them to get it. But look," I say, shaking the empty box, "*someone* ate the last one!"

I glare at Jeff, but then vaguely remember eating the last one yesterday at four in the morning.

"Damn," I say, "I want to be mad at you. It would be so much easier than the mess of stuff I'm feeling. I'm sad that our son will never know his grandpa. My dad was such an amazing person; our little guy will never know this first-hand. And I watched the news today – so many children have been blown up by bombs or hurt by pedophiles. There's so much pain. I miss my dad . . . he had a way of making sense out of things. And I can't stop thinking of my stepmom and how alone she is. One day you'll die, and I don't know how I will live without you. I might die before you, and then I worry you'll be alone, which is even harder to bear than the thought of me being alone. . . . But you know, this mess of stuff I'm feeling isn't all bad. In such a big way, it makes me feel how much I love you and this little guy I carry inside me."

Jeff shuts the freezer door and wraps his arms around me, careful to leave room for my belly.

"How about I run to the store and buy you some more Popsicles?" Jeff asks.

*****

On the anniversary of my dad's death, my sister sends me an email.

> I was thinking of Dad a lot . . . remembering all those 'short' hikes he took us on that turned out to be five hour extravaganzas that involved spectacular mountain views. I realized, now I'm a mom, that he always knew exactly where he wanted to take us. He held back telling

us it would take five hours to get there, because he knew we would moan and groan about the length of the trip if he told us the truth. Remember how he used to pour over those maps and trail guides? Suddenly I realized that it was no accident when he said "let's go just a little further and see what's on the other side of that ridge."

My dad and I were both explorers and adventurers, even though we both explored and adventured in such completely different ways. Maybe the art of living is to become an adventurer and explorer of one's own life in a manner that is uniquely your own. Maybe the most important adventure of all is to love fully and then to grieve fully when your love is lost. *Long Live* helped me do just that.

Chapter 5

THE ART OF SENSATION

Through physical sensation, we know that we are alive and where our body stops and where the world begins. Physical sensations let us know what is out there, and warn us when we are in danger. There is a rare genetic condition known as Congenital Insensitivity to Pain with Anhidrosis (CIPA), in which children are born without the ability to feel physical pain. While feeling no pain might sound like a wonderful predicament, it is, in fact, life threatening. Ashlyn Blocker, a child with this disease who lives in Patterson, Georgia, would chew her lips bloody in her sleep, bite through her tongue while eating, and once even stuck a finger in her mouth and stripped flesh from it.[80]

Sensation not only connects us to the textures of the world out there, but also connects us to our internal world. When we experience internal sensations such as a fluttery stomach, a heavy heart, or a tight throat, we are brought home to our emotions. Emotions do not occur somewhere in our psyche, but are a body-based experience.

Just as physical pain lets us know not to put our hands in fire, body-based emotional sensations let us know to avoid things that threaten our psychological well-being. If we are not connected to internal body-based signals, how do we know, for instance, when we've been pushed too far by someone, or whether a relationship is healthy or abusive? Without connection to sensation, our emotions are left to flounder in a vacuum. We lose connection to ourselves, the earth, and others.[81]

None of us can be aware of sensation 100 percent of the time. We distance ourselves from sensation because it can be a difficult reminder that we are vulnerable physical beings. When we experience intolerable suffering, we dampen our experience of sensation in order to survive. Even

174

everyday life can sometimes be too intense, and we need to find moments of escape. I have experienced this myself when I "numbed-out" watching television after a really bad day, or when I planned to have a natural childbirth and then unexpectedly found myself begging for the relief of an epidural.

It's human reflex to distance ourselves from challenging sensations, but when we distance ourselves too completely, we lose the gifts that sensation has to offer. During the worst of my labour, if someone had offered me a magic pill that would take away all sensation forever, I might have been tempted to take it just to escape the pain. If I had, I would never feel the soft touch of my son's cheek against mine or know what it feels like to hug him. My epidural was certainly a relief, but I'm glad it wore off. No matter how comforting or relieving numbness is, when it is used as a long-term coping mechanism, it takes away the feeling of being alive that makes living worthwhile.

There are many ways to feel alive and engaged in one's sense. Some people, like my dad for instance, do so through the sensation of "doing" – hiking, rescuing people from the sea, and mountain climbing. I feel alive by connecting to the cues my body gives me and the dance moves they inspire. I am well practiced in feeling alive by accessing the wisdom of inner body sensation, emotions, and actions – concepts I explained in Chapter 2. I have made it my life's work to be a guide for others who have chosen this path. It is not for everyone. Some people choose other ways to embrace life. Clients who choose me as their therapist, however, have chosen to enliven their lives by playing with the emotions, shapes, movements, and images that arise through awareness of what they feel inside their skin.

MY SIX STEP METHOD

Over the past ten years, I have developed a method of working with inner body sensation and the arts. This method can be described in six distinct steps:

1. Notice the Sensation
2. Describe the Sensation
3. *Stay-With* the Sensation
4. Find a Simple Shape or Movement that Matches the Sensation

5. Amplify and Intensify the Sensation
6. Harvest

I developed this method by following my intuition, and gradually doing more of the things that just felt right. During this process, I became familiar with the works of Clyde Ford,[82] Pat Ogden,[83] Peter Levine,[84] and Arnold Mindell,[85] each of whom pioneered methods in which awareness of sensation and the following of one's body cues are the main focus of therapy. Reading about their approaches affirmed my developing method. My approach differs, in that my clients intensify the physical and emotional qualities of internal sensations through the arts. Artistic creation is not just one tool of many in the therapy toolbox. It is instead considered to be the main therapeutic event that allows the body's voice to be clarified and focused by the powers of spontaneous artistic expression.

You have already seen many examples of the six steps in action throughout this book – my own stories, the stories of my clients, and Allen's story. I will now explain in a more transparent manner how the process unfolds.

1. Notice the Sensation

Clients often begin their sessions with a body scan. This involves starting at their feet and checking-in with physical sensation as they draw their attention upward, towards their heads. They will talk about simple things, such as how their socks feel or whether they feel hot or cold. They will talk about vague sensations, such as a funny feeling in their stomachs or a hard-to-describe feeling of heaviness. Often, a certain body sensation will draw their attention more than others. It could be a physical pain, or the manner in which a client's body is holding tension. It could be a sensation that feels good (lightness in one's breath), mildly irritating (a scratchy throat), or disconcerting (chronic pain).

I also draw clients towards internal sensations by asking them to notice the physical sensations that accompany strong emotions. I will ask, "What's the physical sensation in your body that lets you know whether you are sad, happy, or angry?" Through descriptions such as a knot in one's belly or a warm feeling in one's heart, a person becomes aware that their emotional world has a kinesthetic home in their body.

Clients also move from image to sensation. When a client creates a painting or sculpture, I will ask them to take a moment and notice the inner sensations they feel in reaction to their artwork. If they cannot name a sensation, I will ask them to physically emulate shapes they see in their creation. They may make a circle shape with their arms emulating a circle in their painting or shape their body to emulate their sculpture. This physical embodiment of their image connects them to an internal sense of their artwork.

2. Describe the Sensation

Once a specific sensation has been named, I ask the client for more descriptive details. I want to find out as much as possible about the sensation in order to clarify its voice. At this point, I am like a research scientist collecting data before going ahead with the experiment. If a client tells me that he feels tension in his throat, I will ask him, "Is the area of tension small or big? Does it go all the way around your neck like a band, or concentrate in one area? Does it have a colour? Is it prickly or smooth? Does it push in on itself or push out? Or is it still?" By offering diverse options, I avoid leading the client to answers that may not be right for them. My "tray" of options is the jumping-off point that the client can use to find their own voice.[86]

3. *Stay-With* the Sensation

In Chapter 3, I wrote about the therapeutic benefit that occurs when a therapist *stays-with* a client without trying to change their state. Now I will speak of the therapeutic benefit of helping a client learn to *stay-with* his or her own challenging feelings.[87] Clients often enter therapy with the desire to lessen their suffering and transform towards healing. If I help them jump too quickly towards their goals, they may fail to get to know who they are in their current state. Also, any pressure I apply to encourage transformation conveys the message that the person he or she is in that moment is not okay with me. I help my clients practice *staying-with* where they are at by asking them to notice body sensations that are related to challenging emotions, thoughts, or images without trying to change or fix them. I ask clients to focus their attention on a sensation by saying, "Lean up against it, put your ear to it, put your hand upon it. Tell this sensation that you are not going to try to change it or fix it, but that you're just going to *stay-with* it for a moment." The sense of "being" that is encouraged by this act then becomes the planting ground for an organic transformative process. Starting anywhere else would be like trying to grow leaves without soil or roots.

While *staying-with* a sensation may not at first seem to change anything, it can have a powerful transformative effect. When we disassociate from challenging memories and emotions and the sensations that represent them, we begin to feel that something is missing. These aspects of self are still a part of us and when we push them away, we feel their distance. The further someone runs away from their exiled parts, the more these parts feel like foreign entities that are chasing them. These aspects can even begin to feel like monsters or demons. By *staying-with* our "monsters," we are inviting them back in the house and letting them stay for dinner . . . and by the time dessert comes, we might even see that our guest is not a monster after all. It's just a part of ourselves that wants to come home.

Staying-with a challenging sensation can also calm the sensation, in much the same way that my son's crying is soothed as soon as I pick him up. He cries to get my attention; when he knows he has it, he calms down. Internal sensations are trying to communicate important wisdom to us. When we don't listen, the cries become louder and more intense. When we finally stop to listen, it's like our inner body sighs with relief because it has finally been heard. The intensity of the sensation will often lower a notch, feeling less frantic or overwhelming. The result can be so therapeutic that no further exploration might be needed. It can also make exploring the message of the sensation more tolerable because the "volume" of the sensation no longer hurts one's ears. Earlier, we saw how Allen *stayed-with* the feeling of the beached whale by lying on the floor and concentrating on the sensation of wanting to disappear. He did this over a period of months, as I wondered whether anything productive was happening. When Allen told me how good it felt to just show up and be exactly who he was, I was reminded of the therapeutic power of *staying-with* sensation.

When I write about the value of *staying-with* challenging sensations, I do not necessarily refer only to ones that are typically considered negative. I once had a client who had just fallen in love and was overwhelmed by the wonderful feelings he was experiencing. He said that his heart felt like it might burst open from too much feeling. He was worried that he might try to sabotage the relationship so that he could get back to the heart he was used to. Helping him *stay-with* and learn to tolerate the sensation of being in love was important work that could help him embrace his new heart. Sometimes we need to practice *staying-with* happiness. Sometimes we need to be with our sadness or our anger. It is all equally important work.

4. Find a Simple Shape or Movement that Matches the Sensation

Clients will often use their hands in an effort to describe a sensation, in a manner similar to how we speak and use hand gestures to help illustrate our words. A client describing tightness in her belly might clench her fist and draw it in towards her. Hand gestures are common in such descriptions, but movements that describe sensations may also be done with a shrug of the shoulders, a shake of the head, or a tap of the foot. Clients often do these movements unconsciously, and my aim is to help my clients become conscious of them so that they can play with the physical themes that are naturally arising. I will say something like, "I noticed you just drew your shoulders in. Does that shape help describe what the sensation feels like? Would you like to try it again?"

Sometimes there aren't any obvious descriptive movements to start with. In this case, I will directly ask a client to show me, through body movement and shape, what the sensation feels like. If they are confused by this question, I will provide a tray of options in the same way I did when helping them with their initial verbal description of the sensation.[88] I will say something like, "I'm going to give you three examples, and you tell me which matches the sensation the closest." I will move my hand up with a lot of tension and ask them if it presses up, or I will press my hands together and ask them if it presses in. I will make a fist and ask if it is like a ball of tension. The client is usually quick to name which one matches best, and then by experimenting, they change the offered body movement and shape to suit them.

Through a clenched fist or a shake of the head, clients are starting to outwardly express their internal world through body movements and shapes. That, for me, is the start of a dance. It's a simple and humble dance that is like witnessing the miracle of a butterfly emerging from its cocoon and tentatively opening its wings for the first time.

In Chapter 3, I described how therapeutic it can be for someone to create and/or witness art that matches how he or she feels inside. However, when that happens, the body and its sensations are not necessarily the focus or starting point. For instance, someone could create a drawing that matches his or her sadness without placing attention to an embodied sense of their sadness. In this sensation-based approach, a client is specifically trying to find shapes and movements that match inner body sensations. In order to move to the next step of amplification, one needs to know what he or she will be amplifying.

5. Amplify and Intensify the Sensation

The fifth step is to amplify the sensation, which involves building upon the simple shape or movement the client has found in a manner that will intensify the experience. There is no pre-determined goal involved. It is simply about giving the body a *voice* and seeing what happens.[89] Someone who clenched his fist as representation of tightness in his belly may amplify the sensation by moving around the studio while punching his fists in the air. Amplification can sometimes make the sensation itself more intense, but it can also be a discovery and expression of the emotional qualities of the sensation. While creating *Long Live*, I felt a sense of panic building as my dad approached death. This panic felt like a fluttering in my chest. I amplified this sensation when I demonstrated to Suzanne a dance in which I asked her to tremble and shake. These movements captured and intensified my panic.

Amplification is similar to the process of finding a shape or movement that matches internal sensation, but it is different in that it can involve a greater range of body movements as well as other art forms. It is a *match plus*, in which the aim is to intensify and dig more deeply into body-based experiences. The *plus* part of amplification can be especially therapeutic. It can make habituated patterns more noticeable and easier to name. For example, we don't notice the force of gravity continually pressing down upon us, because we are so habituated to it. Holding a brick over our heads, however, will help to amplify the feeling of gravity, which makes it easier to notice. This same phenomenon can occur with any pattern of being that we have become habituated to. All patterns of being leave an imprint on our bodies, which is shown through our posture, our muscle position, or how we breathe. By amplifying the sensation of these imprints, we can see things about ourselves to which we were previously blind. Sometimes we need to make something bigger in order to see it clearly.

Making a sensation bigger by amplification often needs to happen in incremental steps in order for it to be tolerable for the client. I often suggest several small takes of the same amplification to divide up the experience into tolerable bites. A *take* involves entry into an experience, *staying-with* the experience for some time, and then coming back out of said experience.[90] The first take is often what I call a "toe-dip." It involves the practice of putting one's metaphorical toe into the murky lake of challenging feelings and then taking it right back out. To ensure that a client can enter a toe-dip and retreat successfully, a tight frame is often necessary. A frame, as discussed previously, can be the planned duration or size of movement, and can also involve my participation in a dance alongside the client as a way to help make the experience tolerable. A client might toe-dip by doing a dance that lasts for only ten seconds, uses only one hand and includes me dancing with them. The client and I often will share the job of holding the frame. For example, the client might be in charge of containing his movement, while I might be in charge of timing the take and letting him know when it is over. Allen frequently did toe-dip takes, especially at the start of his therapy. One example is the take in which he briefly imagined hitting the wall with a pillow. By visiting expression of anger in a safe toe-dip, he realized that doing the real version might be okay.

Sometimes the initial toe-dip can be overwhelming for the client, because he or she does not have the necessary resources or practice in dealing with the "hard-to-be-with" stuff emerging. When this happens, the client needs to build resources before proceeding with another toe-dip. Resource building can include such things as practicing a cleansing exhale, learning to sweep away the experience with one's hand, or exploring what physical objects or images bring a feeling of safety. Clients can find comfort in holding a certain pillow or stone, or imagining a familiar scene. Resource building can also involve approaching the material in even smaller, less-intense increments, which provides a chance to practice the in-and-out of each toe-dip take in a less anxious state.

I often tell my clients that doing a toe-dip is like building up muscles. The first time, it's really hard and you can only do it for a few seconds. But over time, it gets easier and easier as you get better at it through practice.

Having resources that allow one to exit a take successfully is vital because it gives clients confidence in their ability to traverse their challenging material. Without this skill, there is a possibility that a client will become stuck in an overwhelmed state without the ability to disengage. The result can be traumatizing. The toe-dip serves as the test to tell me whether the focus of a particular client's session work needs to be placed on resource building or whether it's time to dig more deeply into the material.

The takes that follow a toe-dip often involve an expansion of the frame, with the client choosing the manner in which this occurs. This puts the client in charge of pacing themselves. The client will say, "I think I'm ready for a longer take, with bigger movements," or, "I'll do the take again, but I'll end on my own time."

The repetition of takes can increase the therapeutic potential of amplification. Clients have the opportunity, through a process of trial and error, to add more of this and less of that until they find the perfect outward expression of their sensations. Numerous takes that each explore the same challenging issue can be done over a period of weeks or months. When this happens, a client's comfort level with his or her material has the chance to gradually increase with practice. In Chapter 3, I discussed how repetition of a new experience helps to ingrain new neural pathways, similar to how walking through a forest over time will shape definable paths. Repetition of takes helps to solidify the new feeling, doing, and thinking pathways that are forming. Moving from take to take also provides time for discussion or game planning in the space in-between.

In the process of amplification, the client's sensation or his or her reaction to the sensation often changes. The initial sensation leads the client on a journey, with one new thing leading to another. It's a discovery process in which action, inspired by sensation, takes the lead. As a woman moves around the studio, a tight feeling in her belly may start to feel warm. An image of a fire might come to her, which inspires a frenzied dance. After her energy is spent, she may collapse on the floor for a rest. When she checks in with her belly, it might feel calmer. These types of changes might happen within one take, but they may also occur over a series of takes. It is also common that the sensation not only changes, but moves to a different location. Tension in the belly can move up to the throat or head. These shifts in quality and location of the sensation provide opportunity for an organic transformative process.

A client once told me that he felt as if he carried the weight of the world on his shoulders. When I asked him to show me what it felt like, he pressed down on his shoulders with his hands. He admitted that it was not effective because it did not actually add any extra weight to his body. I suggested that I place my exercise ball on his shoulders and press down so that he could really get a sense of what it felt like to carry the weight of the world. He joked with me, saying, "All you want to do is amplify my suffering. What type of therapist are you?" We went ahead with my plan. After we finished, he said, "Yes, that's exactly how it feels. Can we try it again?" He ended up doing several more takes with my exercise ball pressed down onto his shoulders. At first, I did not feel any movement from him, but with subsequent takes, he became less passive. By the last take, he was pushing against the ball with his hands. He told me that when I initially pushed the ball into his shoulders, he felt a crushing heaviness in his sternum, but then as the takes progressed, he started to feel a desire to fight against the ball and his arms became energized with this feeling. It was similar to how one instinctually pushes against a pillow put on one's face. Sometimes one needs an oppressive force to realize how much one wants to live. At the end of the session, he said, "It felt so good to meet the heaviness so concretely. It's always been like a ghost haunting me, and now I finally got to touch it." A ghost is always scarier than something you can touch and get to know.

Changes during the amplification can lead someone down a path towards inner knowledge. However, when changes happen quickly and jump around in ways that don't seem to connect, it can feel like trying to pin down a slippery watermelon seed with your thumb. If I notice such a pattern over time, I become curious about the pattern itself. I wonder how this pattern might play out in the client's everyday life. To explore my curiosity, I might say, "I notice your focus moves around your body quickly from one spot to another. What is that like for you? Would you like to explore amplifying the sensation of never being able to catch something?" The great part about working with sensation is that when a "roadblock" comes up, the job then becomes to explore the physical experience of said roadblock.

Amplification frequently involves several art forms that are layered in or shifted to. The addition of other art forms helps to deepen the expressive experience, because each new art form offers a different quality or perspective. A client might layer a vocal component into his dance, or he might shift to a new art form by drawing a picture or creating a poem inspired by his dance. Sometimes amplification might not involve movement at all. It may be done entirely through another art form. This is often the case when *staying-with* a sensation draws forth clear visual images that beg to be caught on paper rather than in a dance.

I once worked with a man who was depressed. I encouraged him to connect with the internal sensation of his depression. With one hand on his chest and the other on his belly, he described a feeling of being in a dark, constricting cave. I was curious about what this cave looked like and asked him if he could show me through a drawing. He spent the session creating a large painting of his cave. In the next session, I placed his painting in the center of the room. After sitting on the couch and telling me about his week, he leaned towards the image and said, "I guess it's time to see what's in there." He explored his cave through movement and poetry over several sessions. What he found were emotions, such as sorrow and anger that he had pushed into this cave, because he felt that they were not appropriate for a man to express. Visiting these emotions incrementally over time with the arts as a holding container allowed him to gain comfort with them. Several months later, with his depression receding, he cut apart the image of the cave and created a collage that represented his recovery.

Amplification can also be accomplished through decentering – moving away from the center of the problem. Once someone has become aware of a sensation and *stayed-with* it, he or she can move away from focusing his or her attention on it, and just create art without any intentional goal. Even though they are not concentrating on the sensation they have named, the themes related to it are already in the room and tend to slip into the space provided.

I worked with a client who was anxious, because her mother was moving into a nursing home and selling the house my client grew up in. She was tasked with the job of deciding what to give away and what to keep. Her inclination was to keep almost everything, but she worried that her small apartment would be overflowing with stuff. I took a book off my shelf and asked her to imagine that it was one of her mother's books, while I put a garbage can by my feet. I threw the book in the garbage and then rescued it. She concentrated on the physical sensations this caused her. She described a tension in her stomach when the book was thrown out and a sense of relief when it was rescued. After a few minutes of this, she told me that she'd had enough of this experiment and she wanted to do some art. She explored the art cupboard until she settled on modeling clay, with which she sculpted a kitchen table and chairs. When I asked her about the sculpture, she said that many people had sat in these chairs. Some had been happy, and some sad. She described how the chairs were alive with so many stories. This led to a discussion about ways to keep the stories of her childhood alive that did not involve hoarding her mother's belongings. When she had focused directly on sensations related to getting rid of treasured belongings, she experienced anxiety. Decentering by dropping the focus on this sensation and just doing art was, therefore, a relief. Themes that were too hard to work with in an embodied manner arrived in the art she created. Sensation was still getting its voice; it was just in a more indirect manner.

The process of amplifying sensation can take a person back in time to relive events that caused the sensations they are working with to be imprinted on their body. This might sound like something one would want to avoid. Certainly, retraumatizing someone with an embodied recapitulation of a horrific event can worsen the effect of the trauma, but revisiting the embodied sense of a trauma, when done incrementally, take by take, and at a pace decided upon by the client, can provide an opportunity to process the experience. Clients can gain a sense of mastery over their traumas as they learn to dip in and out of them. Using the arts as a holding container helps them to avoid feeling overwhelmed. For someone whose trauma involves his or her body being subjected to another's will, taking charge of healing can be an important step in taking back the right to make choices about his or her body.

I often sense when a client has "travelled back in time" to a traumatic event or period in their life through changes in their stance, tone of voice, or pacing. I do not always know the details of the trauma, but from changes in sensation that occur in my own body in reaction to the client, I am able to understand the emotional quality of it. I frequently say to clients experiencing a regression, "Do or say the thing you did not get to do or say back then." They are often unsure of what that might be. I then tell them, "Don't ask your thinking brain what needs to be done, but instead follow your body's cues. Your body knows what it needs to do."

Peter Levine, author of *Waking the Tiger, Healing Trauma*, states that our body has a built-in response that helps us deal with trauma that involves a flight or fight response and then a recovery period, in which pent-up energy is discharged through reactions such as trembling, crying, breathing deeply, sweating, or laughing. He uses the example of a deer that takes time to tremble after the threat of the lion has passed. Peter Levine believes that when people have trouble recovering from trauma, it is likely because they have become frozen somewhere in the midst of their trauma response and are unable to complete the cycle.[91] They are stuck holding on to the trauma. The toll on the body and psyche can be enormous. The tension of such a hyper-body state can cause a range of different sensations, such as numbness, tightness, fatigue, and pain. In my work, I help people amplify these trauma-based sensations so that they can experience an embodied "going back in time" that allows them to take care of unfinished business.

I worked with a woman whose parents were so strict when she was a child that she never felt comfortable crying for fear of punishment. She experienced the standard childhood traumas, such as scraped knees, but never let herself cry or show weakness afterward. She carried this pattern into adulthood. In the process of exploring sensation in my studio, she realized that her body was frozen with tension. She began with amplifying this sensation, which took her through a journey of shifts and changes that eventually led her to many sessions in which she trembled and cried. She was completing a trauma response that she never allowed herself to complete when young.

Another example of going back and taking care of unfinished business is finally saying a swallowed "no." Many times, a person was not able to say no to a traumatic event that occurred or to the person who perpetrated it. They often did not say no because they feared for their safety, were frozen with fear, or felt so much shame that they thought they were to blame. They swallowed their no, and their body got stuck chronically holding onto it, causing tension and pain. When they amplify these sensations of pain and tension, they are led back to that unsaid "no" that needs discharging. When I ask a client who has been sexually or physically assaulted to do or say the thing he or she did not get to do or say when the trauma occurred, the first words are often, "no," or, "stop." That "no" that was frozen inside his or her body is now flowing. Their attackers might never hear these words, but that does not prevent the survivors from saying them and finding a greater sense of ease in their body from doing so. Going forward, they may also be better able to say no to situations that they are not comfortable with, which helps reduce the risk of further traumatizing events.

In my own story, I wanted to say no to the National Ballet Company's demand that I be dangerously thin, but suppressed this no in order to keep my job. This suppression made me feel as if there was a boot on my chest. In therapy, I worked extensively with this feeling, describing it and *staying-with* it. This led me to finally scream an animalistic no in my therapist's office. My *no* set me free. It removed the metaphorical boot pushed against my chest. From then on, I was more capable of saying no to things I did not want.

Allen *stayed-with* the sensation of sadness he felt for his mom, which led to a series of amplifications. He went back in time by painting the monster/boy, an amplification of the dynamics that caused four-year-old Allen to choose food as a solution. In a regressed state, four-year-old Allen was able let his mom know that he was no longer going to hold her sadness for her. This was Allen's no. It was the final step in dismantling the compulsive eating and depression that had plagued him for years.

During amplification, images of death or a feeling of dying often come to the clients I work with. Coming close to challenging sensations instead of running away from them is the death of an old way of being, so that a new way can take its place. A woman who was on the precipice of amplifying a challenging sensation she had avoided feeling for most of her life once said to me, "It might sound strange, but if I were to make that shape with my body, it feels as if something in me would have to break, or even die."

I said to her, "Yes, you're exactly right. Something will have to die. We humans resist the danger of change. We have all sorts of defenses and alarm bells to make sure we continue to do exactly what we have always done. In the seconds before you lift your arm to make that shape, all your alarm bells will go off, warning you of imminent danger. Your adrenaline will rush in. Your fight-or-flight response will be active, because every cell in your body will know that you are going to override conditioning in order to do something dangerously new and personally taboo. You *will* be facing death – the death of an old way of being to make room for the new. This takes a lot of bravery!"

The sensation of disassociated emotions, thoughts, and memories clients once ran from can become the "monster" they bravely play with through amplification. Through play, they can gain comfort with their monster. Their monster may even begin to transform through the process of amplification, like a plant kept in a small, dark container that blossoms once it has enough light and space to grow. Clients may even discover their "monster" is not a monster after all, but a part of them that wants to be acknowledged and allowed to come home. One day, as clients go through the process of naming, describing, *staying-with,* and playing with their monster, they may look into its eyes with compassion and love and realize they are looking at themselves.

6. Harvest

The harvest is the bounty that the client receives by turning towards sensation rather than away from it.[92] The harvest is the life-invigorating feeling, being, or thinking pathways that the client takes from therapy into his or her everyday life. I've identified several ways by which the harvest tends to arrive:

   a) Dialogue
   b) Image and Art-Based Messages
   c) New States of Being in the Inner Body

Arriving at the harvest in sensation-focused therapy is like peeling the layers of an onion to find the core. At the outermost level, the harvest is often a lot of "figuring things out" to come to understand oneself. This usually occurs through the process of analytical dialogue. As a client gets closer to the core, the harvest will often move to image-based messages where the body starts to speak through metaphors that imply feeling states. This is a movement from complexity to simplicity. At the more complex outer layer, the harvest might involve a woman realizing she is anorexic because she is trying to be perfect in order to please her mother. Whereas, when she goes down a layer to the simpler, more body-based message, the harvest might be an image of being cradled in a way that implies unconditional acceptance and love. If she reaches the core of the issue, the final harvest most probably will be an embodied sense of self-acceptance that needs few words to explain or validate. This represents a movement from complexity to simplicity in which, reaching the simple core harvest is the aim of my therapeutic process. It is normal and helpful for clients to shift between the three types of harvest as they make their way towards the core harvest. I will begin by explaining how this process unfolds, starting at the outer layer.

a) Dialogue

Internal sensing does not work in a linear manner, like our thinking brain does. It is a knowing that lives in us; we just need to put our attention towards it to become aware of it. When we do, the knowledge that arrives sometimes does not make sense or seem to connect to our everyday lives. This is because intuitive knowing skips over connecting the dots, and goes right to the answer part. Talking can be a way of making sense of intuitive knowledge. It can help people to connect the dots together so they gain a more complete picture of their issue.

There are various forms of dialogue that encourage this. The first is the dialogue between the client and the therapist that often occurs during *staying-with* and amplification. In this case, the aim is not to draw clients out of the experience they are having, but to ask questions that encourage them to stay in the experience and talk about what they notice. Simple questions, such as, "What do you feel?" or, "What does this remind you of?" or, "What do you need to do next?" are effective, because they encourage a client to tell me what is happening as it happens. In response, a client will say, for instance, "I feel like I'm ten years old again and I remember a time when . . ." or, "This way I'm restricting my breath, I realize I do it all the time, whenever. . . ." Embodied and intellectual learning are occurring simultaneously. The client is having a body-based experience, and taking their thinking brain along for the ride so it can follow along and help figure things out. This helps to create a therapeutic synchronicity between feeling and thought, in which the mind and the body are no longer on divergent paths. What I feel in my body, my thoughts can sort out and what I know in my head, my body agrees with.

Dialogue can happen between therapist and client, but it can also occur between the artist and his or her sensation-inspired art object. In Chapter 3, I explained how clients can dialogue with the art they create by shifting between talking to their art object and talking as if they are the art object. The only difference between that approach and the one I discuss now is that the art the client creates will have arisen from following the cues of internal sensations. Thus, even though the dialogue is happening between the client and his or her art, sensation is still getting its voice. In describing amplification, I told the story of the client who created the cave painting to represent how his depression felt. The creation of this art object provided opportunity for dialogue to occur between the cave and the client. He spoke to his cave drawing, saying, "You follow me everywhere I go. I'm tired of having you always around. I wish you would go away. I want to enjoy life again."

He then pretended to be the cave drawing and responded, "I'm lonely. No one ever comes to visit, not even you. The world needs darkness just as much as it needs the sun."

The client responded by saying, "I'm sorry I've stayed away so long." The harvest was a greater sense of acceptance of the "cave" part of himself.

Similar to the process of "dialoguing" with the image, a client can also speak as if she is the sensation. I might suggest that she use a lead-in phrase such as, "I am Kim's tight shoulder, and I want to tell you. . . ." I often suggest that clients repeat such lead-in phrases many times, until words float in to complete the sentence. Given space, Kim's tight shoulder might eventually say, "I am Kim's shoulder, and I want Sundays off from work so I can lie in the park and enjoy the sun."

b) *Image and Art-Based Messages*

In the process of dialogue, I encourage these types of "fantasy wishes," which help sensation have a voice through metaphor and image. I will say, "Don't worry if what your shoulder wants to say doesn't make sense. Maybe the tightness in your shoulder wants to climb a mountain or build a castle, or run through a cornfield."

These images are informative metaphors that give one's body a voice in the language it knows best. Inner-sensing wisdom is intuitive; it is knowing without knowing how one knows. It is a form of intelligence that is not always easily expressed in analytical words. It speaks best through images and metaphors that elicit a feeling of being there in the moment. The analytical message might be, "Kim, you're a workaholic and need to do less." But when working with sensation, however, it's more likely that the message will arrive with Kim saying, "I want to run naked on the beach and skinny dip whenever I want." A desire for more time to play is implied through a sense-oriented image that leads to a more embodied sense of the message.

Images that provide a rich harvest do not just occur in the imagination or through dialogue but can make their way into Kim's artwork. The sense of freedom Kim craves might arrive when she makes the sound of waves and splashing while creating a sound score or through a playful dance that reminds her of children playing at the beach. When this happens there is the chance that the art itself can be so clear with its message that it becomes a fully realized harvest. Allen's monster/boy painting is an example of such a happening.

c) New States of Being in the Inner Body

When someone peels back his or her layers of complex defenses he or she will find the core harvest, a new state of being in his or her body. New sensations are felt – breath flows with greater ease, weight is lifted off one's shoulder, and an ownership of one's body is felt. When such shifts in inner body states happen, few or no words are needed. For example, the practice of expressing oneself can, over time, strengthen one's ability to put up boundaries against outside influence. The harvest here is an embodied sense that one can stand in the world as a unique person, and all the sensations that come with this. One does not need to explain this in words to make it true.

Allen experienced an embodied harvest when he *stayed-with* and amplified the awkward sensation of trying to club dance by doing the fussy dance. By heading straight for the discomfort, he became more comfortable with it. He ended the fussy dance by lying on the floor with outstretched arms and a relaxed, peaceful smile. He then amplified this sense of comfort by creating an imaginary bubble with his voice. His harvest was an embodied sense of safety that he had never felt before. He did not necessarily know how or why he arrived at this state of being, but that did not matter. His body knew it was possible to be safe without having to be the biggest person in the room. He will likely be able to intuitively find his way back to that sense of safety again.

Softening and yielding towards self-love is another example of an embodied harvest that needs no analytical figuring in order to be therapeutic. Allen had such an experience when he felt a welling of love for his monster/boy. His monster/boy was an amplification of the internal feeling of wanting to eat without stopping as a way to deal with the sadness in his family's home. Turning towards his monster/boy instead of running away was an act of unconditional self-acceptance. Although we talked a little bit about the painting, we did not pick it apart and try to figure it out intellectually. The harvest was an embodied sense of love and nothing else needed to happen other than that profoundly therapeutic happening.

This brings me to my final considerations. I believe that for any harvest to be truly life-transforming, it needs to include a shift in body state. When a client knows his or her transformation is true and real because he or she feels it in their breath, muscles, cells, and blood, that is the moment when this work is occurring at a deeply profound and life-changing level.

HOW THE SIX STEPS WORK TOGETHER

The six phases involved in my sensation-based approach do not occur in a neat and sequential order. Clients choose their own way through. A client may not describe or *stay-with* a sensation and instead jump naturally into amplification, or a client may focus on *staying-with* the sensation, because he or she finds this step therapeutic on its own.

Sometimes, over several sessions, a pattern of avoiding one particular step emerges. In this case, I may say, "I notice you jump right into intense expressive material. How about trying an experiment that involves *staying-with* a body sensation in a quiet, internal way, just to see what happens?" or, "I notice that you shy away from expanding upon this sensation through movement. How would it feel to do a really short toe-dip into some movement, and just see what happens?" There is no right or wrong way that I have in my head. There are just curiosities about where new possibilities might take someone. My form of therapy is about helping people expand their repertoire, so that they have a better chance of stumbling upon the healing path that will work for them.

Clients also jump back-and-forth between steps. During amplification, they might shift back to *staying-with* whenever a change in sensation occurs. For example, a client performing a dance may pause, put a hand on her belly, and say, "Wait . . . something is shifting, and I want to *stay-with* this new feeling for a moment." Frequently, the harvest does not occur at the end of the six steps, but throughout the process over several sessions, or even years. The harvest might be a subtle and permanent shift in one's body stance that occurred gradually. There also can be many small harvests through the therapy process, which culminate in a surprising "ah-ha" moment. The most bountiful harvest of Allen's therapy happened with great speed over three sessions, but only after two years of work.

In creating *Long Live*, the most intense amplification was the public performance, which occurred after eight months of work. The immediate harvest was that it allowed me to practice what lay ahead. Editing the video footage into a film was another amplification that stretched and strengthened my grief muscle to the point that I felt safe to let my grief flow. This created a change in body state, in which my emotions flowed through me like a river with nice high banks that I trusted would prevent a devastating flood. There was also a harvest that came much later in my process when the door that had been opened a crack by *Long Live* gradually opened fully and helped me arrive at a new understanding of my dad and me.

Everyone is different and will lead him or herself through the dance between sensation and art in a unique manner.

As my clients dip in and out of the different steps I have described, I often give them homework assignments to help the work we are doing have a life outside my therapy studio. There is little point to therapy if the new thoughts, feeling, and body states do not sustain themselves in a person's everyday world. Initially, I often invite clients to practice very short *staying-withs* during their day. I will ask them to spend ten seconds noticing what sensations they feel, whenever they are doing everyday things such as riding on the subway or doing dishes. I will then ask them to spend another ten seconds *staying-with* those sensations, and then carrying about their day as usual. In doing this homework, clients are strengthening their connection to internal wisdom in their everyday lives, in short increments that are not too overwhelming. Towards the end of therapy, the homework suggestions often involve *staying-with* and amplification exercises that take the client into deeper experiences. This helps clients have faith that they can be present in their bodies successfully, without my presence. The end goal of the therapeutic process is to foster a resiliency that is not contingent on my presence in their lives.

I will now correlate my six step method with the forms of wisdom described in Chapter 2. The first three steps (noticing, describing, and *staying-with* sensation) directly access inner body wisdom. Increased awareness of internal sensations connects people to the wisdom of their emotions. The meditative qualities of the first three steps can also foster an opening towards spirit. Steps three and four (finding a shape or movement that matches sensation and amplifying sensation) add the wisdom of one's actions into the mix. The physical nature of these steps

further intensifies emotional expression and stimulates imaginative capacities, opening people to new feelings and thoughts. Amplification
also strengthens the voice of spiritual wisdom as therapist and client
share a collective experience of the art created. Physiological wisdom
is present throughout the process. Adrenalin surges as clients face the
unknown. Their heart rate speeds up as they dance. Following physiological wisdom helps people understand when they need to rest. I had
a client who, after doing really intense amplifications, would lie down
and almost fall asleep before another wave of amplification overtook
him. As I stated previously, periods of rest are thought to help "save"
the new neurological pathways that are forming, solidifying positive
transformation. The final step (harvesting) can add an intellectual understanding to one's experience, as well as usher in a fully realised shift
in the inner body. The process is a layered approach in which inner
body wisdom is the root from which other forms of wisdom grow. The
knowing starts at the core of the body and grows out towards the arms,
legs, head, and spirit.

Working with sensation through the arts helps people to enter the
liminal space of their own bodies. The walkabout they experience
through this way of working is a journey through the wilderness of their
muscles, blood, cells, organs. While travelling through their liminal-
body-wilderness, they experience sensations as if they are on a real
walkabout in the wilderness. They meet their "lion" that has been chasing them, and their feet run and their breath speeds up. They forage for
resources and find unexpected survival skills. They arrive at their in-
ner-lake, and see how beautiful it is, and feel a sense of tranquility. They
dip their hands into the lake's water, and a sense of love fills up their
body – love for themselves, others, and the world. The feeling of having really been on a walkabout helps them reach long-lasting transformation, the kind that occurs at all levels of the self. Their mind feels different. Their heart feels different. Their spirit feels different. Their
movements feel different. Their breath and posture and stance all feel
different. They even feel different on a cellular level that affects their
health.

I invite you to go on a walkabout in the liminal wilderness of your
own body. Journey well, my fellow traveler.

FINAL WORDS

In my forties, I am surprised to discover that I am a writer. With my learning disorder, I have struggled with writing my whole life. But a persistent need to document my way of working had been following me, like someone tapping on my shoulder. From the chaos of my dyslexic words, this book gradually emerged and I fell in love with writing. I am the crippled dancer who can no longer leap. I am the crippled writer whose words stumble along for years before finding grace. Through the process of writing this book, the message I discovered and rediscovered again and again, is that our humanity and beauty are in our imperfections. And that's my final "wrod."

NOTES

Introduction

1. This paragraph was inspired by Ellen Levine's discussion about the tension between grounding students in psychotherapeutic methods and cultivating their artistic practices, and how this plays out in their future lives as therapists in: Levine, E. G. (2005). "The Practice of Expressive Arts Therapy: Training, Therapy, and Supervision." In Knill, P., Levine, E. G. & Levine, S. K. *Principles and Practice of Expressive Arts Therapy: Toward a Therapeutic Aesthetics.* Jessica Kingsley Publishers Ltd.: London, England. pp. 172–173.

Chapter One: Becoming a Therapist

2. Williamson, M. (1993). *A Woman's Worth.* Random House Inc.: New York, USA. p. 6.

3. Quote is from: Citron, P. (1996). Toronto Fringe Festival 1996 Reviews. *Dance International Magazine.*

4. Quote is from: Trowbridge, B. (1996). *The Hidden Meaning of Illness: Disease as a Symbol and Metaphor.* Association of Research & English Press: Virginia Beach, Virginia, USA. pp. 186–187.

5. Norman Doidge discusses synesthesia in his book: Doidge, N. (2010). *The Brain That Changes Itself: Stories of Personal Triumph From the Frontiers of Brain Science.* Scribe Publications Pty Ltd.: Melbourne, Australia.

6. To read more about synesthesia, see: Seaberg, M. (2011). *Tasting The Universe: People Who See Colors in Words and Rainbows in Symphonies: A Spiritual and Scientific Exploration of Synesthesia.* Career Press: Pompton Plains, New Jersey, USA.

7. To read more about Descartes' philosophy as it relates to expressive arts therapy, see: Levine, S. K. (2005). "The Philosophy of Expressive Arts: Poiesis as a Response to the World." In Knill, P., Levine, E. G. & Levine, S. K. *Principles and Practice of Expressive Arts Therapy: Toward a Therapeutic Aesthetics.* Jessica Kingsley Publishers Ltd.: London, England. pp. 18–21.

8. Information taken from the article *Frontal Lobes* (Online). www.neuroskills.com/tbi/bfrontal.shtml (retrieved October 2009).

Chapter Two: A Map of Human Experience

9. A children's science website (Online). www.yucky.discovery.com (retrieved September 2009).

10 This description of how neuropeptides work is partially summarized from the

theories of Candace Pert, one of the leading scientists in neuropeptide research. You can read more about Dr. Candace Pert's theories and findings in her book: Pert, C. (1999). *Molecules of Emotion: The Science Behind Mind-Body Medicine.* Touchstone: New York, USA.

11. Dr. Clyde W. Ford, a chiropractor and psychotherapist, wrote the book *Compassionate Touch: The Body's Role in Emotional Healing and Recovery.* In Chapter 2, "The Neurobiology of Compassionate Touch," he cites several studies that support and explain connections between our psyches and our bodies. He states that these findings move us away from the Descartian ideology, in which there is thought to be a separation between the psyche and the body, with the psyche (especially the intellectual process) having a higher value. Ford discusses at length the work of Candace Pert and her colleagues, whose research is validating the connection between biology and emotions. Pert discovered that neuropeptides (receptor sites originally thought to only exist in the brain) actually exist in our spinal cord, around organs, and in muscle tissues. Ford refers to Pert's work, because he believes that it both gives validation to healing methods that support a close connection between the mind, body, and emotions and begins to explain how our bodies can be a source of wisdom. To read further, see: Ford, C. W. (1999). *Compassionate Touch, The Body's Role in Emotional Healing and Recovery.* North Atlantic Books: Berkeley, California, USA.

12. I attended a lecture in which Norman Doidge explained how neuropeptides function. My explanation of neuropeptides in partially taken from my lecture notes. Doidge, N. (2010). "The Brain That Changes Itself: The Neuroplasticity Revolution for the Helping Professions." Leading Edge Seminars. Toronto, Canada.

13. Deepak Chopra, in his book *Quantum Healing: Exploring the Frontiers of Mind Body Medicine*, writes, "The discovery of neuropeptides was so significant because it showed that the body is fluid enough to match the mind. Thanks to messenger molecules (neuropeptides), events that seem totally unconnected – such as a thought and a bodily reaction – are now seen to be consistent. The neuropeptide isn't a thought but it moves with thought, serving as a point of transformation. . . . A neuropeptide springs into existence at the touch of a thought . . . a transformation of non-matter into matter." Chopra, D. (1990). *Quantum Healing: Exploring the Frontiers of Mind Body Medicine.* Bantam Books: New York, USA. p. 95.

14. Psychologists Suzanne Segerstrom and Gregory Miller did a meta-analysis of 293 studies conducted over the past 30 years in July of 2004 and found the following: Short-term stress, like the fight-or-flight response, temporarily boosts the immune system, while chronic, long-term stress suppresses the immune system. The longer the stress lasts, the more the immune system shifts from the positive adaptive changes seen in the fight-or-flight response to more negative changes. When facing long-term stressors, the negative changes occur at a cellular level first, and then move to broader immune functions. Stress that seems to be beyond a person's control, or seems endless, results in the most global suppression of immunity. Segerstrom, S. C. & Miller, G. E. (2004). "Psychological Stress and the Human Immune System: A Meta-Analytic Study of 30 Years of Inquiry." *Psychological Bulletin,* Vol 130(4), Jul 2004, 601–630.

15. A study that correlates loneliness and lack of community to depressed immune responses: Pressman, S. D., Cohen, S., Miller, G. E., Barkin, A., Rabin, B. S., & Treanor, J. J. (2005). "Loneliness, Social Network Size, and Immune Response to Influenza Vaccination in College Freshmen." *Health Psychology,* 2005, Vol. 24, No. 3, 297–306.

16. Read more about Dr. Candace Pert's theories and findings in her book: Pert, C. (1999). *Molecules of Emotion: The Science Behind Mind-Body Medicine.* Touchstone:

New York, USA.

17. Christiane Northrup, author of *Women's Bodies, Women's Wisdom: The Complete Guide to Woman's Health And Wellbeing*, is a medical doctor who relates emotional and psychological conditions to health problems. She states that our psychology forms our bodies; women cannot hope to reclaim bodily wisdom until they understand how society influences the way they think and care about themselves. Her feminist perspective describes the patriarchal systems that influence women's health. She encourages women to work with their bodies rather than against them. She then lays the groundwork for her "mind/body" style of practice by stating that intellectual decisions occurring in the brain are not the only form of wisdom that we have. She believes that the brain is not just a discrete organ, but is connected to our entire body. She believes that this is evident in the fact that brain chemicals are created by, and are present in, all of the body's organs, affecting the way in which we think and feel emotions. She believes, therefore, that wisdom is gained through the entire body. To read further, please see: Northrup, C. (1995). *Women's Bodies, Women's Wisdom: The Complete Guide to Women's Health and Wellbeing*. Piatkus Publishers Ltd.: London, England.

18. Deepak Chopra, in the foreword of Dr. Candace Pert's book *Molecules of Emotion*, states that, "Candace has taken a giant step towards shattering some cherished beliefs held sacred by Western scientists for more than two centuries. Her pioneering research has demonstrated how our internal chemicals, the neuropeptides and their receptors, are the actual biological underpinnings of our awareness, manifesting themselves as our emotions, beliefs, and expectations, and profoundly influencing how we respond to and experience our world. Her research has provided evidence of the biochemical basis for awareness and consciousness, validating what Eastern philosophers, shamans, rishis and alternative practitioners have known and practiced for centuries. The body is not a mindless machine; the body and mind are one." To read further, please see the foreword of: Pert, C. (1999). *Molecules of Emotion: The Science Behind Mind-Body Medicine*. Touchstone: New York, USA.

19. Quote is from: Halprin, A. (2002). *Returning To Health With Dance, Movement and Imagery*. LifeRhythm: Mendocino, California, USA. p. 30.

20. Quote is from: Gendlin, E. T. (1978). *Focusing*. Bantam Books: New York, USA. pp. 32–33.

21. Quote is from: Blakeslee, S. & Blakeslee, M. (2007). *The Body Has a Mind of Its Own: How Body Maps in Your Brain Help You Do (Almost) Everything Better*. Random House Trade Paperbacks: New York. p. 11.

22. Thomas Moore writes about illness as a poetic expression of our souls. To read further, see: Moore, T. (1994). *Care of the Soul: A Guide for Cultivating Depth and Sacredness in Everyday Life* (Rev. ed.). Harper Perennial: New York, USA.

23. I read about the Diana Effect in: Anderson, J. & Anderson, M. (1997). *The Diana Effect*. (Online). http://www.wayfareronline.com/articles/emotions.htm#The Diana Effect (retrieved in November 2003).

24. I read about the Diana Effect in: Morgan-Jones, R., Smith, K., & Oakley, P. (1998). "The 'Diana Effect': Hospital Experienced a Decrease In Number of Admissions For Trauma." *British Medical Journal*, 1998 June 6, 316 (7146), 1750–1751.

25. During a lecture at the European Graduate School, expressive arts therapist Paolo Knill stated that psychological illness was, for the most part, a failure of the imagination. When we cannot imagine a way through our suffering, he explained, we feel lost and boxed in. Life can become intolerable with no hope of change. If we can expand our imaginative capacities, we become better at imagining our way through to the other side of suffering. He essentially states that the expressive arts therapist's

job is to help people develop and expand their abilities to imagine as a cure for their suffering. The paraphrasing was taken from my lecture notes. Knill, P. (2000). Lecture. European Graduate School, Sass-Fee, Switzerland.

26. In the lecture I mentioned above, I remember that Paolo Knill said that psychological illness was a failure of one's imagination. In his essay *Foundations for a Theory of Practice*, he presents a similar idea but focuses more on one's capacity to play rather than on imagination. I have added this endnote just in case I interpreted his lecture incorrectly. To read more see: Knill, P. (2005). "Foundations for a Theory of Practice." In Knill, P., Levine, E. G. & Levine, S. K. *Principles and Practice of Expressive Arts Therapy: Toward a Therapeutic Aesthetics.* Jessica Kingsley Publishers Ltd.: London, England.

27. My writing about emotional intelligence in this paragraph is inspired by the article "The Intelligence of Emotional Intelligence." To read further, please see: Mayer, J. D., & Salovey, P. (1993). "The Intelligence of Emotional Intelligence." *Intelligence,* 17 (4).

28. My understanding of spiritual wisdom was crystallized through reading psychologist Stephen Gilligan's article, *The Experience of "Negative Otherness": How Shall We Treat Our Enemies?* My description of spiritual wisdom is partially paraphrased from the following quote: "It's important to recognize that people know the experience of a relational field in different ways. You may know it through walking in the forest, and call it nature. You may know it by joining with others in social justice, and call it community. You may know it through athletic performance, and call it the zone. You may know it through prayer, and call it God. You may know it through intimate relationship, and call it love." To read further, please see: Gilligan, S. (2003). *The Experience of "Negative Otherness": How Shall We Treat Our Enemies?* (Online). http://www.shentaostudio.com/theexperienceofnegative/ (retrieved in January 2004).

29. I first read about this study on meditation in: Tammet, D. (2009). *Embracing the Wide Sky: A Tour Across the Horizons of the Mind.* Simon and Schuster Inc.: New York, USA.

30. I then read the study itself: Lutz, A., Brefczynski-Lewis, J., Johnstone, T. & Davidson, R. "Regulation of the Neural Circuitry of Emotion by Compassion Meditation: Effects of Meditative Expertise." *PLoS ONE.* 2008; 3(3):e1897.

31. EXA therapist Majken Jacoby, in her article "The Necessity of Form," writes about philosopher Logstrup's view of the senses: ". . . human nature has a sensory basis: our senses, Logstrup maintains, seeing, hearing, touch, and so on, are an actual entry to the world, not only a mirroring of ourselves. There is something out there, and our senses create a bridge to it and intertwine us with all that is around us." To read further, please see: Jacoby, M. (1999). "The Necessity of Form: Expressive Arts Therapy in the Light of the Work of K.E. Logstrup." In Levine, S. K. & Levine, E. G. (Eds.) *Foundations of Expressive Arts Therapy: Theoretical and Clinical Perspectives.* Jessica Kingsley Publishers Ltd.: London, England. p. 55.

32. This paragraph is inspired by Dr. Donald Bakal, who writes about the state of wellness as an integrated psychobiological state that includes emotion, cognition, and physiological factors that are tightly bound in the experience of the self and the world. To read further, please see: Bakal, D. (1999). *Minding the Body: Clinical Uses of Somatic Awareness.* The Guilford Press: New York, USA.

33. This paragraph is inspired by EXA therapist Shaun McNiff, who, in his book *The Arts and Psychotherapy*, states: "Health . . . involves a rhythmic synchrony within the self together with an ability to synchronize with the movements of others and the environment." To read further, please see: McNiff, S. (1981). *The Arts and Psychotherapy.*

Charles C Thomas Publisher: Springfield, Illinois, USA. p. 35.

34. This story is based on a conversation I had with someone after a dance improvisation event. Details have been changed to protect the person's anonymity.

35. To read further about complexes, please see: Sedgwick, D. (2001). *Introduction to Jungian Psychotherapy: The Therapeutic Relationship*. Brunner-Routledge: Hove, East Sussex, England.

36. The following study describes how playing piano at a professional level ingrains neural pathways differently than in control subjects who were not professional piano players: Krings, T., Topper, R., Foltys, H., Erberich, S., Sparing, R., Willmes, K., & Thron, A. (2000). "Cortical Activation Patterns During Complex Motor Tasks in Piano Players and Control Subjects. A Functional Magnetic Resonance Imaging Study." *Neuroscience Letters*. 2000, Jan 14, 278 (3), 189–193.

37. In the following book, there is a description of how years of playing piano at a professional level ingrain neural pathways that control hand dexterity: Blakeslee, S. & Blakeslee, M. (2007). *The Body Has a Mind of Its Own: How Body Maps in Your Brain Help You Do (Almost) Everything Better*. Random House Trade Paperbacks: New York, USA. pp. 56–58.

38. This article describes how being a taxi driver ingrains neural pathways: Maguire, E., Gadian, D., Johnsrude, I., Good, C., Ashburner, J., Frackowiak, R. & Frith, C. (2000). "Navigation-related Structural Change in the Hippocampi of Taxi Drivers." *PNAS*, April 11, 2000, vol. 97 no. 8, 4398–4403.

39. To read more fascinating stories about how experience ingrains neural pathways, please see: Doidge, N. (2010). *The Brain That Changes Itself: Stories of Personal Triumph From the Frontiers of Brain Science*. Scribe Publications Pty Ltd.: Melbourne, Australia.

40. To read more stories of how experience ingrains neural pathways, please see Chapter 1 of: Tammet, D. (2009). *Embracing the Wide Sky: A Tour Across the Horizons of the Mind*. Simon and Schuster Inc.: New York, USA.

41. The article "The Biology of Trauma: Implications for Treatment" discusses the correlation between trauma and the changes in body physiology and biology that persist well after the trauma has passed. It explains that psychological trauma disrupts homeostasis and can cause both short-term and long-term effects on many organs and systems of the body. To read further, please see: Solomon, E. P. & Heide, K. M. (2005). "The Biology of Trauma: Implications for Treatment." *Journal of Interpersonal Violence*, January 2005, vol. 20, no. 1, 51–60.

42. The article "Homeostasis, Stress, Trauma, and Adaptation" describes the effects of early childhood trauma. The authors explain that a traumatic experience can result in the persistence of fear-related neurophysiologic patterns affecting emotional, behavioural, cognitive, and social functioning. To read further, please see: Perry, B. D. & Pollard, R. (1998). "Homeostasis, Stress, Trauma, and Adaptation: A Neurodevelopmental View of Childhood Trauma." *Child and Adolescent Psychiatric Clinics of North America*, 7 [1], 33–51. 1998.

43. The concept that we become numb as a response to a lack of beauty and the intolerable realities of our world is taken from EXA therapists Paolo Knill, Helen Nienhaus Barba, and Margo Fuchs, who write: "We have a special challenge in confronting the anaesthetizing mechanism in the world of today. Could it be that genuine beauty has become absent from our life to such an extent that we have to anaesthetize in order to protect ourselves from sensing abusive realities?" To read further, please see: Knill, P., Barba, H. N., & Fuchs, M. N (1995). *Minstrels of Soul: Intermodal Expressive Therapy*. Palmerston Press: Toronto, Canada. p. 72.

44. This paragraph on the tendency we have to estrange ourselves from embodied experience is inspired by the writing of expressive arts therapist Shaun McNiff. In his book *The Arts and Psychotherapy*, he explains how: ". . . emotional conflict originates in feelings of separation between consciousness and the body . . . All forms of personality splits and emotional fragmentations grow from the disunity of the body and mind. We fear the body – its mortality, its potential for diseases and pain, its unattractiveness, etc. – and thus constantly estrange ourselves from it . . . So it appears that we must begin to embrace and appreciate our bodies, their movements, weaknesses, strengths and idiosyncratic qualities if we are to establish an underlying unity and balance of behaviour." To read further, please see: McNiff, S. (1981). *The Arts and Psychotherapy.* Charles C Thomas Publisher: Springfield, Illinois, USA. pp. 112–113.

45. Quote is from: Meyer, M. A. (1999). "In Exile From the Body: Creating a 'Play Room' in the 'Waiting Room'." In Levine, S. K. & Levine, E. G. (Eds.) *Foundations of Expressive Arts Therapy: Theoretical and Clinical Perspectives.* Jessica Kingsley Publishers Ltd.: London, England. pp. 242–243.

Chapter Three: Healing Through the Arts

46. Louis Cozolino writes about the brain as a continually changing organ that is affected by shifts in life experience. To read further, see: Cozolino, L. (2002). *The Neuroscience of Psychotherapy: Building and Rebuilding the Human Brain.* W.W. Norton and Company, Inc: New York, USA.

47. Norman Doidge discusses the conditions that jumpstart our brains' neuroplastic abilities in: Doidge, N. (2010). *The Brain That Changes Itself: Stories of Personal Triumph From the Frontiers of Brain Science.* Scribe Publications Pty Ltd.: Melbourne, Australia.

48. I attended a lecture in which Norman Doidge listed the conditions that he theorized are needed to jumpstart our brains' neuroplasticity. This information is taken from the lecture notes I made during his presentation. Doidge, N. (2010). "The Brain That Changes itself: The Neuroplasticity Revolution for the Helping Professions." Leading Edge Seminars. Toronto, Canada.

49. Paolo Knill, in his essay *Foundations for a Theory of Practice*, presents a spread sheet that describes the frames that different art modalities provide. Knill, P. (2005). "Foundations for a Theory of Practice." In Knill, P., Levine, E. G. & Levine, S. K., *Principles and Practice of Expressive Arts Therapy: Toward a Therapeutic Aesthetics.* Jessica Kingsley Publishers Ltd.: London, England. pp. 101–103.

50. The following study correlates the expression of anger between married couples with life expectancy. It was found that couples who demonstrated a pattern of anger suppression lived shorter lives than those who did not. Harburg, E., Kaciroti, N., Gleiberman, L., Julius, M., & Schork, A. (2008). "Marital Pair Anger-Coping Types May Act as an Entity to Affect Mortality: Preliminary Findings from a Prospective Study (Tecumseh, Michigan, 1971–1988)." *Journal of Family Communication*, Volume 8, Issue 1, 2008, 44–61.

51. Some of the concepts in this paragraph about imagination are inspired by Ellen Levine's writing. In her book *Tending the Fire: Studies in Art, Therapy & Creativity*, she states that images are the primary material of the imagination and are the building blocks of art making. She believes that without imagination, we are lost in a world of appearances and condemned to reality. She further states that imaginative capacities are essential for our experience of the world and give us access to that which is hidden from us. To read further, see: Levine, E. G. (1995). *Tending the Fire: Studies in Art,*

Therapy & Creativity. Palmerston Press: Toronto, Canada.

52. Some of the descriptions of the attributes of different art forms in this paragraph are inspired by the writing of EXA therapists Paolo Knill, Helen Nienhaus Barba, and Margo Fuchs. In their book *Minstrels of Soul: Intermodal Expressive Therapy,* they state that each art form enhances the process of self-expression in a unique manner. For instance, visual arts tend to be created in isolation and stand still through time, while music and movement often enhance social communication and relationship-building, but are more ephemeral in nature. To read further, please see: Knill, P., Barba, H. N., & Fuchs, M. N. (1995). *Minstrels of Soul: Intermodal Expressive Therapy.* Palmerston Press: Toronto, Canada.

53. Paolo Knill writes about the therapeutic benefit of transferring between different art modalities in: Knill, P. (2005). "Foundations for a Theory of Practice." In Knill, P., Levine, E. G. & Levine, S. K. *Principles and Practice of Expressive Arts Therapy: Toward a Therapeutic Aesthetics.* Jessica Kingsley Publishers Ltd.: London, England.

54. This quote is from: Levine, S. K. (2005). "The Philosophy of Expressive Arts: Poiesis as a Response to the World." In Knill, P., Levine, E. G. & Levine, S. K. *Principles and Practice of Expressive Arts Therapy: Toward a Therapeutic Aesthetics.* Jessica Kingsley Publishers Ltd.: London, England. p. 45.

55. My definition of play is partially paraphrased from Johan H. Huizinga's definition of play in his article: Huizinga, J. (1971). *Homo Ludens: A Study of the Play-Element in Culture.* Beacon Press: Boston, Massachusetts, USA.

56. This quote is from: Brown, S. (2009). *Play: How it Shapes the Brain, Opens the Imagination and Invigorates the Soul.* Penguin Books: London, England. pp. 32–34.

57. Sue Jennings and Mooli Lahad, in their explanation of the effectiveness of play therapy, explain that play is an essential component in a child's psychological development. To read further, please see: Jennings, S. & Lahad, M. (1999). *Introduction to Developmental Playtherapy: Playing and Health.* Jessica Kingsley Publishers Ltd.: London, England.

58. This discussion is inspired by the quote "We suffer when there is no play-space, no gap between what we are and what we can be" in: Levine, S. K. (2005). "The Philosophy of Expressive Arts: Poiesis as a Response to the World." In Knill, P., Levine, E. G. & Levine, S. K. *Principles and Practice of Expressive Arts Therapy: Toward a Therapeutic Aesthetics.* Jessica Kingsley Publishers Ltd.: London, England. p. 71.

59. To read more about expanding one's capacity to play through expressive arts therapy, see: Knill, P. (2005). "Foundations for a Theory and Practice." In Knill, P., Levine, E. G. & Levine, S. K. *Principles and Practice of Expressive Arts Therapy: Toward a Therapeutic Aesthetics.* Jessica Kingsley Publishers Ltd.: London, England.

60. *I Love Lucy* is a well-known American sitcom that starred Lucille Ball, Desi Arnaz, Vivian Vance, and William Frawley. It ran from October 15, 1951 to April 1, 1960 on CBS. Lucy, the main character, was always getting involved in hilarious endeavours that inevitably ended in disaster despite her best efforts.

61. This quote is from: Jacoby, M. (1999). "The Necessity of Form: Expressive Arts Therapy in the Light of the Work of K.E. Logstrup." In Levine, S. K. & Levine, E. G. (Eds.) *Foundations of Expressive Arts Therapy: Theoretical and Clinical Perspectives.* Jessica Kingsley Publishers Ltd.: London, England. p. 64.

62. Norman Doidge writes about how love-related brain chemicals are thought to increase the plasticity of our brain, recreating for a period of time the capacity for rapid restructuring of neural pathways. To read more, see: Doidge, N. (2010). *The Brain That Changes Itself: Stories of Personal Triumph From the Frontiers of Brain Science.* Scribe Publications Pty Ltd.: Melbourne, Australia.

63. I attended a lecture in which Norman Doidge explained his theory of how oxytocin and dopamine play a role in neuroplasticity. Doidge, N. (2010). "The Brain That Changes Itself: The Neuroplasticity Revolution for the Helping Professions." Leading Edge Seminars. Toronto, Canada.

64. Some of the descriptions of honest beauty in this paragraph are inspired by the writing of EXA therapists Paolo Knill, Helen Nienhaus Barba, and Margo Fuchs. In their book *Minstrels of Soul: Intermodal Expressive Therapy*, they explain that the more honest and sensitive expression is, the more it becomes beautiful. This understanding allows expression through the arts to be accessible to all of us because traditional artistic skill is not needed in the pursuit of artistic beauty. They refer to this approach as the "low skill, high sensitivity" approach; clients are encouraged to find the expression that invigorates them without worrying about technical skill. To read more, see: Knill, P., Barba, H. N., & Fuchs, M. N. (1995). *Minstrels of Soul: Intermodal Expressive Therapy*. Palmerston Press: Toronto, Canada.

65. The Golden Ratio is a principle in visual arts composition that states that compositions divided into a certain ratio (roughly 1:1.618) are believed to be more visually beautiful than compositions that do not meet this criterion.

66. EXA therapists Paolo Knill, Helen Nienhaus Barba, and Margo Fuchs discuss the process of crystallization that occurs in art making when out of the blur of colours and emerging images, a crystal-clear image begins to form that leads to a sense of inner clarity. To read further, see: Knill, P., Barba, H. N. & Fuchs, M. N. (1995). *Minstrels of Soul: Intermodal Expressive Therapy*. Palmerston Press: Toronto, Canada.

67. Paolo Knill also writes about the process of crystallization in expressive art therapy in: Knill, P. (2005). "Foundations for a Theory of Practice." In Knill, P., Levine, E. G. & Levine, S. K. *Principles and Practice of Expressive Arts Therapy: Toward a Therapeutic Aesthetics.* Jessica Kingsley Publishers Ltd.: London, England.

68. Many of the concepts described in this paragraph describing beauty are inspired by: Jacoby, M. (1999). "The Necessity of Form: Expressive Arts Therapy in the Light of the Work of K. E. Logstrup." In Levine, S. K. & Levine, E. G. (Eds.) *Foundations of Expressive Arts Therapy: Theoretical and Clinical Perspectives.* Jessica Kingsley Publishers Ltd.: London, England.

69. The following article explains how dopamine surges occur only when the reward is unexpected. Spitzer, M. (2006). *Better Than Thought: Learning, Dopamine and Neuroplasticity.* (Online). Center for Educational Research and Innovation (CERI). http://www.oecd.org/document/57/0,3746,en_21571361_49995565_37073145_1_1_1_1,00.html (retrieved August 2011).

70. In explaining slot machine addiction, this article explains how dopamine surges occur only when the reward comes unexpectedly, without warning. Lehrer, J. "Your Brain On Gambling: Science Shows How Slot Machines Take Over Your Mind." *The Boston Globe*, August 19, 2007.

71. My understanding of the therapeutic qualities of honest beauty is inspired by participating in Paolo Knill's workshops at ISIS-Canada and European Graduate School over many years. He works in an art-focused manner, pursuing a humanistic sense of beauty with great passion. He writes about aesthetic responsibility in: Knill, P. (2005). "Foundations for a Theory of Practice." In Knill, P., Levine, E. G. & Levine, S. K. *Principles and Practice of Expressive Arts Therapy: Toward a Therapeutic Aesthetics.* Jessica Kingsley Publishers Ltd.: London, England.

72. Some of the concepts mentioned in this paragraph that describe liminal space are inspired by Lisa Herman's writing: Herman, L. (2007). *Liminal Space.* From Lisa Herman's personal library of papers.

73. This quote is from Levine, E. G. (2005). "The Practice of Expressive Arts Therapy: Training, Therapy and Supervision." In Knill, P., Levine, E. G. & Levine, S. K. *Principles and Practice of Expressive Arts Therapy: Toward a Therapeutic Aesthetics.* Jessica Kingsley Publishers Ltd.: London, England. p. 197.

74. The description of liminal space is paraphrased from: Herman, L. (2007). *Liminal Space.* From Lisa Herman's personal library of papers. p. 7.

75. I learned this "fussy-baby" dance from Nina Martin, a contact dancer who teaches a method called Ensemble Thinking. Ensemble Thinking was developed by *The Lower Left Collective,* of which Nina Martin is a member. They developed a series of exercises that help break a dancer's physical tendencies and movement patterns. After studying with Nina Martin, I started to use some of the exercises I learned with clients. I did so because I felt that they helped people break through movement and thought patterns interfering with well-being. Martin, N. (2006). Dance Workshop. Workshop hosted by Pam Johnson. Toronto, Canada.

76. This quote is from: Levine, S. K. (1992). *Poiesis: The Language of Psychology and the Speech of the Soul.* Palmerston Press: Toronto, Canada. p. 114.

77. The sentence, "At the core of unconditional acceptance is the energy of love, which opens a sky wide enough to hold the entire rainbow of self" is paraphrased from: Knill, P., Barba, H. N., & Fuchs, M. N. (1995). *Minstrels of Soul: Intermodal Expressive Therapy.* Palmerston Press: Toronto, Canada.

78. The epilogue for Allen's story that I had written was edited out of the body of the book: I open the cabinet and see that I forgot to take out the recycle bin. Looking into it, I see monster/boy's face looking up at me from the pile of papers. I think to myself, *if people knew your story, it could help them.* I "accidentally" forget to take out the recycling for yet another week. I find myself "writing" Allen's story in my head as I ride the subway. I consult with my supervisor, who is encouraging. She tells me, "Sometimes, it can be a moment of pride for a client to know that their story of recovery can reach out and help others." I phone Allen and say, "I am writing a book, and I think your story can inspire others and help describe how expressive arts therapy works. If you are game, I will change lots of details so your anonymity is protected, and you can read it before it's published and give me the okay." "Yes, start writing," Allen answers. "I trust you. Just make sure to give me a cool name."

Chapter Four: The Art of Grief

79. The song Tom sings in the father's death in *Long Live* was "Father Death Blues" by Allen Ginsberg.

Chapter Five: The Art of Sensation

80. The story of the girl who could feel no pain was downloaded from http://www.msnbc.msn.com/id/6379795/ns/health-kids_and_parenting/t/rare-disease-makes-girl-unable-feel-pain/ (retrieved August 2011).

81. This description of what happens when we lose connection to the sensation of our inner body is partially inspired by the conclusion to: Levine, P. (1997). *Waking the Tiger: Healing Trauma.* North Atlantic Books: Berkeley, California, USA. p. 266.

82. Dr. Clyde W. Ford is a pioneer in the field of psychodynamics and therapeutic touch. He is the author of several books, including *Compassionate Touch* and *Where Healing Waters Meet.* He was the 2006 recipient of the Hurston/Wright Legacy Award.

Clyde is a much sought-after public speaker and has appeared on the *Oprah Winfrey Show* and *New Dimensions Radio*. He believes that our bodies are a source of wisdom in the healing process. He explains that through attention to body sensations (triggered through therapeutic touch), we can uncover hidden messages from our physical pain and discomfort that lead us to emotional resolution. To read further, see: Ford, C. W. (1999). *Compassionate Touch: The Body's Role in Emotional Healing and Recovery.* North Atlantic Books: Berkeley, California, USA. Ford, C. W. (1992). *Where Healing Waters Meet: Touching Mind and Emotion Through the Body.* Hushion House: Toronto, Canada.

83. Pat Ogden is the founder and director of the Sensorimotor Psychotherapy Institute, an internationally recognized school that specializes in training psychotherapists in somatic/cognitive approaches for the treatment of trauma, developmental, and attachment issues. Sensorimotor Psychotherapy is a form of psychotherapy that works directly with sensation and motor function as a way to resolve the limitations in behaviour, thinking, and feeling that trauma can cause. To read further about Pat Ogden's work, see: Ogden, P. (2006). *Trauma and The Body: A Sensorimotor Approach to Psychotherapy.* W. W. Norton & Company: New York, USA.

84. Peter Levine understands trauma through the lens of our basic animal nature. Animals have an organic and primitive response to trauma that involves releasing the trauma after the danger has passed. He uses the example of how the deer trembles for a few minutes after the threat of the lion has passed. He believes that we have an ability to think and talk about things because of our higher brain function, but this ability can interfere with our natural physical response to trauma. By talking and thinking, Peter Levine thinks, we do not allow the physical release of the trauma and, therefore, get stuck holding onto it. This can cause anxiety, flashbacks, nightmares, and intrusive memories. Healing in his approach involves allowing our animal selves to lead in an embodied release that we did not complete when the trauma occurred. To read more, see: Levine, P. (1997). *Waking the Tiger: Healing Trauma.* North Atlantic Books: Berkeley, California, USA. Levine, P. (2005). *Healing Trauma: A Pioneering Program for Restoring the Wisdom of Your Body.* Sounds True, Inc.: Boulder, Colorado, USA.

85. Arnold Mindell believes that meaning can be found through awareness and attention given to bodily processes such as body sensations, pains, habitual gestures, and even chronic illnesses. Whereas some therapies attempt to eradicate or ignore these processes, especially the ones considered negative or undesirable, Mindell's approach is to amplify and follow them until they reveal their hidden messages. He states that the desire to heal (or eradicate suffering) can potentially be destructive, because by side-stepping disturbances or passing them off as pathological signals, we may miss their messages and force them to "act-out" more vigorously in order to be noticed and appreciated. To read more about Arnold Mindell, see: Bodian, S. (1990). "Field of Dreams, An Interview with Arnold Mindell." *Yoga Journal.* March/April, 1990. Mindell, A. (2001). *Working With the Dreaming Body.* Lao Tse Press: Portland, Oregon, USA.

86. In Dr. Pat Ogden's Sensorimotor Psychotherapy approach, clients are provided with a menu of options in a similar manner to how I offer a diverse set of options on a "tray." I was using my "tray approach" before I became familiar with Pat Ogden's work. Discovering this similarity in a different genre of therapy was affirming of my method. To read further about Pat Ogden's work, see: Ogden, P. (2006). *Trauma and The Body: A Sensorimotor Approach to Psychotherapy.* W. W. Norton & Company: New York, USA.

87. Daria Halprin, a well-known expert in movement and dance based expressive arts therapy and a teacher of mine at the European Graduate School, once asked my class to draw portraits of ourselves as realistic as we could. I was accustomed to drawing in an expressive, rather than realistic manner, and not being a trained visual artist, my portrait was distorted in an unsatisfying manner. Daria then requested that we stand in front of our own portrait for forty-five minutes and just *stay-with* the image. This *staying-with* was at first very uncomfortable. I was mad because I had thought that this was going to be a class in which I would learn about dance therapy. But instead I was just standing around, not moving! I transferred this anger to the image. I detested it. To me it was ugly, plain and unexpressive. But as I continued to stand and look at it, something happened. I started to see things I had not noticed before. I started to feel warmth towards the image – a kind of compassion one would feel for a child at a party that no one wants to play with. By the end of the forty-five minutes I no longer felt angry or sorry for the image. What shone through all that *staying-with* was the beauty of the image in all its imperfections. From this exercise, I learned about the value of *staying-with* discomfort. To read more about Daria Halprin's style of therapy see: Halprin, D. (2003). *The Expressive Body in Life, Art and Therapy: Working With Movement, Metaphor and Meaning.* Jessica Kingsley Publishers Ltd.: London, England.

88. As described above, my tray approach is similar to how Dr. Pat Ogden's method provides a menu of options. To read further about Pat Ogden's work, see: Ogden, P. (2006). *Trauma and The Body: A Sensorimotor Approach to Psychotherapy.* W. W. Norton & Company: New York, USA.

89. My understanding of amplification is inspired by Arnold Mindell's work. In his books *Dreambody: The Body's Role in Revealing the Self, and Working with the Dreaming Body*, he defines amplification as increasing the strength of physical signals. He believes that amplification is a somatic approach to consciousness in which the body is allowed to express itself. To read more about amplification, see: Mindell, A. (1998). *Dreambody: The Body's Role in Revealing the Self* (2nd edition). Lao Tse Press: Portland, Oregon, USA. Mindell, A. (2001). *Working With the Dreaming Body.* Lao Tse Press: Portland, Oregon, USA.

90. Paolo Knill in his essay "Foundations for a Theory of Practice" describes the practical application of "takes" in expressive arts therapy sessions. I have also witnessed Paolo Knill work with "takes" at ISIS-Canada and European Graduate School and came to appreciate their therapeutic potential. Knill, P. (2005). "Foundations for a Theory of Practice." In Knill, P., Levine, E. G. & Levine, S. K. *Principles and Practice of Expressive Arts Therapy: Toward a Therapeutic Aesthetics.* Jessica Kingsley Publishers Ltd.: London, England.

91. To read more about Peter Levine's methods in helping people recover from trauma, see: Levine, P. (1997). *Waking the Tiger: Healing Trauma.* North Atlantic Books: Berkeley, California, USA.

92. Paolo Knill explains harvesting in expressive arts therapy as dialogue that occurs towards the end of a session in which the client, having returned from an altered reality (the art making), is able to find new perspectives. My approach to harvesting is inspired by Paolo Knill's vision. To read further see: Knill, P. (2005). "Foundations for a Theory of Practice." In Knill, P., Levine, E. G. & Levine, S. K. *Principles and Practice of Expressive Arts Therapy: Toward a Therapeutic Aesthetics.* Jessica Kingsley Publishers Ltd.: London, England.

BIBLIOGRAPHY

Anderson, J., & Anderson, M. (1997). *The Diana effect.* (Online). http://www. wayfareronline.com/articles/emotions.htm#The Diana Effect (retrieved in November 2003).

Bakal, D. (1999). *Minding the body: Clinical uses of somatic awareness.* New York: The Guilford Press.

Blakeslee, S., & Blakeslee, M. (2007). *The body has a mind of its own: How body maps in your brain help you do (almost) everything better.* New York: Random House Trade Paperbacks.

Bodian, S. (1990). Field of dreams, An interview with Arnold Mindell. *Yoga Journal.* March/April.

Brown, S. (2009). *Play: How it shapes the brain, opens the imagination and invigorates the soul.* London: Penguin Books.

Chopra, D. (1990). *Quantum healing: Exploring the frontiers of mind body medicine.* New York: Bantam Books.

Citron, P. (1996). Toronto Fringe Festival 1996 Reviews. *Dance International Magazine.*

Cozolino, L. (2002). *The neuroscience of psychotherapy: Building and rebuilding the human brain.* New York: W. W. Norton.

Doidge, N. (2010). *The brain that changes itself: Stories of personal triumph from the frontiers of brain science.* Melbourne: Scribe Publications Pty Ltd.

Doidge, N. (2010). *The brain that changes itself: The neuroplasticity revolution for the helping professions.* Toronto: Leading Edge Seminars.

Ford, C. W. (1992). *Where healing waters meet: Touching mind and emotion through the body.* Toronto: Hushion House.

Ford, C. W. (1999). *Compassionate touch, the body's role in emotional healing and recovery.* Berkeley, CA: North Atlantic Books.

Frontal Lobes (Online). www.neuroskills.com/tbi/bfrontal.shtml (retrieved October 2009).

Gendlin, E. T. (1978). *Focusing.* New York: Bantam Books.

Gilligan, S. (2003). *The experience of "negative otherness": How shall we treat our enemies?* (Online). http://www.shentaostudio.com/theexperienceofnegative/ (retrieved January 2004).

Halprin, A. (2002). *Returning to health with dance, movement and imagery.* Mendocino, CA: LifeRhythm.

Halprin, D. (2003). *The expressive body in life, art and therapy: Working with movement, metaphor and meaning.* London: Jessica Kingsley Publishers Ltd.

Harburg, E., Kaciroti, N., Gleiberman, L., Julius, M., & Schork, A. (2008). Marital pair anger-coping types may act as an entity to affect mortality: Preliminary findings from a prospective study (Tecumseh, Michigan, 1971–1988). *Journal of Family Communication,* Volume 8, Issue 1, 44–61.

Herman, L. (2007). *Liminal space.* From Lisa Herman's personal library of papers.

Huizinga, J. (1971). *Homo Ludens: A study of the play-element in culture.* Boston: Beacon Press.

Jacoby, M. (1999). The necessity of form: Expressive arts therapy in the light of the work of K. E. Logstrup. In S. K. Levine & E. G. Levine (Eds.), *Foundations of expressive arts therapy: Theoretical and clinical perspectives.* London: Jessica Kingsley Publishers Ltd.

Jennings, S., & Lahad, M. (1999). *Introduction to developmental playtherapy: Playing and health.* London: Jessica Kingsley Publishers Ltd.

Knill, P. (2000). *Lecture.* European Graduate School, Sass-Fee, Switzerland.

Knill, P. (2005). Foundations for a theory of practice. In P. Knill, E. G. Levine & S. K. Levine (Eds.), *Principles and practice of expressive arts therapy: Toward a therapeutic aesthetics.* London: Jessica Kingsley Publishers Ltd.

Knill, P., Barba, H. N., & Fuchs, M. N. (1995). *Minstrels of soul: Intermodal expressive therapy.* Toronto: Palmerston Press.

Krings, T., Topper, R., Foltys, H., Erberich, S., Sparing, R., Willmes, K., & Thron, A. (2000). Cortical activation patterns during complex motor tasks in piano players and control subjects. A functional magnetic resonance imaging study. *Neuroscience Letters,* Jan 14, 278 (3),189–193.

Lehrer, J. (2007). Your brain on gambling: Science shows how slot machines take over your mind. *The Boston Globe,* August 19.

Levine, E. G. (1995). *Tending the fire: Studies in art, therapy & creativity.* Toronto: Palmerston Press.

Levine, E. G. (2005). The practice of expressive arts therapy: Training, therapy and supervision. In P. Knill, E. G. Levine & S. K. Levine (Eds.), *Principles and practice of expressive arts therapy: Toward a therapeutic aesthetics.* London: Jessica Kingsley Publishers Ltd.

Levine, P. (1997). *Waking the tiger: Healing trauma.* Berkeley, CA: North Atlantic Books.

Levine, P. (2005). *Healing trauma: A pioneering program for restoring the wisdom of your body.* Boulder, CO: Sounds True, Inc.

Levine, S. K. (1992). *Poiesis: The language of psychology and the speech of the soul.* Toronto: Palmerston Press.

Levine, S. K. (2005). The philosophy of expressive arts: Poiesis as a response to the world. In P. Knill, E. G. Levine & S. K. Levine (Eds.), *Principles and practice of expressive arts therapy: Toward a therapeutic aesthetics.* London: Jessica Kingsley Publishers Ltd.

Lutz, A., Brefczynski-Lewis, J., Johnstone, T., & Davidson, R. (2008). Regulation of the neural circuitry of emotion by compassion meditation: Effects of meditative expertise. *PLoS ONE.* 2008, 3(3):e1897.

Maguire, E., Gadian, D., Johnsrude, I., Good, C., Ashburner, J., Frackowiak, R., & Frith, C. (2000). Navigation-related structural change in the hippocampi of taxi drivers. *PNAS,* April 11, 2000, vol. 97 no. 8, 4398–4403.

Martin, N. (2006). Dance Workshop. Workshop hosted by Pam Johnson. Toronto, Canada.

Mayer, J. D., & Salovey, P. (1993). The intelligence of emotional intelligence. *Intelligence, 17* (4).

Meyer, M. A. (1999). In exile from the body: Creating a 'play room' in the 'waiting room'. In S. K. Levine & E. G. Levine (Eds.), *Foundations of expressive arts therapy: Theoretical and clinical perspectives.* London: Jessica Kingsley Publishers Ltd.

McNiff, S. (1981). *The arts and psychotherapy.* Springfield, IL: Charles C Thomas.

Mindell, A. (1998). *Dreambody: The body's role in revealing the self* (2nd ed.). Portland, OR: Lao Tse Press.

Mindell, A. (2001). *Working With the Dreaming Body.* Lao Tse Press: Portland, Oregon, USA.

Moore, T. (1994). *Care of the soul: A guide for cultivating depth and sacredness in everyday life* (Rev. ed.). New York: Harper Perennial.

Morgan-Jones, R., Smith, K., & Oakley, P. (1998). The "Diana Effect": Hospital experienced a decrease in number of admissions for trauma. *British Medical Journal,* June 6, 316 (7146), 1750–1751.

Northrup, C. (1995). *Women's bodies, women's wisdom: The complete guide to women's health and wellbeing.* London: Piatkus Publishers Ltd.

Ogden, P. (2006). *Trauma and the body: A sensorimotor approach to psychotherapy.* New York: W. W. Norton.

Pert, C. (1999). *Molecules of emotion: The science behind mind-body medicine.* New York: Touchstone.

Perry, B. D., & Pollard, R. (1998). Homeostasis, stress, trauma, and adaptation: A neurodevelopmental view of childhood trauma. *Child and Adolescent Psychiatric Clinics of North America, 7* [1], 33–51.

Pressman, S. D., Cohen, S., Miller, G. E., Barkin, A., Rabin, B. S., & Treanor, J. J. (2005). Loneliness, social network size, and immune response to influenza vaccination in college freshmen. *Health Psychology,* Vol. 24, No. 3, 297–306.

Seaberg, M. (2011). *Tasting the universe: People who see colors in words and rainbows in symphonies: A spiritual and scientific exploration of synesthesia.* Pompton Plains, NJ: Career Press.

Sedgwick, D. (2001). *Introduction to Jungian psychotherapy: The therapeutic relationship.* Hove, East Sussex, England: Brunner-Routledge.

Segerstrom, S. C., & Miller, G. E. (2004). Psychological stress and the human immune system: A meta-analytic study of 30 years of inquiry. *Psychological Bulletin,* Vol 130(4), Jul, 601–630.

Solomon, E. P., & Heide, K. M. (2005). The biology of trauma: Implications for treatment. *Journal of Interpersonal Violence*, January, vol. 20, no. 1, 51–60.

Spitzer, M. (2006). *Better than thought: Learning, dopamine and neuroplasticity.* (Online). Center for Educational Research and Innovation (CERI). http://www.oecd.org/document/57/0,3746,en_21571361_49995565_370 73145_1_1_1_1,00.html (retrieved August 2011).

Tammet, D. (2009). *Embracing the wide sky: A tour across the horizons of the mind.* New York: Simon and Schuster.

Trowbridge, B. (1996). *The hidden meaning of illness: Disease as a symbol and metaphor.* Virginia Beach, VA: Association of Research & English Press.

Williamson, M. (1993). *A woman's worth.* New York: Random House.

INDEX